"This is a timely book, as Adoption Services are structurally and bureaucratically being reorganised. In the confusion and chaos that inevitably follows, it is easy to forget that adoption is ultimately a relational experience. This well researched book looks at the attachment relationships, for all parties involved. Attachment is the touchstone of that experience and Prophecy adds depth, history and neuroscience to enrich our understanding of that experience. She also adds her clinical experience and that of others, to add to the narrative. A very rich and rewarding read."

Alan Burnell. Co-founder and Director of Family Futures

"This remarkable book provides a riveting historical account of British society's evolving understanding of not only mothers' but also fathers' painful experience of giving up a child to adoption. Prophecy Coles has succeeded yet again in vividly conveying the emotional impact of being a child existing for 9 months in a mother's womb only to face anxieties of separation from her and the father and placed in the care of others. It seems imperative that professionals and both natural and adopting parents and their offspring develop an understanding of adoption which this important book provides."

Jeanne Magagna. Former head of Psychotherapy Services at
Great Ormond Street Hospital and former Consultant to
Family Futures Adoption and Fostering Consortium

"With wisdom, and deep clinical and life-experience, Prophecy Coles has delivered an evocative and thought provoking text on the important subject of adoption. Her unique personal voice shines though, as she weaves tales which are moving and peppered with understandings from literature, history, politics and psychotherapy, and most importantly, are infused with a heartfelt and compassionate appreciation of the complex issues that adoption raises."

Graham Music. Consultant and Child Psychotherapist at the Tavistock and
Portman Clinic

"This sensitive book by an experienced psychoanalytic psychotherapist, Prophecy Coles, extends her fascination with the sad chances the newborn infant can suffer. It is extraordinary that early disruption has for so long been overlooked as a serious life event for the infant, and for the child and adult that he/she becomes. Such long-term effects have perhaps been intuitively known — as the book conveys a cow losing its calf is a crisis even a child can know deeply. Coles does face us with the stunning disadvantage and prolonged distress of adoption. We want so much to create an advantage for the dispossessed that the disturbance gets silently shoved away into a dark cupboard and can only with long persistence be taken out and looked at again. This book can help keep the difficult-to-face in front of us and recognise how profoundly we have always wanted to hide it. Surely all care workers need to use it in the care they provide for people they support."

Bob Hinshelwood. Fellow of the British Psychoanalytic Society,
former Emeritus Professor in the Department of Psychosocial and
Psychoanalytic Studies, University of Essex

Psychoanalytic Perspectives on Illegitimacy, Adoption and Reproduction Technology

In this book, Prophecy Coles traces the existential history of the unwanted child with particular attention to the illegitimate child, linking myth, literature and clinical practice in the historical and legal context of adoption.

From the time of the Reformation in the sixteenth century until the early twentieth century the lives of such children were short-lived. The Adoption Act of 1926 did much to change the moral climate and the fate of the illegitimate child. It provided the child with a legal family and a name. There follows some unexpected difficulties that emerged after World War Two. Adopted children did not necessarily thrive, and young mothers who had been forced to give up a child born out of wedlock revealed their suffering. The sealed records of the illegitimate child's origins became an issue. Today, the children who are available for adoption are older and may be distressed by several years in care. Fundamental to helping these adopted children and their families there needs to be a multi-disciplined therapeutic approach to try and mitigate the damage that has often been done to the early infant brain through trauma. This book brings to life some of the adoption issues through the study of personal memoirs. Each chapter considers adoption from a different angle: the adopted child, the birth mother, the birth father, foster parents and adopting parents. The final chapter discusses some of the problems around adoption that have arisen again with reproductive technology and surrogate mothering.

This book will be of value to all those who have been involved in or affected by adoption. It will be of special interest to those adopting parents who have not been properly prepared or supported in their magnificent work of taking on some of the most troubled children in our society.

Prophecy Coles is a retired psychotherapist. In all she has written she has been pursuing the idea that the relationships we have with those other than our parents can leave a lasting impression on the patterns of our adult life. Her publications include, *The Importance of Sibling Relationships in Psychoanalysis, Sibling Relationships, The Uninvited Guest from the Unremembered Past, The Shadow of the Second Mother* and *Psychoanalytic and Psychotherapeutic Perspectives on Stepfamilies and Stepparenting.*

Psychoanalytic Perspectives on Illegitimacy, Adoption and Reproduction Technology
Strangers as Kin

Prophecy Coles

LONDON AND NEW YORK

First published 2021
by Routledge
2 Park Square, Milton Park, Abingdon, Oxon OX14 4RN

and by Routledge
52 Vanderbilt Avenue, New York, NY 10017

Routledge is an imprint of the Taylor & Francis Group, an informa business

© 2021 Prophecy Coles

The right of Prophecy Coles to be identified as author of this work has been asserted by her in accordance with sections 77 and 78 of the Copyright, Designs and Patents Act 1988.

All rights reserved. No part of this book may be reprinted or reproduced or utilised in any form or by any electronic, mechanical, or other means, now known or hereafter invented, including photocopying and recording, or in any information storage or retrieval system, without permission in writing from the publishers.

Trademark notice: Product or corporate names may be trademarks or registered trademarks, and are used only for identification and explanation without intent to infringe.

British Library Cataloguing-in-Publication Data
A catalogue record for this book is available from the British Library

Library of Congress Cataloging-in-Publication Data
Names: Coles, Prophecy, author.
Title: Psychoanalytic perspectives on illegitimacy, adoption and reproduction technology : strangers as kin / Prophecy Coles.
Description: New York : Routledge, 2020. | Includes bibliographical references and index. |
Identifiers: LCCN 2020006206 (print) | LCCN 2020006207 (ebook) | ISBN 9780367367428 (paperback) | ISBN 9780367367411 (hardback) | ISBN 9780429351099 (ebook)
Subjects: LCSH: Illegitimacy. | Adopted children--Psychology. | Birthmothers--Psychology. | Foster parents. | Adoptive parents. | Stepfamilies--Psychological aspects.
Classification: LCC HQ998 .C65 2020 (print) | LCC HQ998 (ebook) | DDC 306.874--dc23
LC record available at https://lccn.loc.gov/2020006206
LC ebook record available at https://lccn.loc.gov/2020006207

ISBN: 978-0-367-36741-1 (hbk)
ISBN: 978-0-367-36742-8 (pbk)
ISBN: 978-0-429-35109-9 (ebk)

Typeset in Times
by Taylor & Francis Books

Contents

Acknowledgments		viii
Introduction		1
1	Some of the myths surrounding illegitimacy and adoption	10
2	Bastardy	21
3	The prelude to the Adoption Act of 1926	33
4	Birth mother, illegitimacy and adoption	46
5	Fathers and their illegitimate sons and daughters	59
6	Foster carers	75
7	The adopted child	86
8	Adopting parents today	104
9	Reproductive adoption	125
Index		141

Acknowledgments

This book could not have been written without the contributions of the following people: Silvia Biggs, David Black, Sue Boyd, Adrian Briggs, Adam Burnell, Faye Carey, Karen Ciclitiva, Coline Covington, Sophie Fletcher, Angela Foster, Kath Gott, Sarah Hadland, Melanie Hart, Anna Hopewell, Bob Hinshelwood, Maggie Huntingdon-Whitleley, Penny Jacques, Dennis Judd, Dorothy Judd, Jeanne Kaniuk, Kate Langley, Jeanne Magagna, John Mason, Graham Music, Lucy Peppiat, Eilish Quinn, Ann Scott, Laurie Slade, Jennifer Silverstone, Kate Springford, Jill Steward, Tanya Stobbs and Annabel Tarrant.

I also wish to thank Alan Hall from the Wandsworth Library who was able to borrow all the books I needed. Without the continuing support of Kate Hawes, the Commissioning Editor of Routledge, this book would not have been written. I also wish to thank Hannah Wright who has overseen the production of this book and Lusana Taylor who has meticulously edited the script.

Thank you to all my family who have taken an interest in my endeavour. I dedicate this book to Walter, whose support, through the many transcripts that I have asked him to read, has been tireless.

Introduction

When I came to the end of my last book on stepchildren and stepparents my daughter-in-law Tanya Stobbs asked me a far-reaching question: 'Are there similarities between being a step-child and an adopted child?'[1] Her question jolted me into thinking how little I knew about the adopted child. Did they travel the same or a different path to that of a stepchild? If their path was different where did it lie? As I have researched this book, I have discovered a world that the adopted child uniquely encounters and which carries an historical legacy that is quite different to that of a stepchild. In answer to Tanya's question I try to show that the adopted child experiences a world that has few similarities to that of a stepchild.

My lack of knowledge about the difficulties of adoption and the consequences upon a person's life is well reflected in a clinical example from the days when I was training to be a psychotherapist. I worked in a clinic that offered once a week therapy for one year only. This was in the early eighties. I saw a lonely fifty-year-old unmarried man, whom I shall call Kenneth, and with my supervisor, we called him 'the man who wasn't there.' He had been referred for mild depression and anxiety that his drinking was getting out of control. Why we called him 'the man who wasn't there' was that his presence seemed evanescent even though he complied with all the rules, such as arriving on time and talking freely. He would give a detailed account of his week, and the amount of alcohol he had drunk and then turn to me for my supposedly therapeutic insight. For my part I came to dread making any comment on what he said because he would leap to agree with me and, in doing so, I knew he was leaving himself behind. We tip-toed around his early life and he vehemently maintained that his adoption at a few months old was of no consequence and he was not in the least bit interested in thinking about his natural parents. It needs to be remembered that he was adopted in the 1930s when birth records were sealed. So my understanding of the difficulties an adopted child might face as he or she grew up was effectively 'sealed off' from me when I encountered Kenneth, and I made no substantial contribution to his understanding of his mild depression and drinking problems.

It is only with hindsight that I have realised that one reason he 'wasn't there' was because his adoption had left him with a fragile sense of belonging anywhere. This meant that a therapy, that was already bound by an ending after one year, seemed to confirm his profound non-verbal belief that he was not wanted

2   Introduction

and therefore it was too dangerous to be present. My lack of understanding was compounded by the fact that I did not work with children, where adoption issues were more likely to appear. The Tavistock Clinic had set up a specialist team dealing with adoption and fostering in the Child and Family Department in the 1980s, but I did not come across their work until I began to do research for this book.[2] It is from the position of ignorance about the psychic impact of Kenneth's adoption that I have set out to understand better the consequences on all who are part of this process. On this journey I shall hope to show the benefits that adoption has provided for couples who could not have children. It will also become clear that adoption has been a creative solution for most of the children whose parents cannot look after them. However, I have also learned that adoption is not in all cases the ideal solution that is hoped, and an adopted child who has experienced early infant trauma may be very distressed and even violent and this can lead to a breakdown in some adopting families.

Before I begin it is perhaps important to state some of the ideas and beliefs that underpin my exploration. My formative years were spent in the depths of the country on a farm and far from schools or shops. My constant companions were my siblings, but my other allies were the animals that surrounded us and that I loved. Looking back on our early childhood I believe I drew strength from the relationships with all those who lived around us, but I was also comforted by the enduring natural and animal world that sustained our way of life. Nevertheless, there was symbolically a darker side to the life that went on around me. There was the experience of hearing a cow's distressed lowing for her calf, if it was taken away, that embedded itself in my mind. I was made aware that a farmer's actions could upset the 'natural' order of things, or in my childish mind, mothers and their young needed each other. I don't want to impugn the particular farmer that I am referring to, as he was one of the kindest and most stable men I knew in my childhood. He was like an enduring oak tree. But the actions that led him into taking the calves away from their mothers was symbolic of a system that was capitalising upon providing more milk that would make him more money. This was little comfort to a child, and the pain I felt as I heard the distressed cows calling for their calves left a long-lasting memory. I have been reminded again of the sound as I have learned about how young unmarried girls were forced to give up their child for adoption and their babies were left in the arms of strangers. In the agonised words of Anne Sexton (1964) 'You sense the way we belong/... You will not know me very long.'[3]

There came a change, as I turned away from farm life in adolescence, and I discovered on the book shelves of my parents' extensive library, Joanna Field's (1934) *A Life of One's Own*. [4] This book awoke me to the challenging possibility that I had an inner world that I knew little about and Field seemed to provide a way of discovering its contours. This approach gradually allowed me to develop a way of thinking about what I had found so distressing about cows being separated from their calves, and, in time, this led me to enter the psychotherapy world. There I eventually found a door had been opened about the importance of mothering, and I stepped easily into the shoes of Bowlby's psychobiological attachment theory.

Introduction   3

I have always felt that Bowlby's attachment theory redressed an imbalance in the delicate demarcation between the conceptualisation of the inner and outer world of psychological theory. It makes sense that the need to feel physically safe and held is the primary experience if one is to survive well. It follows from this view that the way a child is treated is the place to start understanding psychological anxiety and the patterns of relating. At the same time this theory also embraces the importance of the mother's state of mind. A securely attached mother will treat her baby in such a way that he or she will become in turn securely attached. Disturbance in the early months of life with a mother who is herself disorientated or distressed will have the effect of disrupting the relationship with the baby. This has led to a deeper understanding of the way intergenerational patterns of behaviour are laid down from the earliest days of mental life, not only from 'father to son' but now from mother to child as well.

When it comes to understanding some of the anxieties surrounding the experience of adoption the expansion of Bowlby's attachment theory into the world of neuroscience has been most illuminating. Neuroscientists have discovered a vital link between the synchrony of the infant brain and the brain of the mother, rhythmically beating together, as it were. This has led to the mapping of the stages of infant brain development and, through the use of brain scans, we can see the disruptive effect that early trauma has upon this delicate structure. The evidence shows that the developing brain can be damaged if the child is left alone too long in an unmanageable state of fear or anxiety. A mother or caretaker is essential to soothe or contain the infant state of mind and without this continuing experience the infant develops a reactive response of fight/flight or disengagement, or in the words of Emily Dickinson (1830–1886) 'There is a pain – so utter/ It swallows substance up – /Then covers the abyss with trance/ So memory can step/Around – across.'[5] These insights of neuroscience become increasingly important when it comes to understanding the difficulties of adopted children who have faced several years of broken attachments.

Finally, one of the most important insights that attachment theory has given me is the belief that children are not born delinquent or neurotic and their wills do not need to be broken, but they can become dis-functional when the conditions of their upbringing are chaotic and unstable or cruel. When my eldest child was born in the late 1950s an elderly acquaintance visited me and with great conviction she assured me that I would be laying up any amount of trouble for myself in the future if I did not break his will. I must never respond to his cries. What might have happened to him if I had followed her belief? Remembering the cows and their calves on the farm of my childhood, what I have valued above all in attachment theory is that the belief that the way we treat each other is cardinal in understanding all our behaviour. There is an important caveat to that idea; there is research evidence, such as in the work of Rutter (1985), that has shown that there are some children who in spite of a chaotic upbringing are resilient and manage a creative life. Resilience is an important concept that needs to be valued and remembered, yet those with this capacity are a minority. The majority of young people in remand homes and prison today have travelled the road of unstable

4   Introduction

care. So to return to the exhortation I was given to break the will of my eldest son, it made me aware not only of how different this elderly woman's beliefs about child care were in comparison to mine, but it has led me to try and understand the underlying beliefs and values that are given to child care by a particular society at a particular time. In the end I have been led to conclude that if there is any universal truth to be discovered about human behaviour it is more likely to be discovered by the way we bring up our children.

How to begin? I have always found it easier to understand a problem by asking myself about its historical antecedents, so I have structured this book along an historical trajectory. I begin in Chapter One with three myths about adopted children: Moses, Ion and Oedipus. The point I wanted to make about Moses was that adoption did not crush him; on the contrary he rose above his experience and became a hero. In that sense he became an iconic figure for the success of adoption and this must surely have played into the expectations and cultural beliefs that adopted children can flourish and triumph. The next hero is less well-known and yet his fictitious life is much nearer to the real experiences of adopted children. Ion is the hero of the Euripides' play of the same name. In this play Euripides explores the conflicting emotions that a young mother experiences when she gives up her illegitimate son; at the same time Euripides describes the complicated emotions that an adopted person can have when he meets his mother in adulthood. There is pain and there is murderous rage and disillusionment, on both sides, but a creative resolution is possible. The final myth I consider, with some trepidation, as he is the shibboleth of psychoanalytic theory, is the tragedy of Sophocles' *Oedipus*. I was struck by the contrast to the Euripides myth of Ion and I found the most chilling aspect of the Oedipus myth is that his whole royal Theban family dies out, there are no more progenitors and there is no future for that family. What was Sophocles telling us? The moral I want to draw from this myth is that the destruction begins when Oedipus' parents wanted to get rid of him. It is this murderous wish and the ensuing lies that accompany Oedipus' survival that lead to the final tragedy. This is certainly not a myth that embraces the success of adoption, but its power propels us to confront the fact that some parents can have murderous wishes towards their children and if these wishes are acted upon there can be unintended and destructive consequences. From these three myths I wanted to show that there have been heroic myths about adopted children, who went on to flourish and become leaders, and this has been important in sustaining the positive belief in adoption. There is a middle road, as we saw in the myth of Ion, where there are profound psychological difficulties but they can be resolved. Finally, there can be a darker side to adoption, as exemplified in the myth of Oedipus, that still casts a shadow.

In Chapter Two I follow the darker fears that have accompanied the illegitimate child and show how they became particularly acute following the Reformation in the sixteenth century. For about four hundred years there was no economic help for an unmarried woman with an illegitimate child and so she would be impelled to place her child in a Workhouse, where its chances of survival were slight. The

Introduction 5

mother's plight, and that of her child, was compounded by common law that stated her child was a *'filius nullius'* or a child of no man, and so in this way the father of an illegitimate child had no legal or financial responsibility to care for his child. The published *A Memoir of Robert Blincoe*, born in 1792, and Dickens' *Oliver Twist*, all too painfully record the child slavery that was inflicted upon the unwanted child if it managed to survive.

In Chapter Three I follow the life of the illegitimate and unwanted child that begins to change for the better by the end of the nineteenth century. The two Great Wars forced the nation to recognise that the way they had treated their poorest children meant that there were not enough healthy and strong young men to defend the nation; in response, a lot of new legislation was brought in, such as compulsory education, school meals and a Ministry of Health. The Adoption Act of 1926 pioneered by the philanthropist Clara Andrew promoted a new way of looking after the illegitimate child; it should be adopted by a couple who were unable to have a child of their own. In contrast Lettice Fisher founded the National Council for the Unmarried Mother and her Child (the N.C.U.M.C.) and she set up homes for unmarried mothers and children. She advocated that adoption should only be the last resort if a mother could not look after her own child. At the time of this debate the Tavistock Clinic was founded to deal with traumatised soldiers returning from the war in 1920. Gradually it added radical ways of thinking about children. Freud's ideas about early childhood, Klein's ideas about mothers and babies and Bion's theory of the emotional containment provided by the mother, were all helping to develop new ideas about the significance of early childhood. It was, in particular, Bowlby's observations on the importance of the attachment of mothers and babies that helped to change the focus of attention upon the trauma of broken attachments in early childhood. The future for the illegitimate child began to undergo a radical change for the better.

There was still a lot to understand about the complexity of adoption, and the area that had been most neglected was the emotional experience of the unmarried mother who, through social pressures, was forced to give up her child for adoption. She was seldom thought about in the rush to implement these new ideas that followed the Adoption Act of 1926, except to imagine she was relieved to be free of her responsibility. Chapter Four explores the unrecognised suffering of the birth mother, who was morally condemned and at the same time expected to hand over her baby to an adoption agency. To add to her pain, it was assumed that she had no maternal feelings towards the child she was expected to give away. The suffering that these young birth mothers experienced was at its most extreme in the Irish Magdalene Laundries, but even Protestant Mother and Baby Homes exacted their punishment. Happily, by the late 1960s research was beginning to recognise that birth mothers had suffered and at the same time these mothers were finding a space to voice their suffering.

The publishing of the memoirs of birth mothers and the opening up of the sealed records in 1976 in the UK brought about another surprising and positive change: a few fathers began to ask questions about their illegitimate children. This is the theme of Chapter Five. I had been outraged that the common law in

6   *Introduction*

the UK had allowed fathers of illegitimate children to escape and take no responsibility but I was relieved to discover that throughout history some fathers have behaved honourably towards their illegitimate children, such as Benjamin Franklin and Lord Chesterfield. But what became clear was that the oppressive prejudice against illegitimacy still strangled the most liberal father, and in the eighteenth and nineteenth centuries, their illegitimate sons were crushed by the prejudices that were held against them. It was not until the beginning of the twenty-first century that fathers began to express their feelings about having had an illegitimate child. Two writers that I look at, Gary Clapton (2003) and Gary Coles (2004), describe a sense of being connected to their unknown child by an invisible thread. Both fathers found, ironically, that the belief that an illegitimate child is a 'child of no man' counted against them because they were never expected to put their name on their child's birth certificate. They could only find their child through the mother. What is most significant about these two memoirs is that they token an important shift in the recognition that fathers have always had feelings about the children they have fathered, and the more liberal societies across the world are beginning to recognise that a birth father and his child are emotionally connected, however tenuous the actual connection may be.

The adoption triangle has been the image that has been used by most research, but it is clear as the years have gone on that more than three people – the birth mother, the adopted child and the adopting mother – are involved in adoption. It was suggested in Chapter Five that the father now needs to be included in any consideration, and in Chapter Six I describe a crucially important figure in the adoption circle, namely the foster mother. I had already cited Pythia the foster mother of Ion in the Euripides' play, in Chapter One, and I suggested she was one of the earliest iconic figures of the loving foster mother. On the other side the foster mother has had another unfortunate image. Historically, she often exploited her position when she took in the illegitimate child of a desperate young mother who had nothing with which to support her child, and this child usually met an early and premeditated death. Today the foster mother has an unimaginably difficult role to play in the unfolding life of an adopted child. She may be expected to look after a new-born baby, who has had to be taken away from its mother for reasons of the child's safety. She may nurture this child for two or three years before an adoption order can be made and then the attachment is broken. The irony is that the way foster parenting is set up, it fosters broken attachments. I look at some significant work that has labelled this irony as a 'blind spot' and much innovative work is afoot to change the way foster carers are thought about. It needs to be noted that I have not dealt with the role of social workers in adoption.

In Chapter Seven I ask the question as to how the adopted child feels about its adoption. I look at some of the earliest research on that question undertaken by Mary McWhinnie (1967) in the 1950s. At the time it was an unwelcomed question to be asking but other research followed in the 1970s, and what gradually emerged was that all was not quite as well as had been hoped and some adopted children had not flourished. David Kirk (1985) in the US suggested that rather than shuffle the adopted child's records out of sight, society needed to recognise that the kinship structure of a family with adopted children was different from the usual family structure with naturally born children. Other voices began to be heard, not least adopted children asking why they were not allowed to know about their origins. The spearhead for this approach came again from the US, with such writers as Jean Paton (1968), Florence Fisher (1973) and Betty Lifton (1975). The flood gates opened and adopted children began to insist that it contravened their human right to be denied knowledge of their ancestral history. In 1976 the sealed records were opened in the UK. The accounts that began to emerge revealed unsuspected difficulties. Not all birth mothers were overjoyed to be found by their adopted children, especially if they had lived with the denial of the child's birth all their life. The child, now an adult, had to face the fantasies about the lost maternal object. Perhaps the most significant and controversial point that was being suggested was that a baby even adopted within a few weeks of birth suffered a 'primal wound' if it was separated from his or her mother. I end the chapter with Jeanette Winterson's (2011) book on her adoption, *Why Be Happy When You Could Be Normal?;* it stands as one of the most searing accounts of the difficulties that an adopted child can face.

Chapter Eight is concerned with the experience of adopting parents. Adopting a child today is quite different to the days when the Adoption Act came into force in the 1920s; apart from anything else the stigma of illegitimacy no longer holds sway and so young mothers are not under social pressure to give up their child. The children that are available for adoption within the UK, unless one is prepared to go overseas to find a baby for adoption, are older and described as 'hard to place'. The strain that is put upon adopting parents to nurture these children is often hard to bear. The children will have experienced a chaotic early life of broken attachments. This is where the work of Bowlby and the development of attachment theory has been crucially important in helping everyone understand how to deal with these damaged children. I take Ann Kimble Loux's (1997) book *The Limits of Hope* as an example of the difficulties of late adoption. This is a painful account of the author adopting two sisters whose background she knew nothing about. She faced little help and seeming ignorance about the damage that had been done to these two sisters before they were adopted. I contrast this book with the work that was starting to be done in the UK in the 1980s by several adoption societies who were recognising the difficulties adopting parents faced with these troubled children. In particular, I look at the work done by an organisation called 'Family Futures', and there we see a remarkable long-term multidisciplined approach to helping adopting parents and these troubled children. Their work supports the thesis of Graham Music (2019) who wrote, 'we are on the cusp of a paradigm shift in therapeutic work, one requiring an integration of multiple orientations, from neurobiology, attachment theory, psychoanalysis, systemic thinking and more.'[6]

8 *Introduction*

In Chapter Nine, my final chapter, I touch on the adoption of children who have been born through reproductive technology. What arrested my attention was the fact that fertility treatment has been dealing with some of the same anxieties that had arisen in the earlier days of adoption. Now the problem was expressed in the language of sperm donors and egg donors, but the question remained the same: should these donors remain anonymous and unknown to their future children? I discovered an even more complicated issue that arose in the case of surrogate mothers. In this situation, if an infertile couple resorted to contracting a surrogate mother to bear their child, the surrogate mother was legally the 'natural' mother and this child that she had carried for nine months, had to be adopted by the 'other' infertile mother. The emotional ramifications on everyone are still unfolding and little seems to have been remembered about the earlier conflicts around adoption and the existential problems for the child of having two mothers. Accompanying surrogate mothering, there is another issue that needs more research, and was well described by a surrogate mother Elisabeth Kane (1988). When the surrogate baby she had carried for nine months was given away to the infertile couple, the disappearing baby had a devastating effect upon her three children. Was it dead? Had she killed it? Why could they not see it? Wasn't it their brother? The family was never the same again and the children developed profound psychological anxieties. We are at the foothills of the new kinship structures that are created when children are adopted today through assisted reproduction, and the psychological consequences and implications are yet to be discovered. To answer Tanya's question, I hope I have shown that at the very least the life of an adopted child is very different to that of a stepchild.

Notes

1 Coles (2018)
2 Kendrick, Lindsey & Tollemache (2006)
3 Sexton (1964) I need to thank Jeanne Magagna who directed me to Sexton's anguished poem, 'Unknown Girl in a Maternity Ward.'
4 Joanna Field was the pseudonym that Marion Milner assumed at the time of this publication.
5 quoted in Nafisi (2010) p. 129.
6 Music (2019) p.2.

References

G. Clapton (2003) *Birth Fathers and their Adoption Experiences*. Philadelphia/London: Jessica Kingsley Publishers.
G. Coles (2004) *Ever After. Fathers and the Impact of Adoption*. South Australia: Clova Publications.
P. Coles (2018) *Psychoanalytic and Psychotherapeutic Perspectives on Stepfamilies and Stepparenting*. London/New York: Routledge.
J. Field (1934) *A Life of One's Own*. London: Little, Brown Book Group.
A. Fisher (1973) *The Search for Annie Fisher*. New York: Arthur Fields Books, Inc.

Introduction 9

S. Freud (1923) *The Ego and the Id*. S.E. 19. London: Hogarth Press.

E. Kane (1988) *Birth Mother*. San Diego/New York/London:Harcourt Brace Jovanovich.

J. Kendrick, C. Lindsey & L. Tollemache (eds) (2006) *Creating New Families: Therapeutic Approaches to Fostering, Adoption and Kinship Care*. London: Karnac Books.

A. Kimble Loux (1997) *The Limits of Hope*. Charlottesville/London: University of Virginia Press.

H.D. Kirk (1985) *Adoptive Kinship: A Modern Institution in Need of Reform*. US/Canada: Ben-Simon Publications. B. Lifton (1975) *Twice Born: Memoirs of an Adopted Daughter*. New York: McGraw Hill.

M. Main & R. Goldwyn (1988) Predicting rejection of her infant from mother's representation of her own experience: Implication for the abused-abuser intergenerational cycle. *International Journal of Child Abuse and Neglect*. 8. 203–217.

M. McWhinnie (1967) *Adopted Children: How They Grow Up: A Study of Their Adjustment as Adults*. London: Routledge & Kegan Paul.

G. Music (2019) *Nurturing Children: From Trauma to Growth Using Attachment Theory, Psychoanalysis and Neurobiology*. Oxford/New York: Routledge.

A. Nafisi (2010) *Things I Have Been Silent About*. London: Windmill Books.

J. Paton (1968) *Orphan Voyage*. New York: Vantage Press.

M. Rutter (1985) Resilience in the face of adversity and protective factors and resistance to psychiatric disorder. *British Journal of Psychiatry*. 147. 598–611.

A. Schore (1994) *Affect Regulation and the Origin of the Self*. New Jersey: Lawrence Erlbaum Associates.

A. Sexton (1964) *Selected Poems*. Oxford: Oxford University Press.

J. Winterson (2011) *Why Be Happy When You Could Be Normal?*London: Jonathan Cape.

1 Some of the myths surrounding illegitimacy and adoption

Lady Bracknell in Oscar Wilde's *The Importance of Being Earnest* was most concerned when Jack, her prospective son-in-law could not give any account of his parentage. '... to be born, or at any rate bred, in a handbag, whether it had handles or not, seems to me to display a contempt for the ordinary decencies of family life that reminds one of the worst excesses of the French Revolution,' she remarked.[1] Wilde's satire on the fate of the illegitimate child was an immediate success. It highlighted the absurd myth that an illegitimate child was seen as a child of nobody and had no name, but it also brought to the audience's attention the more subversive fear that the birth of an illegitimate child was a threat to the proper ordering of polite society.

The deep-seated fear of the illegitimate child has run uneasily through the social history of child-care. The anxiety became more acute in Western society following the Reformation in the sixteenth century, and from that moment on, the illegitimate child was seen to be a pariah in society, with no legal status or inheritance rights. As if that was not enough, the child was also tarnished by a belief that it was a disruptive force threatening the stability of family life both ethically and economically. I am going to suggest that the idea that the illegitimate child is innately flawed seems to hover in the shadows of our cultural imagination, whether East or West, and the ever-present ghosts of the child's heredity and the uninvited guests of the child's 'natural' parents are seldom laid to rest.[2] With this thought in mind, I am going to look at some of the early myths that have surrounded the illegitimate or unwanted child as I believe such tales can help us to see more clearly the way that this ancient anxiety still lingers and clouds our thinking about illegitimacy and adoption.

Moses was the son of Israelite slaves born in Egypt. The ruling Pharaoh, anxious about a potential Israelite uprising, ordered all first-born sons to be killed. Moses' mother, as is well known, hid him in a basket in the bulrushes, where later he was discovered crying by the Pharaoh's daughter. It seems that Moses' mother must have been lingering nearby because she was told by the Pharaoh's daughter to feed him and look after him, and then bring him to her. Soon after this incident the Pharaoh's daughter, who was childless, adopted him, but Moses' mother continued to look after him and feed him. When Moses grew up, he got into conflict with Egyptian society as he never forgot that he was a Hebrew being

Myths surrounding illegitimacy and adoption 11

brought up as though he were an Egyptian. In *Exodus*, we learn that on one occasion 'he spied an Egyptian smiting a Hebrew ... he slew the Egyptian.' It quickly followed that 'When the Pharaoh heard of this he ruled that Moses must be killed.' Moses fled and was eventually called upon by God to bring the Israelites out of Egypt into the 'land flowing with milk and honey.' And thereby found a state for the Jews.[3] For the Jews it was a most significant tale, for the Egyptians it was more humiliating.

One of the arresting features of this myth is that it is a tale about how an adopted child can threaten the society in which she or he grows up, especially if he or she is of another race or tribe. Moses, who knew he was the child of an Israelite slave, never forgot the way the Egyptians could treat these people. He could not take on the identity of an Egyptian, even though he had been adopted by one and brought up as though he was one. I think here one can catch a glimpse of a belief that has run through most societies, namely the importance of genetic inheritance. In this myth Moses makes us aware that he has a different blood line, and such a fact does not fit in easily with the otherwise ordered system of inheritance and succession of his Egyptian upbringing.

This iconoclastic potential of the adopted child has been deeply disturbing in the cultural history of both East and West. At the very least it turns upside down the altruistic intention of the adoption, namely to nurture an unwanted child. The Pharaoh's daughter had found Moses supposedly abandoned in the bulrushes, crying, and had immediately responded with care and concern. It follows that the adopted child is expected to be grateful, but that is often not so. In the myth about Moses, furthermore, we have an adopted child who threatens the old order by his behaviour. He is filled with conflict and this is enacted in a murderous rage when he sees an Israelite slave being maltreated. This murderous rage that can be ignited when an act of injustice is felt, is an important emotional reaction that besets many adopted children, as we shall see in the two following myths I consider. My intention here is to do no more than suggest that in this myth Moses presented a challenge for all concerned, not least because it involved clashes of race and class and the blood line.

I am now going to turn to Euripides' (480–406 BC) play *Ion* because it illustrates the way in which an adopted child's family history, or blood line, is pivotal to the complexities and anxieties of adoption.[4] This is a play about the mythical history of Ion who was abandoned by his mother and was brought up 'fatherless and motherless.'[5] I shall not detail all the twists and turns of the play as I want to keep to the central insight that Euripides had about mothers and their illegitimate children. The background to the play was that the heroine, Creusa, was raped by Apollo when he saw her picking flowers in a field. She felt full of shame and could not tell her parents, so she hid her baby son in a cave. When she returned a few days later he had disappeared and she imagined he had been devoured by wild animals. In fact, he had been rescued by Apollo and taken to Delphi where he had been brought up by Hermes and Pythia.

The play begins when many years later, Creusa and her husband Xuthus come to consult the Delphic Oracle about Creusa's infertility. As they arrive

12 *Myths surrounding illegitimacy and adoption*

they meet Ion, now a handsome young man, who is sweeping the steps. There is a moment of recognition between mother and son as they look at each other and wonder why they are both so stirred. This tension now radiates the play as we wonder whether and by what means they can discover that they are indeed related. There were no legal documents for the handing over of Ion to be adopted by Hermes and Pythia, the Prophetess of the Delphic Oracle, and no-one dares question Apollo. This dilemma is strangely reminiscent of the difficulty illegitimate children have had because their birth documents were hidden from them until the late twentieth century in the UK.

The play now moves into the somewhat improbable drama of Ion's stepfather, Xuthus, who tried to claim that he was Ion's father. Gilbert Murray's translation of the play that I have followed, makes the point that Xuthus is a blundering figure of fun who served to highlight Euripides' belief that there is a 'cry of blood' that exists between biologically related people.[6] Creusa and Ion knew intuitively that they were connected because of this blood kinship, whereas Ion remained coldly detached from Xuthus. He was asked to believe that Xuthus may have conceived him at a Bacchanalian feast sometime in the past and grudgingly he is forced to accept this possibility. The false connection that Xuthus tries to impose upon Ion has a dramatic consequence that leads both Creusa and Ion into a murderous rage with each other.

We can assume that Creusa's rage about her rape had been simmering in the cauldron of her imagination since Ion's birth, but now when Xuthus asserts that he is Ion's father, she is incandescent at his self-deception that threatens to push her again into a position where her pain and knowledge is ignored. She knows how Ion was conceived and for Xuthus to claim the rights of paternity dismisses her experience and turns her into a blind rage. She plots to poison Xuthus for being so mendacious, but she also plans to poison Ion for believing this lie.

Her plot fails, but not before Ion also gets in touch with his own murderous rage when he learns that Creusa is plotting to poison him at the feast that is to celebrate Xuthus' paternity. Ion decides to stone her to death. Here we see that Ion's violent wish is linked to his existential sense of loss and disappointment. He had suffered a lifetime of ignorance about his family history, and now, just within grasp of discovery, his life is threatened by the very person with whom he had felt some empathy and warmth.

The possible tragedy of both mother and son killing each other is saved in a dramatic way. Pythia, the woman who had raised Ion, appears. She was Ion's foster mother, as we would call her today, as she had brought him up, and it was clear that Ion loved her. 'Mother, though not in flesh, mother in love!'[7] At this moment in the play when Creusa and Ion's rage threaten their lives, Pythia brings in the cradle that Ion had been put in by his mother. Pythia had kept other tokens including the 'childish sampler' that Creusa had sewn for him. In other words, Pythia had preserved something of Ion's biological history, and this was long before written records were made. These tokens served to confirm that Creusa was Ion's mother and both mother and son could now safely embrace each other. But what is so moving in terms of contemporary history is that the discovery of

Myths surrounding illegitimacy and adoption 13

Creusa's sampler links to the 'tokens' that have often been left with an abandoned child. For instance, in the Museum of the Coram Foundling Hospital, in Coram Fields in London, founded in the eighteenth century by Thomas Coram (1668–1751) there are cases of 'tokens', sometimes no more than a half button, left by anguished mothers. Whatever the token, it represented an enduring link between mother and child, and in the case of the half button, the mother would keep the other half in the hope that one day she might be able to claim back her child with this token of identity. That day seldom dawned.[8]

In the closing pages of the drama, Creusa and Ion are reconciled, but it is only the beginning of another journey. Ion is left with many of the complicated feelings that orphaned and adopted children have expressed. 'Thinking of her, my mother, stealthily-wise/wedded, who sought to expel me far away/ unwanted; never on her breast I lay;/A slave's life, nameless, in god's house I had.' He continues to be dismayed that a mother could have behaved as she did and he is angry at the deprivation he has suffered, adding '… All the time I should/have lived enwrapped in happy babyhood,/and known life's joy, I was cut off, exiled/ From the fond life a mother gives her child.' In the end however he reflects that his mother had suffered as well. 'Poor mother, too! She likewise from her boy/she had born cut off, n'er knew a mother's joy.'[9]

This is only a partial resolution for Ion because he is still left with questions about his paternity, as indeed are most of the children who were adopted before the possibility of seeing their birth records. The ending is ambiguous. Ion has a message from Apollo not to be angry even though Ion can never have it confirmed that Apollo is his father because Apollo is a god and must remain secret.[10] This may seem disappointing, but culturally the problem of paternity goes beyond gods and mortals. The problem that has always beset men is the question 'how can I be sure that this is my child?' What I have taken from this strange ending is that if we take Euripides' play as a paradigm about adoption, then as Rachel Bowlby (2007) suggests, '… the desirability of openness … of origin may … divide a child who comes to know or is presented with different and mutually jarring stories.'[11] Or put a slightly different way Euripides is bringing to our attention that the child, who is brought up in a family that is not his own, will have a hard time reconciling himself to his complicated experiences of two mothers and two fathers; in Ion's case, Pythia and Creusa, and Xuthus and Apollo.

What is so arresting about this play is that it is not just about an abandoned child, it is also about the agony a mother feels when she is forced by external circumstances to give up her child. Euripides understood, two thousand years ago, something that we have only recently begun to acknowledge, namely the complexity of emotions that a mother feels when she has to give up her baby. What he also understood was that a child has a perilous sense of identity if she or he does not know who his or her parents are. Euripides also observed that a mother who gives up her child can suffer from subsequent infertility and that is quite central to the play. This type of infertility, that one might call emotional infertility, is now an accepted possibility and some women, who give up their

14 *Myths surrounding illegitimacy and adoption*

children at birth, later find themselves infertile even though there is no biological reason.[12] Euripides understood this and many other things about the emotional hazards of being a woman with an unwanted pregnancy. It is for this reason that Euripides has appealed to many women. Euripides was born into a fiercely paternalistic Greek society, yet he was critical of the way men have treated women who conceive their illegitimate child. He had no fear of voicing the view that society has turned a blind eye to men's irresponsible behaviour towards such women. Not surprisingly this play has been read as one of the earliest feminist tracts.[13] In the words of Creusa, ''Ah, women still/Are born to suffer, gods to work their will!/How else? What help is there, when those who do/The wrong that slays us are our judges too?''[14]

I think it is also worth returning to Pythia in the role of the foster mother, as such women are often the unsung heroes of adoption. The foster mother may step in and look after a new-born baby that has been taken away at birth from a mother who is unable to manage, or when a mother decides to hand over her child to an adoption agency. In many cases she is literally a life-saver, and can make an everlasting imprint upon the psyche of the child she has looked after, especially if her care has lasted several years in earliest childhood. The foster mother stands in an intermediate position of being as Ion said, a mother 'not in flesh' but a mother 'in love.' She is, one might say, the custodian of the child's history. And in the case of Pythia it is her knowledge of Ion's birth history that calms the tempestuous emotions that are lashing both mother and son.

The last myth that I am now going to consider casts a darker shadow across the adoption process even to this day. It confronts us with the more negative feelings some parents may have towards their children. This is the myth of Oedipus, and though it is not about an illegitimate child it is about an unwanted child who is rejected by his parents and is then adopted. Oedipus is undoubtedly the most famous hero within the psychotherapy world. He holds centre stage for the Freudian theory that 'It is the fate of all of us, perhaps, to direct our first sexual impulses towards our mother and our first hatred and our first murderous wish against our father.'[15] One result has been that within Freudian psychoanalysis the attention has been directed towards the sexual fantasies contained in the inner world of the child as it develops and has been less concerned with the events that surrounded his life. Yet, reading Sophocles' *Oedipus the King* with the idea that Oedipus' adoption and his parents' attitude towards him underwrite the unfolding tragedy, I have found the myth to be a helpful reminder of some of the complicated feelings that can accompany adoption.[16]

I need to add some background information to the Oedipus myth that comes from Aeschylus in his play *Seven against Thebes* and from Euripides' play *The Phoenician Woman*. These plays help to fill out the history of the Oedipus myth by making clear that Oedipus' tragedy rests upon the preceding generational history. Laius' father, who was King of Thebes, had died when Laius was a year old, and he and his mother were turned out of the court by his uncle who took over the throne. As an angry and disinherited young man Laius was staying in the court of King Pelops and had an affair and abducted Chrisippus, the

Myths surrounding illegitimacy and adoption 15

illegitimate son of King Pelops. Chrisippus subsequently died. The affair was considered to be an unforgivable crime because it broke the bounds of courtly behaviour and this incited Apollo's anger. Apollo decreed that if Laius was to have a son, his son would kill him and marry his mother. From these two plays we see that Laius' behaviour as a young man is pivotal to the unfolding tragedy in which all the members of this Theban family are annihilated. It also illustrates the way that the unconscious determination of Oedipus' life rests upon his generational history. This reading of Sophocles' tragedy suggests that the actions of our ancestors are entangled in our family history. However, I am not saying that the background history of an adopted child implies the contravention of a 'natural law', or put another way, I am not suggesting that there is something 'unnatural' about being an adopted child. Nor am I concluding that the adopted child will bring about death and destruction to kinship structures. But Oedipus' journey, as he searches for the truth about his origins, does have close parallels to the difficulties that can accompany adoption when records are sealed and the child is lied to about his or her parentage.

It is well-known that Oedipus was not wanted and was given to two shepherds by his parents, Jocasta and Laius, to be put on a mountain where he might possibly be devoured by wild animals. In fact, the two shepherds, like good social workers, give him to the childless King and Queen of Corinth, Polybus and Merope, and he is adopted. In adolescence he hears that Polybus and Merope are not his parents and when he consults the Delphic Oracle he is told that he will kill his father and marry his mother. He flees from Corinth towards Thebes in order to avoid this fate, but on his journey he does kill his natural father Laius at a crossroads and marries his mother, Jocasta, the widowed Theban Queen. The plague returns to Thebes after sixteen years of Oedipus' rule as King of Thebes, and Oedipus is forced to face the truth of the Oracle. Jocasta kills herself and he blinds himself with her brooch and is led from the scene by his daughter Antigone.

If we take this myth as concerned with adoption, then it does illustrate a destructive history that may surround an adopted child. Oedipus' mother Jocasta had wanted a child and in order to achieve that end she has to seduce Laius when drunk, however, when she learned that Apollo had decreed that if Laius had a son he would be compelled to kill his father, she gave Oedipus away. What was her state of mind? She did not leave him with any loving 'tokens' that might link him back to her; instead she left him with deformed feet that had been pierced by a nail and tied together. So we could assume that, unlike most mothers who give up their child, she was angry. She might even be said to be revengeful. This attitude she maintains to the very end when she lies to Oedipus and denies she had any part in getting rid of him. So, in comparison to the myth of Ion and his mother, the Oedipus myth illustrates a very different maternal state of mind and one in which the mother (Jocasta) and Laius must have hoped that their son would not survive.

The play also highlights another consequence that can follow the lies and denial about an adopted child's origins. Incest becomes a possibility. From this

16 *Myths surrounding illegitimacy and adoption*

point of view, the myth is pointing to the necessity of knowing one's parentage if incest is to be avoided. There is a surprising lack of concern historically about the incestuous taboos being broken if a child's early history is denied or remains hidden. By the middle ages it was believed to be better to keep the child's 'bad blood' unrecorded so he or she could start again. It was only in 1975 that UK adoption agencies opened their sealed records and a child could find the original birth certificate and the name of his or her mother. Many adoptees over the centuries have not only felt an impotent anger at being blocked from knowing the truth about their lineage, but others have mockingly challenged the secrecy with the threat that they may well be in an incestuous relationship for all they know.[17] This anxiety was well expressed as long ago as the second century AD by an early Christian, Clement of Alexandria (150–216). In a quite matter of fact way he wrote, 'How many fathers, forgetting the children they have abandoned, unknowingly have sexual relations with a son who has become a prostitute or a daughter become a harlot?'[18] So we see that lies and denial about the blood ties between a child and its parents does raise the real possibility of incestuous acts, as the myth suggests. We are no longer in the realm of fantasy but in a much more unbounded realm of possibility.[19]

There is another important insight that the Oedipus myth illustrates. There is much greater acceptance today that the impact of cruelty or trauma affects a child's brain development and mental state. If a child is adopted there will have been events that preceded the adoption that can affect the child's emotional response to other people. One of Oedipus' earliest experiences will have been of agonising pain as a nail was put into his feet. This was then followed by being given away. If we imagine him as a child today then these traumatic incidents must have disturbed Oedipus' psyche and left him with many distressing feelings, in particular an inarticulate rage at the pain he suffered. On this account, as he developed we could imagine Oedipus as an angry and anxious young man and this state of mind will have been augmented by the failure of his adopting parents to tell him the truth about his origins when he asked. If they had done so, he would not have had to leave them and make his journey to Thebes.

Like many other adopted children, Oedipus' doubts about his identity begin to take a firm hold in adolescence following a drunken incident in which he heard that he was not the true child of his supposed parents.[20] There have been many well documented case histories of adopted children who, when they reach adolescence, begin to ask questions about their origins. They may be told by their companions at school that their parents are not their real parents, and this may confirm their suspicions. They then feel compelled to go on an Oedipus-type journey because they may know unconsciously that they have been deceived and this gives them the energy and desire to find out who they really are.

This way of understanding the Oedipus myth contradicts many psychoanalytic accounts that have interpreted the myth as confronting Oedipus' self-deception. It has been suggested he must have wondered about his damaged feet and he must have thought about the man he murdered at the crossroads. And then what was in his mind when he married a woman who was old enough to be his mother?[21] These are some

Myths surrounding illegitimacy and adoption 17

of the arguments that are brought to bear on the idea that the Oedipus myth follows the fate of self-deception. An alternative argument is to suggest that the foundation of self-deception is the result of being deceived as a child. How can you be sure of anything if the very foundation of your life has begun on a truth being denied you? Who can you trust? Where indeed does the truth lie? The myth of Oedipus helps us to understand that his adoption had tragic consequences because he was deceived. Today we believe that a child should know who his or her parents are and be helped to face the truth of why he or she was given up for adoption, otherwise as Murray (1958) said, a 'moral offence' is committed and a 'monstrous human pollution' may be let loose.[22] That is not to say that Oedipus' parents, or any other parents who cannot manage to love and care for their children, are entirely to blame. The myth also suggests that we all carry the legacy of our ancestral past and this can deform our capacity to look after our children well enough. What we can say about this myth is that the ancestors will come back and haunt the generations to come if a child is lied to about her or his birth.[23]

These three myths that have an abandoned child at their centre hold up a mirror to many contemporary families who have adopted children. The tales can bring comfort and reassurance to parents who have given up their child for they can hope that the child will have a better life and achieve fame and fortune. On the darker side, more difficult questions can appear. Who are these children? And embedded within that query there lurks another one. Who were their parents? Do these children come from 'good blood' or are they from 'bad seed'? Finally, and at the extremity of these anxious thoughts, there lies the one we most wish to disavow. Does the adopted child threaten the 'natural' order of things? A metaphorical illustration of what I mean is the cuckoo. Lurking in the shadows of the adoption process there may be an anxiety that the adopted child may turn out to be like the cuckoo who throws out the other eggs in the nest. In other words, the hidden fear is that the adopted child may bring disruption to the 'natural' family. 'No child of mine would behave as you are behaving now!' has been the response of some adopting parents when confronted by a troubled adolescent.

Adopted children have been of concern to all civilisations and they hold an important place in our cultural imagination and inflect our unconscious anxieties. In the three myths that I chose, their histories can be heard mingling with the hopes and the anxieties surrounding adoption. These myths help us to understand some of the complicated fantasies that adopted children can entertain, as well as some of the anxious emotions that birth parents and adopting parents can have towards their children.

Notes

1 Wilde (1894/2008) Act 1. p. 267. I have to thank my granddaughter Allegra for reminding me of this play. She was studying it at school just as I was writing this chapter.
2 Bowlby (2007). 'I am taking mythologies to be both inescapable and ubiquitous: they are the implicit explanatory stories through which we make sense of the world.' p. 8.

18 *Myths surrounding illegitimacy and adoption*

3 *Exodus*. 2. vs 11–2 & 3. v.8.
4 I have used Gilbert Murray's (1954) translation of Euripides' *Ion*.
5 Murray (1954) p. 17.
6 Murray (1954) suggests that the attraction that Euripides so skilfully portrays between mother and son is a 'cry of blood,' and goes on to suggest that though such an idea is 'discredited in modern times' in Euripides' time 'family feeling was so much stronger and more vitally important than it is now.' (n. p. 119)
7 Murray (1954) p. 24.
8 Coles (2015).
9 Murray (1954), p. 103.
10 ibid. p. 100.
11 Bowlby (2007) p. 213.
12 Many women who give up their children for adoption find themselves subsequently infertile. '38% of birth mothers fail to conceive again.' Verrier (2009).
13 Bowlby (2007) '... since the 1960's Ion has been taken up by feminists.' p.199. Also, Rustin & Rustin (2002) '... a remarkably modern play [that has] many contemporary resonances.' p. 49. As Novy (2007) suggests, 'Euripides ... gives full attention to the situation of the separated mother and son.' (p. 51) Also Hall (2001) in her Introduction to Euripides, *Orestes and Other Plays*: 'Euripides has been an existentialist, a psychoanalyst, a proto-Christian with a passionate hunger for righteousness ... But perhaps the most tenacious Euripides has been the pacifist feminist.' p. xii
14 Murray (1954) pps. 112–114.
15 Freud (1909) p. 262.
16 One of the earliest explorations of the adoption trauma in Oedipus was Feder (1974) who suggested that it could lead to angry, revengeful and incestuous behaviour. But even earlier, Jean-Pierre Vernant and Pierre Vidal-Naquet (1972) pointed out that because Oedipus was adopted, he cannot unconsciously have wished his father was dead. In 1977 Weider went further and wrote that incest was a real threat in the absence of biological knowledge of the birth parents. In 1982 Hamilton in *Narcissus and Oedipus* challenged Freud's idea that the myth was a child's phantasy and wrote '... for the adopted child, the family romance is the true story.' (p. 234) In 2003, Canham wrote about the plight of adopted and fostered children and likened them to Oedipus. 'Many of the children who end up in foster care or being adopted do so for reasons very similar to Oedipus – like him they are victims of physical, emotional and sexual abuse.' (p.11) Also Goldberg (2000) 'Some things faced by adults who have been adopted transcend time: the implications of Oedipus' adoptive status and his knowledge or lack of it have resonance now.' (p. 199).
17 For example: Kay (2010), Keating (2009), Maxton-Graham (1983), Melosh (2002).
18 Boswell (1988) p. 3.
19 Boswell (1988): '... literary assumptions about survival agree with moral writings is presupposing that the chief danger attending abandonment is that of incest, a possibility only for surviving children.' n. 101, pps. 392–393. Also, 'A young woman who was adopted as a baby had a frequent dream. She falls in love with a young man and they begin to live together. They decide to look up their family histories and the young man discovers he has a missing sister, who was put up for adoption. She realizes she is the missing sister.' Arms (1990) p. 240.
20 Brodzinsky, Schechter & Henig (1993):'some adoptive parents may watch their teenagers for signs of sexual experimentation as proof that the "bad seed" planted by their teenage birth parents has finally borne fruit.' p. 111.
21 Steiner (1985).
22 Murray (1958) pps. v–vi.
23 Coles (2011).

References

Aeschylus. *Seven Against Thebes*. Trans. P. Vellacott (1961) London: Penguin Books.

S. Arms (1990) *Adoption: A Handful of Hope*. Berkeley: Celestial Arts.

J. Boswell (1988) *The Kindness of Strangers*. London: Penguin Books.

D. M. Brodzinsky, M. D. Schechter & R. M. Henig (1993) *Being Adopted. The Lifelong Search for Self*. New York: Anchor Books.

R. Bowlby (2007) *Freudian Mythologies. Greek Tragedies and Modern Identities*. Oxford: Oxford University Press.

H. Canham (1999) The development of the concept of time in fostered and adopted children. *Psychoanalytic Inquiry*. 19. 2. 160–171.

H. Canham (2003) The relevance of the Oedipus Myth to fostered and adopted children. *Journal of Child Psychotherapy*. 29. 1. 5–19.

P. Coles (2011) *The Uninvited Guest from the Unremembered Past*. London/New York: Routledge.

P. Coles (2015) *The Shadow of the Second Mothers*. London/New York: Routledge.

Euripides. *Phoenician Women*. Trans. R. Waterfield. Oxford: Oxford University Press.

Exodus. *The Holy Bible*. (1912) London: Bagster & Sons Ltd.

L. Feder (1974) Adoption trauma: Oedipus Myth/clinical reality. *International Journal of Psychoanalysis*. 55. 491–493.

S. Freud (1909) *Family Romances*. S.E.IX. London: Hogarth Press.

R. Goldberg (2000) Clinical work with adults who have been adopted. In A. Treacher & I. Katz (eds) *The Dynamics of Adoption: Social and Personal Perspectives*. London/Philadelphia: Jessica Kingsley Publishers.

E. Hall (2001) *Introduction in Euripides. Orestes and Other Plays*. Trans. R. Waterfield. Oxford: Oxford University Press.

V. Hamilton (1982) *Narcissus and Oedipus*. London/Boston/Henley: Routledge & Kegan Paul.

K. Jones (1999) *Catherine Cookson: The Biography*. UK: Constable & Co.

J. Kay (2010) *Red Dust Road*. London: Picador.

J. Keating(2009) *Child for Keeps: A History of Adoption in England, 1918–45*. London: Palgrave Macmillan.

K. Maxton-Graham (1983) *An Adopted Woman*. New York: Remi Books.

B. Melosh (2002) *Strangers and Kin. The American Way of Adoption*. Cambridge, Massachusetts/London: Harvard University Press.

G. Murray (1954) *Ion*. London/New York: Oxford University Press.

G. Murray (1958) *Oedipus*. Trans. G. Murray. London: George Allen & Unwin. M. Novy (2007) *Reading Adoption. Family and Difference in Fiction & Drama*. United States: University of Michigan.

M. Rustin & M. Rustin (2002) *Mirror to Nature: Drama, Psychoanalysis and Society*. London/New York: Karnac.

J. Steiner (1985) Turning a blind eye: the cover up for Oedipus. *International Journal of Psychoanalysis*. 12. 2. 161–175.

Sophocles. *King Oedipus*. Trans. E.F. Watling (1947) London: Penguin Books.

J-P Vernant & P. Vidal-Naquet (1972) *Mythe et tragedie en Grece ancienne – 1*. Paris: La Decouverte/Poche.

N. Verrier (1993) *The Primal Wound. Understanding the Adopted Child*. London: CoramBAAF.

20 *Myths surrounding illegitimacy and adoption*

N. Verrier (2009) *The Primal Wound. Understanding the Adopted Child.* London: CoramBAAF.

H. Weider (1977) The family romance fantasies of adopted children. *Psychoanalytic Quarterly.* 46. 185–199.

O. Wilde (1894/2008) *The Importance of Being Earnest.* Oxford: Oxford World's Classics.

2   Bastardy

I ended the last chapter with the suggestion that an understanding of some of our cultural myths about adoption help to illuminate the legacy, positive and negative, that has accompanied the unwanted or illegitimate child. In this chapter, as I move away from imaginative story-telling, I enter a much darker world in the sixteenth century in Britain in which the illegitimate child was thought to be a child who should not have been born. As this punitive belief towards illegitimacy took hold, the child became known as a 'bastard' and this word denoted an historical shift away from the everyday acceptance of children that were born out of wedlock. Now the illegitimate child became clearly defined and in naming the child a 'bastard' an attitude was taken towards it that was 'shocking to humanity.'[1] To this day an illegitimate child can feel shame about its origins. In a BBC Radio 4 broadcast in 2018 called *Nobody's Child*, two MPs, Caroline Flint and Jess Phillips, who were both illegitimate, ended the programme by saying that they felt that the stigma of 'bastardy' had not gone even though the law has changed.[2]

The history of the word 'bastard' reveals that its origin comes from an association with the modern equivalent of the travelling salesmen. '*Bastum*' in Latin meant packsaddle that the travelling salesman carried with him, so '*basturdus*' came to mean a child left behind by the travelling man, or more figuratively, a 'baggage-child.'[3] This description of a salesman who travelled from village to village suggested he did not stay long in any one place, but what he frequently did leave behind was his 'natural' child or 'bastard.' In medieval French this child became known as '*fil de bas*' or 'one begotten and born out of wedlock' and in Elizabethan England 'bastardy' became associated with fornication.[4] Why the etymology of the word 'bastard' is important is that it reflects the way that illegitimacy was beginning to be thought about from the sixteenth century onwards. In naming the child a 'bastard' the child was carrying a burden that defined not only their character but also the way they would be treated.

Until the sixteenth century the adoption of children had been an unregulated or *de facto* affair. Sir Thomas More adopted Margaret Giggs (1508–1570) when her mother died in 1510. Margaret's parents Olive and Thomas Giggs lived next door to Sir Thomas More and his wife Jane in Cheapside. Olive Giggs had been the wet nurse to Sir Thomas' eldest daughter Margaret, following the birth of

22 Bastardy

her own daughter Margaret. The two Margarets grew up together as though they were sisters. Olive died when her daughter was two and the Mores informally adopted Margaret Giggs and she grew up in their household, loved and cherished and as well-educated as More's daughter Margaret Roper. In fact, Margaret Giggs became a distinguished mathematician and was well versed in medical matters and it was claimed that she cured More when he was with a fever in the Tower.[5]

The unregulated process of adopting an illegitimate child occurred in all classes of society and it was possible to make an illegitimate child legitimate, though there were legal and social constraints on inheritance because of the 'blood line.'[6] Charles II had fourteen illegitimate children, many of whom were given titles and estates, but he was careful to prevent any one of his sons from inheriting the throne lest the royal blood line might be disputed. This easygoing attitude to illegitimate children was prevalent amongst 'the noble and the wealthy [and] continued to be openly acknowledged ... without comment and criticism.'[7]. It was said that Lord Melbourne (1779–1848) and his siblings were 'doubtfully related' but this did not prevent him from holding the office of Prime Minister. Similarly, the behaviour of the Countess of Oxford, Jane Harley (1774–1824) was accepted in society and her many children were humorously called the 'Harleian miscellany!'[8]

This attitude towards illegitimacy was accepted on the estates of the feudal landlord. He might father children from among his peasants, and his peasants might produce children out of wedlock, but all these children would be nurtured in the community without censure. This melting pot of children was accepted by everyone as they could be put to work on the estate. Lest that is seen as painting too rosy a picture of feudal life, all the children of the poor, legitimate or illegitimate, were expected to work from an early age, whether on the land or in the cottage industries of weaving and lace making. Children were not an economic luxury but were seen as important economic contributors to the family. Their life was hard, they worked long hours and the mortality rate was high, but I think it would be safe to say that their life on the land or in the cottages was not as bad as the exploitation of illegitimate children in the cotton mills, the mines and as chimney sweeps, in the mid-nineteenth century when child slavery reached its peak.[9]

The feudal estates began to break up in the late fifteenth and early sixteenth centuries and the social and economic structures that had held the family and their communities together gradually crumbled. This was in large measure brought about by the dissolution of the monasteries that Henry VIII ordered in 1536. Many people had found shelter within the monasteries, such as mothers and their disabled children and old people, and overnight, as it were, they found themselves homeless. At the same time there was another important change taking place associated with the growth of the middle class. They began to move off the land as more lucrative opportunities were beckoning with the growth of early industrialisation. Towns began to develop and the rich built themselves fine houses. Meanwhile the poor desperately followed hoping to find some employment. Such factors brought about a tectonic shift in social structure and the problem of 'bastardy' began.

Bastardy 23

In 1572 the first Poor Law Act came into being in response to the critical problem of the number of people who found themselves without home or work and without any regulated source of help. The nursery rhyme, 'Hark! Hark! The dogs do bark, the beggars are coming to town,' is believed to have been a thirteenth century ballad sung by wandering minstrels, nevertheless in Elizabethan times it came to reflect the anxiety that these 'Rogues, Vagabonds, Sturdye Beggars and other lewde and idle persons' were posing for the stability of society. The question that the Poor Law was attempting to settle was what to do with these people and how should they be looked after. Another difficulty immediately arose as to how to differentiate between the 'Rioter who consumeth all, The Vagabond that Will Abide in No Place and The Idle Person, as the Strumpet and Others.' They were all fit for work and needed to be distinguished from those who were genuinely in need. Unmarried women with an illegitimate child were not seen as in need and no provision was made for their infant. They were believed to have offended 'Gods Lawe and Mans Lawe' and if money was given to support them it would be 'defrauding of the Reliefe of the impotente and aged true poor' and more importantly it would be encouraging 'a lewde Lyef.'[10]

Over the next four centuries there were many issues that the Poor Law Act addressed, but the moral ethos remained unmodified. The general attitude towards the poor was that they were undeserving and women with children born out of wedlock in particular were seen as a drain on the economy. It is interesting to note that an echo of the ethos that the poor are feckless and exploit the goodwill of society can be heard today in the rolling out of Universal Credit in 2018. One anxiety that underpins the concept of Universal Credit is the wish to solve the problem of those who exploit the benefit system, or in other words, 'The Rioter who Consumeth All.' In fact, statistically, benefit fraud makes up 0.8% of those on benefits. As in the centuries of debate since the first Poor Law Act, the Government seems resolutely deaf to the fact that Universal Credit is causing economic hardship to the most deprived, and seems determined to hold fast to what is in effect a new punishing Poor Law Act, while declaring that it is helping more people to get back into lucrative work.[11]

It is easy to attack the intransigence of the Poor Law but what was admirable was the recognition that there needs to be a compulsory poor rate that is levied through tax for those who are unable to find employment and are starving. Where it failed was in its care for the unwed mother and child. All consideration for them foundered on a mixture of high-minded sexual morality intertwined with financial punishment. This can be most clearly seen during the reign of the Stuarts when an edict came from James I in 1610 that declared that 'Every lewd woman who shall have any bastard which may be chargeable to the parish shall be committed to the House of Correction for one year.'[12] The effect of James I's Act was that many women killed their children rather than face a year in a House of Correction, and so another act of 1623 had to be passed to try and prevent the murdering of 'bastard' children, with little success as the centuries unfolded.[13] More importantly James I's edict helped to reinforce the double standards of

24   *Bastardy*

sexual morality that exonerated the man but punished the woman who bore his child out of wedlock. She had to pay the heavy price of being seen as little better than a prostitute whose 'bastard' was tainted with her bad blood.

Once women who had illegitimate children were considered to be no better than prostitutes, it was only a short step for them to be seem as a threat to the moral fabric of society. In the words of Pinchbeck & Hewitt (1973), 'the sixteenth and seventeenth century poor law legislation in which the wanton production of children without families to incorporate them was conceived of as a hazard to internal peace and social organization.'[14] This threat, in turn, reflected the patriarchal marriage laws that were believed to underpin the proper ordering of society. The man kept order and his potentially unruly wife and his children remained legally under his thumb by the marriage law that stated, '... husband and wife are one person, and that person is the husband.'[15] One consequence of such a legal position was that a married woman had no rights to property, inheritance or even custody of her own legitimate children.[16]

The fundamental belief of these stringent marriage laws was that without such control a disordered society would be let loose and the inheritance of property and the natural laws of lineage would be in chaos. It followed on from these concerns that the illegitimate child must have no legal rights and must not upset the proper regulation of society that since feudal times, had defined who was who and where everyone belonged. A rich man such as Charles II, had the wherewithal to give his illegitimate children estates and titles, but at the same time he made sure that they posed no threat to the blood line to the throne. When it came to the less privileged but aspiring middle classes an illegitimate child posed difficulties that could not be so neatly evaded.

I think it is worth pausing here and describing in greater detail the most astounding piece of patriarchal legislation that got around the problem of the illegitimate child of the middle-class man. How could a well-ordered Christian man, while upholding the importance of family life, avoid the difficulty of having, what was euphemistically called, a 'natural' child? The judge William Blackstone (1723–1780) came to the rescue. He pointed out that in common law the illegitimate child is a *filius nullius,* in other words a child of nobody, or more accurately the child of no man. Furthermore, because the 'natural' child is a child of nobody he 'can *inherit* nothing being the son of nobody, ... he cannot be heir to anyone ... he is therefore kin to nobody and has no ancestor from whom any inheritable blood can be derived.'[17] In this way the illegitimate child could be no legal threat to the family of the privileged man who begat him or her, nor could such a child challenge the rules of inheritance. The question then became whose child is the child of nobody? And here is the greatest piece of legislative dishonesty about the illegitimate child that continues to have repercussions upon women and children to this day. It was stated that as the illegitimate child was the child of no man it had to be the child of its mother, and suddenly overnight it seemed the child must have been immaculately conceived. Even more dishonestly, the unmarried mother found herself with custodial responsibility for her illegitimate child, unlike a married mother who had no legal or custodial rights to her child, and the erring father could disappear like the travelling salesman with his packsaddle.[18] In the words of Anne Sexton (1964) '"name of father – none", I hold/you and name you bastard in my arms.'[19]

Blackstone cannot be accused of making the life of an illegitimate child any worse by pointing out this harsh reality; he was only stating what common law accepted and it was an ingenious solution that was meant to uphold the fabric of honourable middle-class family life. However, it left a yawning social and economic black hole into which the unmarried mother and her child fell. She must look after her own child with no financial support from the state and if she suffered economic hardship she was expected to trace the father of her child and get him to pay her maintenance.[20] If she managed to find him, and most slipped away, she had to bring him to court and prove he was the father of her child. This seldom convinced the magistrate, and in the majority of cases the woman would be forced to place her child in the Workhouse or a similar institution and seek work elsewhere.[21]

The child of nobody whose desperate mother placed him or her in the Workhouse, was most unwelcomed by the guardians of the Workhouse who considered the child to be 'a child which ought not to be produced,'[22] and though infanticide was never endorsed, the mortality rate for the illegitimate child in the Workhouse remained obstinately double that of the legitimate child even into the middle of the twentieth century.[23] Furthermore, the illegitimate child was put into a separate category to orphans or other children in the Workhouse and the mother was not allowed to visit her child whereas legitimate children were allowed to be visited and even taken out.[24] As Pinchbeck & Hewitt (1973) put it, the Poor Law 'was intentionally operated in such a way as not only to humiliate the [unmarried] mother but to stigmatise the [illegitimate]child.'[25]

The first Workhouse was built in 1632 in Abingdon and others soon followed. The buildings were over-crowded and unhygienic and filled with homeless adults, including the aged and those with mental disabilities. A description of the Harton Workhouse on the Tyne Dock in the late nineteenth century showed how little had changed little over three centuries. It was a 'free hospital and asylum, last resort for unmarried mothers, orphans, the elderly, the physically or mentally handicapped, the insane, the homeless and the destitute.'[26] The children had to be cared for by the adults in the institution, many of whom were not suitable. The standard of nutrition varied across Workhouses but there was an ethos that the poor should not be fed better than those who were managing outside, lest it might encourage more people to give up work, or so the overseers of the Poor Law believed. The children's clothes were so inadequate that they could not dare to go out of doors in the winter, and as there was no sanitation, disease was rampant. They had no space to play and they probably slept six in a bed. It was a life of 'profound emotional emptiness and economic exploitation.'[27] One philanthropist, the energetic businessman, Jonas Hanway, (1712–1786) highlighted the high infant mortality among the 'bastard children' of unmarried women who were housed in Workhouses. In a publication in 1762 he lambasted the Workhouse as 'the greatest sink of mortality in these kingdoms' through their failure to properly nourish these children.[28]

26 Bastardy

The conditions of the Workhouse remained unchanged over the centuries and at the end of the nineteenth century the illegitimate child was still suffering from inhumane treatment. The suffragette Emmeline Pankhurst (1858–1926) became a member of the Board of Guardians of a Workhouse in Manchester in 1894, where she discovered that it 'was being very harshly administered ... [by] guardians not of the poor but of the rates.' This is a feature that has beset the administration of Poor Law Relief since its inception and continues to this day in the philosophy of Universal Credit. The inmates 'were being very poorly fed' yet there was 'a frightful waste of food' as their diet consisted mostly of bread. The young children were put to work and Pankhurst '... was horrified to see little girls seven and eight years old on their knees scrubbing the cold stones of the long corridors. These little girls were clad, summer and winter, in thin cotton frocks, low in the neck and short sleeved. At night they wore nothing at all, night dresses being considered too good for paupers.' The effect on Pankhurst of seeing the way the nation's poorest children were being treated led her to comment, 'The Poor Law properly administered, ought to give back to the children of the destitute what the upper classes have taken from them, a good education on a self-respecting basis.'[29]

The increase in illegitimacy became particularly acute in the eighteenth century and early nineteenth century due to the many wars that were being fought across Europe.[30] Many men, and these included regular soldiers and mercenaries, moved about the country and in their moments off duty found comfort among the local girls. When the time came for them to leave they left behind many women carrying children. As Pinchbeck & Hewitt wrote, '... troops moved about the country to keep the peace or defend the coast [and] many girls lost touch with the fathers before the child was born.'[31] It was estimated in the mid nineteenth century that there were 'one hundred and ninety-five thousand permanent child paupers [registered] in England and Wales ... in addition there were thousands of street arabs, vagrants and children who lived by their wits.'[32]

'From the security of the twentieth century, it is possible to wonder at a society which could report such events with such composure' wrote Jenny Teichman in 1982.[33] And it certainly seems true that reading the debates that took place and the various reforms of the Poor Law, what seemed to underpin them was the absence of human concern towards these unwanted children. One of the greatest difficulties that had to be overcome, when it came to debates about the care of 'bastards,' was an entrenched belief that the State must not interfere in the protection of children lest it '... impair the principle of solidarity of the family,'[34] as though these children had a family. Yet such debates helped to prolong the lack of care for those most in need. Who was there to protect them? It was certainly not the overseers in the Workhouses who wanted to get rid of the financial burden of these children, as soon as possible. This they could do by selling them on, for a fee of about £5, as an indentured 'slave,' whether to cotton mills or later to the coal mines or as chimney sweeps. In this way the guardians of the Workhouse gained some revenue, and filled their pockets as well, and thereby a profitable trade began in which 'they took to selling batches of children to the factory owners of Yorkshire and Lancashire who as often as not would then literally work them to death.'[35]

Bastardy 27

This was nothing short of legalised child slavery and such treatment was confirmed by Robert Blincoe, who was an illegitimate child born in 1792.[36] He had been placed in the St Pancras Workhouse in 1796 when he was four. He had no memory of his early life and no memory of his mother. One of his most painful feelings was that he had no name to call his own. When he was seven he was indentured for fourteen years to a cotton mill owner in Nottinghamshire and later in Derbyshire. He became well known because he told his story to one John Brown in 1822 and Blincoe's *Memoirs* were published in 1832. It was through this publication, that had on its cover his portrait in black with a crooked body and bent legs, that he came to represent in many people's minds the symbol of the exploited child of the factory system. Blincoe was made to work unendurably long hours, sometimes as much as eighteen in a day. He was beaten unmercifully all through the fourteen years of his indenture and he was so badly nourished that he resorted to eating pig swill on occasions. One consequence of his starvation diet was that his legs became badly bent so that he had difficulty in walking for the rest of his life and he never grew to his full stature.

Blincoe's *Memoirs* of his years of suffering in the cotton mills reached a wide public and prompted a select committee of Parliament to take evidence from workers who had suffered as badly as Blincoe. Nevertheless, nothing was done and throughout the nineteenth century there was a continuing failure to curb the excesses of capitalist greed, and in particular the exploiting of the cheap labour of underage and unwanted children. As there was no-one overall who was concerned for their well-being, no manufacturer took any notice of the Parliamentary Acts of 1802 and 1815 that attempted to shorten the hours children should work. In 1819, as these Acts were being debated and amended it aroused a comment from Sir Francis Burdett, '... has any man a horse that he could think of putting to such toil? It is shocking to humanity.'[37] Shocking to humanity it certainly was, but the hours that children worked continued.

During Blincoe's period of indenture the Slave Trade was being debated. He would have been unaware of it at the time, but nevertheless his *Memoirs* used black slavery as a metaphor to describe the life of the illegitimate child in the mills as 'the home-cotton-slave-trade.'[38] We may have forgotten Blincoe now, but at the time of the publication of his *Memoirs* the emblematic image of this physically damaged man, on the cover of the book, did shock the public. Here was a grown man who was deformed from living his formative years in what was no better than a concentration camp. And the effect of the *Memoirs* was to gradually bring about a new awareness of the physical damage that was being done to children as they worked inhumane hours in the mills, mines and as chimney sweeps.

It has been claimed that Charles Dickens was influenced by Blincoe's *Memoirs,* when he wrote *Oliver Twist* in 1837.[39] Blincoe's life and Oliver Twist's life certainly had similarities. They were both brought up in Workhouses but their experiences diverged. Blincoe longed to be rescued from the Workhouse by being taken on as a child chimney sweep, whereas Oliver Twist pleaded with Mr Gamfield that he should be spared such a fate. Blincoe thought he had been adequately fed at the Workhouse whereas Oliver Twist was severely reprimanded

28 Bastardy

for asking for a second helping. But perhaps what Dickens, unintentionally, helps us to see is that the life of the fictional child, Oliver Twist, was very different from the real life of Robert Blincoe. Underpinning the tale of Oliver Twist's life is the fact that Dicken imagines he is well-born, and so little by little the reader has the comfort of knowing that there will be a redemptive moment when Oliver's true history will be revealed. In contrast Blincoe's life is unsustained by anything beyond his own endurance, and he knows and the reader knows there is no hope of a redemptive moment when he might discover he was well-born or had a parent who was looking for him. His bleak life, that contained nothing but suffering, heightens one's appreciation of the existential black hole that the illegitimate child endured. There was no one to take Blincoe's side and there could be no imaginative sleight of hand by an author who could turn his life around. All he had to rely upon was his own capacity to survive, which he did, unlike many of the children of the Workhouse who went to an early grave.

There was another system of child slavery that had been going on since the late eighteenth century. This was the transportation of unwanted and illegitimate children to the US and the West Indies to work on the tobacco plantations. By 1797 they began to arrive in Australia, Rhodesia, South Africa and New Zealand.[40] The philanthropist Dr Barnardo (1845–1905) became caught up in the need to populate the further reaches of the British Empire with British children, and in the words of Barnardo's biographer, June Rose (1987), 'Barnardo the "Imperialist" has seen himself landscaping the colonies by planting out his children throughout the Empire.'[41] Thousands of children, some no more than four or five years old, were transported. The planting out of these children into an unfamiliar and harsh environment was very different from Barnardo's original vision of providing a home for 'street children.' When Barnardo began, he rescued children who were homeless and living on the streets in London. They may have been illegitimate, or orphans, or simply children who had been turned out onto the streets by parents who could no longer feed and look after them. He had been riven by a belief that a life of green fields and open spaces away from the 'vice, drunkenness and harsh treatment' they experienced at home, would allow them to grow into healthy young people.[42] Initially he set up a system of homes in the country in England or in the suburbs, where a small number of children would live a family life with a 'father and mother.' Many children flourished under this system, but Barnardo was insistent that even if they were not orphaned they should have nothing more to do with their family. He was the family. It was perhaps this belief, that the children of the impoverished flourished better under his system of care, that led to the deportation of thousands of Barnardo children to the Colonies for their own good.

It has been estimated that about 150,000 children were sent to the outposts of the British Empire between 1882 and 1967.[43] From the accounts that have been given of the life of these children in the Colonies, they were treated as indentured servants, often abused, with no-one to protect them and with minimal Government inspection.[44] They were allowed no contact with anyone who might have cared for them at home, and they were certainly not cherished as fine upright British Citizens upholding the values of the Empire.

In retrospect, the emigration of unwanted children that took place from the eighteenth century until twenty-five years after the Second World War, has revealed itself to be a trade in child slavery that was dressed up as 'child migration.' Margaret Humphreys (1995) in an Epilogue to her book *Empty Cradles* wrote that in her seven years of research on child migration to Australia, from 1939 until the child trade ended in 1967, 10,000 children were probably sent to Australia alone.[45] The Government turned a blind eye to the true nature of this exploitation until 2018 when the Department of Health and Social Care said, 'The child migration policy was misguided and deeply flawed' and went on to say that 'Over £9 million has been available to former child migrants.' This followed the Independent Inquiry into Child Sexual Abuse that recommended compensating about 2,000 surviving child migrants who had been sent to some of the Commonwealth Countries after the war.[46]

There had been other systems of caring for unwanted children that had been continuing more silently over the centuries. The system of 'baby farming' was an alternative that desperate mothers had resorted to rather than sending their child to the Workhouse. By the nineteenth century 'baby farmers' would put advertisements in the newspapers saying they would provide loving family life for children for the modest fee of £5. There was no shortage of babies to look after, and the women who ran what came to be known as 'baby farms' prospered. It shows how desperate mothers must have been that they could imagine that £5 would cover the cost of bringing up a child. However, with so little else in the way of economic support the unwed mother had to turn a blind eye if there was to be any hope of survival for both herself and her child. There was no inspection of or regulation over the care that was being provided by 'baby farmers.' In most cases the child was not provided with enough food to live for long. Several scandals about 'baby farming' that rocked nineteenth-century England helped to change this method of caring for unwanted and illegitimate children. In a particularly notorious scandal, which appeared in the popular press in 1870, a Mrs Waters was brought to trial and hanged for the murder of several illegitimate children she was supposedly looking after. In fact, and there were many others who were doing the same, she drugged the babies with opium and failed to feed them and so they died.[47]

Perhaps the most shocking indictment of the lack of moral concern for these children can be seen in the difficulty in getting through Parliament the Prevention of Cruelty to Children Act. In 1835 there had been an Act to prevent cruelty to animals, but it was not until 1889, and through many years of debate, that a comparable Act, The Prevention of Cruelty to Children, was passed. To bring a little light relief to these otherwise bleak accounts of the treatment of the illegitimate child I am going to quote from a story told by a remarkable philanthropist Thomas Agnew (1834–1924) who was a Liverpool-based business man and whose work contributed to the recognition that an Act that prevented cruelty to children was needed. He had long been aware of the appalling poverty in Liverpool and the cruelty that was inflicted on children by their impoverished and often drunken parents and he began to wonder what could be done for these

30   *Bastardy*

children. He was visiting New York in 1881 and he noticed that the US had a Society for the Prevention of Cruelty to Children. He enquired as to how it had come about and he later told the following story:

> A lady visiting the poor in New York found a child whose groans and cries horrified the neighbourhood, but the mother kept the child in her own house under lock and key. The lady applied in vain to the police and the courts; she was told there was no redress. So she addressed her complaint to Mr Burgh, the Secretary of the Society for the Prevention of Cruelty to Animals and reported that an animal was being barbarously treated. Mr Burgh at once sent an Inspector who was completely taken aback when he found the animal was a child ... the mother was convicted and punished.[48]

There is a footnote to this story. When Thomas Agnew returned to Liverpool he wanted to found a comparable society to the one in New York but was met with opposition. In 1882 he was in London and met up with another philanthropist, Sidney Smith. Smith invited Agnew to go along to a meeting that he was addressing about the need for a home for dogs. It was duly passed at which point Smith got up at the meeting and told Agnew's story about how he wanted to form a society for the prevention of cruelty to children in Liverpool. Support was immediately forthcoming, and Agnew went on to found a society for the Prevention of Cruelty to Children in Liverpool in 1883, which led in the end to a National Society for the Prevention of Cruelty to Children in 1889.[49]

As I end this chapter it has been with relief that I could find a moment of levity in an otherwise heart-rending story of the systematic cruelty towards unwanted children since the sixteenth century. But cruelty towards children did not end with this act of 1889. To return to Blincoe and the life of the child 'slaves' in industrial England, it took another hundred years of legislative debate and several Factory Acts before children were protected from exploitation either by their parents, the overseers of the Poor Law or the managers of industry. But, as I shall hope to show in the next chapter, by the end of the nineteenth century the conscience of society was being awakened and there was 'the gradual development of a quickened sense on the part of the community at large of the duty it owes to the Children.'[50]

Notes

1 Sir Francis Burdett in 1825, quoted in Waller (2006) p. 276.
2 BBC Radio 4, October 2018.
3 Teichman (1982) pps. 1–2.
4 Shorter Oxford English Dictionary (1973).
5 cupboardworld.blogspot.co.uk, accessed April 2018.
6 Hopkirk (1949)
7 Pinchbeck & Hewitt (1969) p. 68.
8 ibid. p.222, also Cecil (1969).
9 Hopkirk (1949)

Bastardy   31

10 Pinchbeck & Hewitt (1973) pps. 206–208.
11 www.guardian.com in 2011–2013. See also, the introduction of Universal Credit in 2013 that 'promised that there would be a system of child support which puts the interest of the child first... However, £18b was to be cut from the cost of benefits ... that ... would bring real income cuts to many poorer families.' (quoted in Thane & Evans (2012) p. 199) Also, 'The *Guardian* on 1st May (2018) (p.33) reported that 100,000 children are being pulled into poverty every 12 months, and that 1.5 million children are predicted to be pulled into poverty by 2021 because of benefit changes.' Megee & Alexander (2020) p. 122.
12 Pinchbeck & Hewitt (1969) p. 97.
13 'The mother soe offending shall suffer Death as in the case of murther.' Pinchbeck & Hewitt (1973) p. 209.
14 ibid. p. 206.
15 Teichman (1982) p. 66.
16 Hopkirk (1949)
17 Sir William Blackstone quoted in Pinchbeck & Hewitt (1973) p. 362.
18 'An illegitimate child being at law a filius nullius has not legal guardians, but the mother has a right of custody, though this is more limited than the corresponding right of a father over a legitimate child.' Keating (2009) p.37.
19 Sexton (1964) p.17.
20 There was an ingenious insurance policy that some parishes put into place, against future laxity on the part of young men. 'A payment of a lump sum or composition fee to the parish which released the putative father from future liability was accepted practice.' It was not commonly carried out, needless to say. Pinchbeck & Hewitt (1973) p. 211.
21 Pinchbeck & Hewitt (1973).
22 Hopkirk (1949) p. 42, n 22.
23 Hopkirk(1949) p. 42. See also, Keating (2009), McWhinnie (1967), Teichman (1982).
24 Waller (2006).
25 Pinchbeck & Hewitt (1973) p. 583.
26 Jones (1999) p.14.
27 Waller (2006) p. 25.
28 Pinchbeck & Hewitt (1969) pps. 177–178.
29 Pankhurst (1914/2015) pps. 23–25.
30 In the eighteenth century alone, eight wars were being fought in Europe, beginning with the Nine Years' War from 1688–1697 and including the Seven Years' War of 1756–1763 and ending with the French Revolution of 1792.
31 Pinchbeck & Hewitt (1973) p. 585
32 Hopkirk (1949) p. 83.
33 Teichman (1982) p. 62.
34 Hopkirk (1949) p. 83.
35 Waller (2006) p. 25.
36 Brown (1832)
37 Sir Francis Burdett published a pamphlet in support of the 1819 amendment to two ineffective Factory Acts of 1802 and 1815. Waller (2006) p. 276.
38 Brown (1832) p. 3.
39 Waller (2006)
40 'In 1618 a group of orphaned and destitute children left Britain for ... the US.' Bean & Melville (1989) p.1.
41 Rose (1987) p.105.
42 ibid.
43 Between 1882 and 1967, 30,000 Barnardo children had been sent to the Colonies. (Rose, 1987, p. 82) Other voluntary organisations also sent children overseas, such as the Fairbridge Society, The Church of England Advisory Council on Empire

32 *Bastardy*

Settlement, the Church of England Children's Society and the Catholic Council for British Overseas Settlements. See Bean & Melville (1989).
44 Humphreys (1995).
45 see also, ' ... about 150,000 children were "exported" to outposts of the British Empire' until the final boatload in 1967 (Bean & Melville, 1989 p. 1).
46 *The Guardian*, 'UK child migrants sent to Australia offered $36k compensation,' 2.03.18.
47 Pinchbeck & Hewitt (1973) pps. 587–588.
48 Brack (1983) p.11.
49 ibid.
50 Pinchbeck & Hewitt (1973) p.414.

References

P. Bean & J. Melville (1989) *Lost Children of the Empire. The Untold Story of Britain's Child Migrants*. London/Australia: Unwin Hyman Ltd.

A. Brack (1983) *All They Need is Love*. Liverpool: Gallery Press.

J. Brown (1832) *A Memoir of Robert Blincoe*. Manchester: J. Doherty.

D. Cecil (1969) *The Young Melbourne*. London: Constable.

P. Coles (2015) *The Shadow of the Second Mother. Nurses & Nannies in Theories of Child Development*. Oxon/New York: Routledge.

J. Hopkirk (1949) *Nobody Wanted Sam: The Story of the Unwelcomed Child, 1530–1948*. London: John Murray.

M. Humphreys (1995) *Empty Cradles*. London: Corgi Books.

K. Jones (1999) *Catherine Cookson: A Biography*. London: Constable & Co.

J. Keating (2009) *A Child for Keeps*. Basingstoke/New York: Palgrave Macmillan.

M. McWhinnie (1967) *Adopted Children. How They Grow Up. A Study of their Adjustment as Adults*. London/ New York: Routledge & Kegan Paul.

M. Megee & L. Alexander (2020) The right start in life: The politics of learning and mental health in schools. In J Edwards (ed.) *Psychoanalysis and Other Matters*. Oxon/ New York: Routledge.

E. Pankhurst (1914/2015) *My Own Story*. London: Vintage Books.

I. Pinchbeck & M. Hewitt (1969) *Children in English Society*. Vol 1. London/Toronto: Routledge & Kegan Paul.

I. Pinchbeck & M. Hewitt (1973) *Children in English Society*. Vol 11. London/Toronto: Routledge & Kegan Paul.

J. Rose (1987) *For the Sake of the Children: Inside Dr Barnardo's – 120 Years of Caring for Children*. London: Hodder & Stoughton.

A. Sexton (1964) *Selected Poems*. London: Oxford University Press.

Shorter Oxford English Dictionary (1973) Oxford: Oxford University Press.

P. Thane & T. Evans (2012) *Sinners? Scroungers? Saints? Unmarried Motherhood in Twentieth Century England*. Oxford: Oxford University Press.

J. Teichman (1982) *Illegitimacy*. New York: Cornell University Press.

J. Waller (2006) *The Real Oliver Twist. Robert Blincoe: A Life that Illuminates a Violent Age*. Cambridge: Icon Books.

3   The prelude to the Adoption Act of 1926

By the end of the nineteenth century there was a quickening of concern that the treatment of the children of the poor and the unwanted and illegitimate children in particular needed to be re-considered. Earlier in the century Peel had brought in a Health and Morals of Apprentices Act in 1802. This Act was in response to the concern that there were not enough strong and healthy young men to defend the country against a Napoleonic invasion. 'The nation needed a good supply of fit and able men to drive them back into the Channel,' it was claimed. However, an unwelcomed finding was that the state of health of the children of the lower classes was such that they were too 'decrepit ... and weren't capable of the tough physical labour upon which England's greatness depended.'[1] Peel's Act was little heeded and the exploitation and starvation of child apprentices continued. A shift was nevertheless slowly taking place and in 1870 there was the Education Act which meant that for the first time all children were provided with a space to have a childhood and were free from the expectation that they must contribute economically to the family.[2] But, it was not until the Boer War of 1901 that a more radical shift was forced upon the nation. It was discovered that when recruitment was set up, two out of every five young men were not physically fit to fight, and the Government had to face the extent of its starvation and neglect of its poor children, in spite of its innumerable Poor Law Acts. A convulsive shudder seemed to go through society with the overriding sentiment: 'How are we going to protect the Empire and our future if we neglect our children?'

It is an uneasy thought that it was only when the country faced war that the sensibility of the nation was quickened into thinking about the way it had treated its poorest children; in the telling words of one commentator, 'When a nation is fighting a war or preparing for another ... it must look to its future supplies of cannon fodder.'[3] The 'future supplies of cannon fodder' needed in the first place enough food just to survive before they could be considered strong enough to fight a war. They also needed health checks. Suddenly legislation began to tumble through Parliament. In 1906 school meals were started and medical inspections became part of school routine. There followed health visiting and welfare centres and by 1919 The Ministry of Health was set up. This sudden outcry about the ill health of the poorest children called for a 'National Baby Week.' This was announced in 1917 and the propaganda for this

34 *The prelude to the Adoption Act of 1926*

national day read, 'While nine soldiers died every hour in 1915, twelve babies died every hour, so it was more dangerous to be a baby than a soldier.'[4] The National Baby Week of 1917 was emblematic of the dawning awareness that infant welfare was in a state of crisis.

I have already traced some of the historical reasons for the neglect of the illegitimate child. It had been underpinned by the belief that because the illegitimate child was conceived in sin she or he was best left to die, and this attitude was hard to shift even after the First World War. In the memorable words of Dr Lyster in 1927, '... there was an attitude of mind amongst supposedly Christian people who seemed to regard the high death-rate amongst illegitimate babies as an indication of Divine displeasure, which cause them to be born with a predisposition to death, and that was a quite proper state of things.'[5] But now, following the First World War, there was a more general crisis about infant welfare. There was a falling birth rate of legitimate children while the number of illegitimate children was rising.[6] So the question was, should something be done to try and preserve these unwanted children, especially in the case of other wars? This dilemma was beautifully expressed by Keating (2009) in the following words: 'With the carnage at the Front and the declining birth rate even illegitimate births were seen as increasingly *too precious to squander.*'[7]

Before it was possible to imagine that illegitimate children were 'too precious to squander' a seismic shift in the moral attitude against such children was required. What was also required was a new approach to poverty and state welfare as the Poor Law was still exacting its penitential mission against the young mother and her illegitimate baby. The changes that did eventually take place were brought about by the philanthropic work of many concerned women. Josephine Butler (1828–1906) was one of these remarkable people. She helped to bring attention to the double standards of sexual propriety that had pushed women and their illegitimate babies into extreme poverty. She fought against the masculine standards that men demanded of women, while at the same time pointing out the way men disavowed such constraints upon themselves. One example that outraged her was that it was considered quite appropriate that brothels should be set up in towns where there was a military or naval base. The servicemen needed to be satisfied but the women who were expected to satisfy these men were despised and maltreated. Butler made it her life's concern to expose this double standard and, more importantly, to emphasise that women should be treated by the same standards as men. In the case of prostitution she believed that if women had enough economic support they would not need to resort to this profession. What was important about Butler's work was that she helped to shift the public attitude towards social reform rather than the punishment of women. In 1867 she set up a Home for Rest in Liverpool, pointing out that for 'many women who have married too young to have had any opportunity of learning a trade or practicing for domestic service.'[8] In other words she was an early pioneer in the proper education of women.

It was clear from all the work in which Butler engaged, she should be considered an early suffragette. She was an intimate friend of Millicent Fawcett

(1847–1929), and alongside other early feminists, she believed that there could not be a just society if women did not have the vote and the legal power to challenge male authority. However, in order to be heard, Butler had to weave her way through the sexual duplicity of her time and find the appropriate words to deliver her message. She did not condone sexual immorality but with amazing skill and sincerity, she eventually brought about a change in belief about prostitution in which it was gradually recognised that many women were forced onto the streets through lack of education and poverty.[9] It needs to be noted that her concern was with women who were being sexually exploited rather than woman with illegitimate children. But her work was extremely influential in making society more aware of its double standards of morality in which it was always the poorest women who suffered the most. Her work also helped to counteract the attitude that illegitimate children were the children of prostitutes.

There were other charities and philanthropists in the nineteenth century focusing on young mothers and children, and their work did help to bring about a change of attitude towards vulnerable young women. The London Female Penitentiary had been founded in 1807 in Pentonville where 'penitent young women aged from fifteen to twenty-five who were exposed to crime and destitution,' could find a roof over their head. Miss Burdett-Coutts (1814–1906) with the support of Charles Dickens (1812–1870) founded a rescue home in 1847 in Shepherd's Bush for young girls.[10] And in 1871 the first home that would accept a mother and her illegitimate child was opened under the auspices of a charity called 'The Female Mission to the Fallen' which offered a home and employment.[11]

In spite of the glimmer of concern for these young girls and their babies, most of the rescue homes were grim places with a deeply ingrained religious philosophy of spiritual reform which they continued to enact well into the 1960s, as we shall see in the next chapter.[12] These homes were, however, slightly better than the Workhouse and there was some hope the child might survive. But there was another shadow lurking ready to constrain the mother. If she was to 'fall' again and have another child she might find herself dispensed into a mental asylum and certified under 'The Mental Deficiency Act of 1913 [that] allowed local authorities to certify and institutionalise, generally unmarried, pregnant women.' Dr Lyster, the doctor mentioned above, proposed that this was 'a dangerous suggestion' for if a woman, with a second child, was examined for a '...mental defect ... Many people were all too ready to try to get these women shut for life in mental institutions when there was no sufficient evidence of deficiency.'[13] And many were.

In spite of the murmurings that the death rate of the illegitimate child should be improved, not least so that there should be more young men to defend the nation, the country stumbled against the fear and prejudice that if these ill-conceived children were allowed to survive there would be a decline in the gene pool. One example of this seeming threat was well illustrated in Manchester where there had been an influx of Jewish refugees from the Russian Revolution. They were bringing in children who were in ill health and were said to be potentially 'undermining the health and well-being of society.' But certain brave Jewish

36   The prelude to the Adoption Act of 1926

women in Manchester set about counteracting this fear. In particular there was a young woman called Margaret Langdon (1890–1980), the daughter of a well-to-do philanthropic Jewish family, who set about trying to improve the health of the poorest Jewish children in Manchester. She was keen to show that it was poverty that was the destructive force in society, not the people. In 1922 she opened the Delaware Forest School in the countryside outside Manchester for Jewish children who were too delicate and undernourished to go to school. The children flourished and after a few months of country air and good food they could return to normal schools in good mental and physical health. Langdon's work did much to counteract the Government's concern that the influx of 'poverty stricken Jews ... who were for the most part poor physical specimens, would further weaken the British gene pool.'[14] Again, as in the case of Butler, Langdon was not concerned with the fate of the illegitimate child but nevertheless her work showed that by restoring the health of the nation's poorest children, these children could become strong and creative members of society.

The emerging issue was how to find the best way to look after ill-nourished and unwanted children. One solution that was brought to the attention of the Ministry of Health was that these children should be adopted into loving and caring families. There they would flourish and the ills of the institutional care of the Workhouse could be rectified. One of the people who pioneered this approach was a remarkable woman Miss Clara Andrew (1862–1939). She was born in Exeter and was the daughter of Thomas Andrew, a High Bailiff at the Exeter County Court.[15]

Andrew followed in the footsteps of other notable women philanthropists, and during the First World War she had helped to find homes for 800 child refugees who fled from Belgium when Germany invaded their country. From her experience of finding satisfactory homes for these refugee children, she developed the idea that there were many other unwanted children who could be placed in families successfully. In 1918 she set up a Children Adoption Association in Exeter and this then led her after the war to present herself to the civil service in London as 'an adoption officer.' One of the notable things, as already mentioned, was that by 1919 the Board of Health had been set up to consider ways of dealing with the health of poor children. It followed that Andrew's idea about unwanted children being adopted was a possible solution. But as in all the discussions about sexual morality and illegitimate children, Andrew found herself battling with strong opposition. '... people spoke of the dangers to public morals if the illegitimate child shared in the benefits of this new movement,' she was to write.[16]

The prejudice against the adoption of illegitimate children had always bedevilled the work of the charities trying to find homes for them. Dr Barnardo, who had done so much to help the 'street arabs,' as he called them, had been strongly against adoption. As already mentioned in Chapter Two, he set up his Barnardo Homes with the belief that he was providing the 'family' to which 'his' children belonged and he was the overall father. Barnardo was always in control and he was reluctant to let foster parents adopt any of the children whom they cared for

The prelude to the Adoption Act of 1926 37

in these homes.[17] Barnardo was not the only one who was opposed to adoption. There were endless parliamentary debates about how to deal with the unregulated care of illegitimate children, and there were many who thought that Andrew's adoption ideas were a threat to the health of the nation.

We have seen this concern in the example above of the threat ill-nourished Jewish children in Manchester were seen to pose, and a similar anxiety was being voiced in 1907 by the eugenics movement that later transformed itself into the Eugenics Society in 1926. They believed that the falling birth rate of the legitimate child and the rise of the illegitimacy rates would lead to the degeneration of the next generation.[18] This dovetailed into the widely held belief that illegitimate children carried an hereditary defect and so by encouraging the survival of the poor and illegitimate child the nation was heading towards its physical and mental degeneration. This was the prejudice that Andrew challenged when she said that illegitimate children were not necessarily tainted with some hereditary defect and nurture could be as powerful a force for change as nature. She believed that in many cases it was not the unnatural appetite of the woman that had led her into bearing a child, but the appetite of men. Women were, she stated emphatically, often as 'much sinned against rather than sinning.'[19] This was well expressed a little later by Miss Helen Newill (1895–1941) a member of the Archbishop's Advisory Board for Preventive and Rescue Work, who pointed out, 'We heard a great deal about unmarried mothers and "fallen" women but very little about unmarried fathers or "fallen" men.'[20] Andrew's compassionate attitude did not answer the anxiety about the hereditary defects of the illegitimate child, but it did focus on the fact that men had been largely exonerated from any moral and financial responsibility for an illegitimate child.

Andrew, who remained unmarried throughout her life, was a woman with strong opinions. Following the foundation of the Adoption Society she had set up in Exeter she went on to form the National Children Adoption Association (the N. C.A.A) in London after the war. She was able to attract the attention of the rich and privileged with her enthusiasm. Princess Alice, Countess of Athlone, (Queen Victoria's granddaughter) became the patron and with a grant from the Board of Health, she was able to buy a property in Campden Hill, London. This building was to become the first of many of the hostels that her society founded and which took in children who had been approved for adoption, three quarters of whom were illegitimate. A stringent vetting of suitable children was undertaken; they had to be healthy and no child whose mother had had more than one child was taken on.[21] After they had been chosen, they lived in the hostel for three months before adoption, and even if the adoption had taken place there would be trial period of one month.

A brochure was published to advertise the society and its children, but it had a slightly unfortunate tone. It read like a catalogue from a general goods store. There were photographs of appealing girls, as girls were the more favoured when it came to adoption, and it even went so far as to describe prospective adopting mothers like 'little girls going to a doll's shop.' One adopter, having visited the home, wrote, 'Please send baby before the summer sales are over: it would mean

38 *The prelude to the Adoption Act of 1926*

a great economy of scale.'[22] On the strength of the catalogue alone one can appreciate that some people feared the N.C.A.A. was little more than a glorified 'baby farm.' But it was not, and unlike other adoption societies that came into being at this time, there was no transfer of money over the adoption of a child. In the first year of its life the N.C.A.A. approved 2,310 children for adoption and 448 were adopted.[23]

The work by Andrew undoubtedly helped to pave the way to the Adoption Act of 1926. Adoption now became legalised and an illegitimate child could become the legitimate child of the adopting family. *De facto* adoption still took place, under the counter, but it was no longer the way most adoptions proceeded. The most controversial part of the legal adoption process that was taken on board by the Adoption Act was Andrew's belief that records about the child's natural parents must be kept secret. The natural mother should not know the adopting parents, the child should not know who its original parents were and the adopting parents should be protected from any unwelcome intrusion. This was well expressed by the Vice-Chairman of the N.C.A.A:

> I know a certain number who do feel inclined [to adopt], but who do not do it because ... they cannot get a child without the feeling that the mother or father might break into their drawing room at any moment and claim the child, to the scandal of their neighbours.[24]

This description by the Vice-Chairman of the N.C.A.A. reflects the fact that it was the middle-classes who were adopting illegitimate children, and it was their 'drawing room' that needed protecting from the intrusive demands of the lower classes. But they also needed another more equivocal protection. Historically the illegitimate child has been believed to carry the 'bad blood' of its parents. It followed that these hereditary defects must not creep in and must be put out of view. The slate must be wiped clean and as Sir William Clarke Hall (1866–1932), the reforming Metropolitan Police Magistrate, put it in 1920, 'when a child is adopted, its life from that time should begin *de nove.*'[25] This hope has of course never been achieved and in fact the further we go in understanding infancy and the neuroscience of the brain, the more evident it is that the slate cannot be wiped clean and life cannot begin as *'de nove'* at adoption. But at the time it was believed that this was the most humane way of lifting the innocent illegitimate child out of a situation in which she or he was morally and socially condemned.

This is where another pioneer enters the adoption debate: Lettice Fisher (1875–1956). She was the daughter of Sir Courtenay Ilbert (1841–1924) who was a clerk in the House of Commons, and her philanthropist mother Jessie (1850–1924), a rent collector working under Octavia Hill (1838–1912) and who subsequently trained as a nurse at St Thomas' Hospital. Lettice was educated at Francis Holland School in London and Oxford and then studied economics as a postgraduate at L.S.E. She believed that her knowledge about economics could be used to further the practical needs of the poorest and, following in her

The prelude to the Adoption Act of 1926   39

mother's footsteps, she became a rent collector in East Oxford.[26] She married her tutor, the historian H.A.L. Fisher (1865-1940) who was the Education Minister under Lloyd George's war time Government until 1922. She became a Suffragette and when her husband became Vice-Chancellor of Sheffield University she became involved in voluntary social work with women who were working in the munition factories in Sheffield.

One of the things that Fisher must have seen as she worked with women in the munition factories was that provision needed to be made for working women who might become pregnant and in particular a woman who was having an illegitimate child. The pertinent question was whether she should be sacked and go the Workhouse? These legal and moral niceties had to be foregone during the war lest the workforce be depleted, and miraculously financial provision was found for women with illegitimate children, through the National Relief Fund. This enabled them to find baby care and they could continue working.[27] The duplicity of the thinking that had condemned mothers and their illegitimate children in peace time, was becoming transparent when finance had been found to provide them with child-care when they were needed during the war. This eventually led the Government to face the fact that there was an overwhelming need to help unmarried mothers so that their children could survive and the diminishing birth rate could be counteracted.

A conference was called in 1918 to which almost all the organisations dealing with women's welfare were invited and as a result a committee was set up chaired by Lettice Fisher. Their brief was to reform the Bastardy Act in such a way that fathers could be made to contribute to the upkeep of their illegitimate children. They were also to consider how to 'meet the varying needs of [unmarried] mothers and [their illegitimate] babies' and how to make provision of day care and hostels for both mother and baby for the first two years of the baby's life.[28] This committee transformed itself into the National Council for the Unmarried Mother and her Child (The N.C.U.M.C.) which Fisher chaired until her retirement in 1955. One of the chief concerns was that the mortality rate of the illegitimate child was double that of a legitimate child and so their endeavour was to change the economic conditions and education for young mothers so that more babies might survive.[29] The N.C.U.M.C. could be seen as embracing the philosophy that the illegitimate child 'was too precious to squander' though they never put it like that. But what they did challenge was the Poor Law's punitive belief that no Poor Relief should be given to unmarried mothers because it was 'felt it would provide an incentive for immoral and feckless behavior.'[30]

In contrast to the N.C.A.A. (The National Children Adoption Association) we can begin to see that Fisher and her volunteers in the N.C.U.M.C. were part of a more psychologically informed approach towards mothers and their illegitimate babies. In Fisher's memorable words, 'The unmarried mother should be regarded not as an outcast of society but as injured by society.'[31] With this thought in mind their philosophy embraced the emerging ideas about the physical health and mental well-being of a mother and child. The N.C.U.M.C. was in the forefront of the view that mothers should not be separated from their babies,

40 *The prelude to the Adoption Act of 1926*

whether married or not. This in turn meant that the survival of illegitimate babies rested upon unmarried mothers being given enough economic support to allow them to stay with their baby for at least the first two years of the baby's life. There was not only a psychological appreciation of the importance of the bond between a mother and her baby, but there was also a very practical side to the recommendation that mothers and illegitimate babies should not be separated. It made it possible for the baby to be breast-fed for several months and this would ensure its better health; in Fisher's words: 'The usual plan was to put the babies out to nurse, thus automatically depriving them of their food and enormously diminishing their always slender chance of survival.'[32] Now the task of the N.C.U.M.C. was to raise enough money to provide hostels in order that unmarried mothers and babies could be kept together. By 1926 sixteen hostels around the country had been set up.

It was not surprising that Fisher suffered the same moral condemnation as Andrew when she had set up the N.C.A.A. The N.C.U.M.C was seen as 'encouraging immorality'[33] but Fisher was undeterred and wrote that she had 'a determination not only to build but to amend' and amend in particular the neglect that the nation had inflicted upon the unmarried woman and her child.[34] She was able to call on the great and the good to support the enterprise not least through her husband's Government contacts. Neville Chamberlain became their President from 1928 to 1931 and in the first year of the N.C.U.M.C. 600 cases had been helped and by 1939, 17,403 mothers had passed through their books.[35] These astonishing figures speak for the enormous need that the N.C.U.M.C had tapped into and makes an interesting comparison with Andrew's adoption figures mentioned earlier.

There was a twist to the argument the N.C.U.M.C. put forward for keeping mothers with their babies, and this again illustrates the subtle way these pioneering philanthropists had to steer their course against the moral tide. In the Manifesto of the N.C.U.M.C. they argued that if a mother is forced to give up her illegitimate child she is deprived of 'developing a sense of responsibility' and this will mean that she will resort to 'the line of conduct which has led to the birth of the first child.' She believed that keeping mothers with their babies offered more hope of the 'moral regeneration' of the mother. Fisher later elaborated on this view with a powerful psychological insight. She wrote that if a mother had her child taken away from her 'the result of that course is that there is another child to keep a year or two later.'[36] In other words, a mother who is traumatised by having to give up her baby, will often resort to having another one soon after. This was an important reflection on Fisher's understanding of why some mothers might go on and have another illegitimate child if the first one is taken away.

Though Fisher believed that keeping mothers and babies together was in everyone's best interest, she was not opposed to adoption as long as it was properly legalised. Andrew had insisted that secrecy should surround adoption because one of the besetting difficulties of *de facto* adoption had been that there had been no security for the adopter and the adopted child. The natural parent might reclaim the child when convenient, especially when it had become

The prelude to the Adoption Act of 1926   41

financially viable. There had been an earlier act in 1889 known as the Poor Law Protection Act that had aimed at preventing parents from reclaiming children, but it had been abandoned.[37] Now, in Fisher's opinion a protective law was needed for another reason. In her experience some mothers who had given up their child for adoption could sometimes find that their child was returned by the adopter and this was in no-one's best interest. So though Fisher was not opposed to legalised adoption, she firmly believed that adoption was not the way to deal with illegitimacy and should only be used as a last resort. As late as 1944 she wrote a letter to *The Times* stating that 'adoption is not a solution of the problem of illegitimacy… Only when it is really impossible that the mother should care adequately for the child should adoption be arranged.' And more trenchantly in another letter a few weeks later she went on to say, 'We do not want at all to attack adoption … What we do want to urge is that it must be something less good than real parentage, if only the real parent can be given the right help.'[38]

The views of the N.C.U.M.C. reflected a change that was taking place in society not only about the physical health of the poorest children but a new appreciation of the importance of the relationship of mother and child, supported by the indisputable fact that breast feeding was more likely to ensure the baby's survival. These views were finding support from other areas, namely education and psychoanalytic ideas. Since the middle of the nineteenth century there had been a dawning appreciation of the delicacy and vulnerability of the child's mind, pioneered in particular by Friedrich Froebel (1782–1852). He had observed that a child's physical and mental well-being thrived through play if it was encouraged by the adults who looked after it, and this led him to suggest that a child had an inner life that needed to be nurtured. Froebel's work and the work of others alongside him such as Montessori (1870–1952) led to a flowering of the psychological and social imagination that began to spread across middle-class culture in Europe; by the early twentieth century there was a new appreciation that the early foundations of mental well-being began in childhood. Another source of this creative shift was the influence of the Romantic Movement under the moral gaze of Wordsworth (1770–1850) and Coleridge (1772–1834), who were in the forefront of this change of vision. It has been said that they '… shifted the entire culture around them, and opened up that keen interest in the intense experience of childhood and the remarkable reverence for the insights of the child which still form a part of our outlook now.'[39]

This change in sensibility and the emphasis on studying the mind of the child in early childhood is well reflected in Freud's (1856–1939) and Klein's (1882–1960) psychoanalytic ideas that were gaining popularity in the UK. In 1913 the British Psychoanalytic Society was set up and this was followed in 1920 by the Tavistock Clinic, founded Dr Hugh Crichton-Miller (1877–1959). Under the influence of Freud's theories of trauma, Crichton-Miller established an institution that dealt with the shell-shocked soldiers returning from the First World War. One of the earliest therapists to work with these men was Wilfred Bion (1897–1979) who had fought in the First World War. He brought an understanding of his own traumatic suffering as a Commander in a Tank

42   *The prelude to the Adoption Act of 1926*

Regiment, and in his memoirs of the war, he wrote these unforgettable words, when one of his companions in his tank was killed: 'And then I think he died. Or perhaps it was only me.'[40] This experience of existential agony led him back to memories of his early childhood and to think about the early mother and baby relationship. He concluded that the mother was the earliest potential container of an infant's primitive state of mind and without the experience of being held and soothed and calmed down, the psychological well-being of the infant was compromised and traumatised. A little later the work of John Bowlby (1907–1970) changed the focus towards a more psychobiological theory of the need for a secure attachment between the new-born infant and the mother for the development of psychological and physical health.

It may seem that this detour has taken us away from Fisher and the N.C.U.M. C. but her views and those that were developing at the Tavistock Clinic with Bowlby's concept of attachment, have been enormously influential on the later understanding of adoption and the attachment difficulties that such children can face when they are taken away from their mother. Today, with the accumulating insights from neuroscience, attachment theory is the most widely used explanatory theory to understand the disruptive attachment disorder that many adopted and fostered children suffer. I will return to more detailed discussion of these developments in a later chapter. For the moment it is worth noting an ironic observation about the early clinicians who were working at the Tavistock Clinic made by Bessel van der Kolk in 2014. He commented that

> The scientific study of the vital relationship between infants and their mothers was started by upper-class Englishmen who were torn from their families as young boys to be sent off to boarding schools, where they were raised in regimented same-sex settings ... John Bowlby, Wilfred Bion, Harry Guntrip, Ronald Fairbairn and Donald Winnicott.[41]

This observation is surely true, but van der Kolk's comment helps us to see that traumatised men who had suffered the horror of the First World War and the philanthropic women who were concerned with the way society was treating mothers and their illegitimate children had some common ground. Children were being traumatised, both the most privileged and the poorest; furthermore, van der Kolk's observation helps us to see the truth of Beatrice Beebe's belief that 'most research is me-research.'[42]

In concluding this chapter on adoption and the legal framework that was created for dealing with the problem of the unwanted child, it is important to remember that the work of Andrew and Fisher has influenced all the subsequent thinking about adoption. Since the early days of Andrew and other voluntary adoption societies, there has been the belief that adoption is a good solution to the problem of the child who cannot be brought up in her or his own home; instead of being cast off into an orphanage or Workhouse a child could be adopted by a couple who were unable to have a child of their own. This gave the child a chance to experience a loving and happy family life. In the words of

The prelude to the Adoption Act of 1926 43

Jack Goody (1969) adoption could provide homes for 'orphans, bastards and foundlings' and fulfil the need for adopting parents to acquire 'social progeny' and 'heirs for property.'[43] This dovetailing together of the child who needs care and the childless couples who want 'social progeny' has been one of the much-heralded solutions that adoption has brought to the social problem of the unwanted child.

Nevertheless, the adoption process has not been as easy as it seemed in the days when Andrew set out to regulate it. The belief that the adopted child should have no information about his or her natural parents has been challenged by many adoptees. Now the law has been forced to change and sealed records can be opened. There has also been much concern about the length of time it can take for a child to be finally adopted as in most cases it can take at least two years. Alan Milburn, Secretary of State for Health, in 2001, commented 'Overall the adoption system ... is too slow and bureaucratic, too opaque and too unfair. Children should not be left waiting indefinitely for the perfect family on spurious grounds or a perverse sense of what is politically correct.'[44]

There has also been a powerful lobby that has questioned the efficacy of adoption, as in the case of the N.C.U.M.C pioneered by Lettice Fisher. The idea that a mother and baby will flourish best if they are kept together has found almost universal support in the memoirs that have been written by birth mothers and birth fathers. Yet, in spite of this popular endorsement, the philosophy of the N.C.U.M.C. continually founders on economic problems; 'If only the real parent can be given the right help,' Fisher pleaded. The sad fact is that any economic help that might be given still comes up against the Welfare State that is reluctant to adequately subsidise what are now known as 'single-parent families.'[45] It is hard not to conclude that there continues to be a belief that if a single mother and her child are given adequate provision they will only want more.

Notes

1 Pinchbeck & Hewitt (1973) pps. 613–614.
2 ibid.
3 Dwork (1987) p. 209.
4 Pinchbeck & Hewitt (1969) pps. 177–178.
5 Graham-Dixon (1981) p. 12.
6 In 1914, 37,329 illegitimate children were born and their death rate was 207 per 1,000, compared to 100 per 1,000 of legitimate births. Keating (2009) p.62.
7 Keating (2009) pps. 62–63 (author's italics).
8 Jordan (2001) p. 77.
9 Butler was largely responsible for the repeal of the Contagious Diseases Act of 1886, in which women, without recourse, had been subjected to the physical examination by official men to see if they were carrying venereal disease. Jordan (2001).
10 Hopkirk (1949) pps. 149–150.
11 McWhinnie (1967) note, p.271.
12 Thane & Evans (2012) p. 24.
13 Graham-Dixon (1981) p. 12.
14 Delaware Forest School, www.langdonuk.org. I am very grateful to Jennifer Silverstone for this reference.

44 The prelude to the Adoption Act of 1926

15 There is no official biography of Clara Andrew and there are few references to her in the history of adoption. I have relied on references to her in Keating (2009).
16 Keating (2009) p. 21.
17 Rose (1987).
18 Keating (2009) p. 21.
19 ibid. p. 46.
20 Graham-Dixon (1981) p. 21.
21 It is difficult to know whether Andrew morally condemned women who had more than one child or whether she was bowing to social prejudice.
22 Keating (2009) p. 50.
23 ibid. p. 106.
24 ibid. p. 78. I am grateful to Dorothy Judd's suggestion that adopting parents might have felt guilty at 'taking' another mother's baby, and would therefore fear that the baby might be snatched from them.
25 ibid. p.79.
26 Colpus (2018).
27 Keating (2009).
28 Fisher (1946) quoted in Graham-Dixon (1981) p.21.
29 In 1918, 207 per 1,000 illegitimate babies died. Keating (2009) pps. 22–23.
30 Keating (2009) p. 64.
31 Graham-Dixon (1981) p. 3.
32 Fisher (1946) pps. 3–4.
33 Keating (2009) p. 65.
34 Fisher (1946) p.3.
35 ibid. p. 8.
36 Keating (2009) p. 65.
37 Pinchbeck & Hewitt (1969) pps. 385–386.
38 Keating (2009) pps. 184–185.
39 Guite (2018) p. 18.
40 Bion (1982).
41 van der Kolk (2014) p. 109.
42 ibid. p.109.
43 Goody (1969) p. 57.
44 Keating (2009) p. 1.
45 ibid. pps. 184–185.

References

W. Bion (1982) *The Long Week-End 1897–1918*. Abingdon: Fleetwood.

E. Colpus (2018) *Between Self & Others*. London: Bloomsbury Publishing.

D. Dwork (1987) *War is Good for Babies and Other Young Children. A History of the Infant and Welfare Movement in England. 1898–1918*. London/New York: Tavistock Publications.

L. Fisher (1946) *Twenty-One Years and After. The Story of the National Council for the Unmarried Mother and her Child*. 2nd edition. London: Carnegie House.

S. Graham-Dixon (1981) *Never Darken My Doors. Working with Single Parents & Their Children. 1918–1978*. London, Kentish Town: National Council for One Parent Families.

J. Goody (1969) Adoption in cross cultural perspective. *Comparative Studies in Society & History*. 11.

M. Guite (2018) *Mariner*. London: Hodder & Stoughton.

The prelude to the Adoption Act of 1926   45

M. Hopkirk (1949) *Nobody Wanted Sam. The Story of the Unwelcomed Child. 1530–1948.* London: John Murray.

J. Jordan (2001) *Josephine Butler.* London: John Murray.

J. Keating (2009) *A Child for Keeps. The History of Adoption in England, 1918–1945.* UK: Palgrave Macmillan.

A.M. McWhinnie (1967) *Adopted Children. How They Grow Up. A Study of their Adjustment.* London: Routledge & Kegan Paul.

J. Nicholson (1968) *Mother & Baby Homes*London: Allen & Unwin,

D. J. Patchick (2020) Delamere Charitable Trust. www.delamerecharitableturst.org.uk.

I. Pinchbeck & M. Hewitt (1969) *Children in English Society. Vol 1. From Tudor Times to the Eighteenth Century.* London: Routledge & Kegan Paul.

I. Pinchbeck & M. Hewitt (1973) *Children in English Society. Vol 11. From the Eighteenth Century to the Children Act 1948.* London: Routledge & Kegan Paul.

J. Robinson (2010) *Bluestockings. The Remarkable Story of the First Women to Fight for an Education.* London: Penguin Books.

J. Rose (1987) *For the Sake of the Children: Inside Dr. Barnardo's. 120 Years of Caring for Children.* UK: Hodder & Stoughton.

P. Thane & T. Evans (2012) *Sinners? Scroungers? Saints? Unmarried Motherhood in Twentieth_Century England.* Oxford: Oxford University Press.

J. Teichman (1982) *Illegitimacy: An Examination of Bastardy.* New York: Cornell University Press.

B. van der Kolk (2014) *The Body Keeps The Score.* London: Penguin Random House.

4 Birth mother, illegitimacy and adoption

One of the difficulties that anyone writing about adoption today confronts is that with the psychological knowledge that we now possess, we can have greater confidence in claiming that a mother who gives up her baby at birth suffers an emotional trauma. We are also more certain that her new-born child suffers and carries an inarticulate experience of loss when separated from her.[1] But when the Adoption Act of 1926 came into force those ideas were only beginning to be recognised. As we have seen in the previous chapter, when Clara Andrew set up the N.C.A.A. in the 1920s she and many others believed that the adoption of illegitimate babies, who were placed into childless middle-class families, was the perfect solution to the problem of increased illegitimacy that followed the First World War. It not only ensured their survival but at the same time it increased the legal birth rate and freed the young unmarried mother from her burden. Since that optimistic beginning some jagged edges have appeared as it has gradually become apparent that this solution has caused life-long suffering to the birth mother; or in the words of Triseliotis, Feast & Kyle (2005): 'Rather belatedly, it wasn't until the 1980s that curiosity and concern were expressed about the fate of the birth mothers whose children were adopted.'[2]

It is true that Lettice Fisher heralded an alternative vision when the N.C.U.M. C. was set up; but the idea that it was best for mothers to keep their illegitimate child was hard pressed to be heard against a backdrop of moral and economic prejudice. Even in 2012, Thane & Evans wrote that there has been 'a failure to eradicate prejudice against single parent families and their persistent disadvantage.'[3] And when Jane Robinson in 2015 wrote her book *In the Family Way,* she found 'the stigma surrounding illegitimacy was so intense, so lingering, that the subject is still concealed in shadows' and the people she interviewed insisted on anonymity.[4] They feared to reveal their 'ghastly truth' and this had been compounded by the earlier secrecy and pain and lies that had been forced upon them.[5]

In this chapter I am going to pursue the concern that Triseliotis, Feast & Kyle (2005) raised that we have neglected the birth mothers whose children were adopted.[6] The birth mother was, until quite recently, wiped out of her child's history under the belief that 'If the eyes can be closed to facts, the facts themselves will cease to exist so that it will be an advantage to an illegitimate child

Birth mother, illegitimacy and adoption 47

who has been adopted if in fact his origins cannot be traced.'[7] This extraordinary idea that if the eyes are closed then the facts will cease to exist has had the effect that it really did obliterate the mother.

The social and psychological obliteration of the mother of the adopted child, that began with the Adoption Act in 1926, continued well into the 1970s. Throughout this period a young girl who became pregnant would be sent off by her parents to a Mother and Baby Home during the later months of her pregnancy, usually as far away as possible lest she brought shame upon her family. The institution would often have a religious foundation. There were a few compassionate places, such as those run by the Salvation Army. They provided care for the mother with her baby for a year or two, but they were so few and far between that it was more common for young mothers to be sent to institutions where they were expected to give up their babies for adoption. Once the young mother had given birth she might look after her infant for some days or weeks until he or she was adopted, but by six weeks she would have to sign adoption papers and agree to sever all contact with her child. In most cases she would return to her family home after the adoption and a common story would be told for the benefit of the neighbours. It would be said that she had been away on a visit to a relative, or even that her job had given her a temporary posting abroad. The socially acceptable attitude was that nothing untoward had happened and so of course no-one ever spoke about a baby, whether that was the grandparents or the young mother.

It has only recently emerged, from personal memoirs and governmental reports, that many of these mother and baby institutions were run on extremely punitive lines that had little changed over the centuries. These institutions were accountable to no-one, nor did they leave any records, which has meant that researchers have relied on personal testimony to discover the way they were run. Many of these Mother and Baby Homes, whether in the UK or in Ireland, had originally been Magdalene Convents that looked after prostitutes; they took their name from Mary Magdalene the repentant prostitute. However, by the eighteenth century the name of these institutions was changed to Magdalene Asylums, so that other 'fallen women' as well as prostitutes, such as orphans and young pregnant girls discarded by their family, could be included.

It is noticeable that the philosophy of these Magdalene Asylums differed according to their religious foundation. One of the earliest was founded in Ireland in 1767 and was a Protestant institution with a redemptive philosophy. The philanthropist Lady Arabella Denny (1707–1792) had founded her asylum in Dublin originally for prostitutes. She believed that the inmates could be redeemed by education and work and then they could be returned to society as reformed and able to earn a respectable living. Her asylum expanded and they began to take in young pregnant girls, but their philosophy did not change. These young girls were given encouragement to find work and look after their children. Lady Denny's philosophy of redemption was an astounding example of kindness and understanding. By contrast the Catholic Magdalene Asylums exemplified a punitive outlook on all 'fallen women' that looked in the opposite direction. In 1798

48 *Birth mother, illegitimacy and adoption*

when the General Magdalene Asylum of Donnybrook in Ireland was founded 'The wish and intention of the Sisters is that their inmates should remain with them for life ... The Sisters believe that very few of these who have lost their good name, and generally speaking have contracted habits of intemperance, idleness, and other vices, will be unable to resist temptation if exposed to the rough contact of the world again.'[8] Tragically, in many of these Catholic asylums, young girls found themselves incarcerated for life.

It is worth exploring further why the homes for prostitutes were called Magdalene Convents, as it helps us to understand how young pregnant girls came to be seen as no better than prostitutes. Rebecca Lea McCarthy's (2010) book, *Origins of the Magdalene Laundries* describes the trouble that the image of Mary Magdalene aroused within the hearts and minds of the founding fathers of the Christian Church. Mary Magdalene was believed to have been a repentant prostitute and this was endorsed by Pope Gregory, in the seventh century, who had 'mistakenly identified Mary with the sinner who anointed Jesus with oil. Thus she became the repentant whore.'[9] Whatever the truth of this scholarly debate may be, the important thing is that culturally we have come to accept that Mary Magdalene was a prostitute, and 'her image has penetrated our psyche, our traditions, and history' and she has come to represent 'a role model' for 'any woman who was seen to challenge society's moral code.'[10] As a consequence, when the Magdalene Convents became the Magdalene Asylums there was a silent assumption that a young pregnant girl who entered one of these institutions was associated with prostitution; and if it was a Catholic asylum she was expected to remember for the rest of her life the shame of her sexual sins.

Over the centuries as the Magdalene Asylums grew to accommodate unmarried mothers there was another surprising category of women who were believed to be in moral danger. This category of women, found only in Catholic Ireland, were young girls who were considered too beautiful! They might find themselves incarcerated for no other reason than their looks, though it was unclear as to whether it was thought that they were more vulnerable to temptation because of their beauty or whether they needed to be hidden lest they tempted men. The asylums, whether they were enclosing beautiful girls or not, came to be known as 'houses of correction' for 'unchaste young women ... On unforgiving principles.'[11] They were little better than the Workhouse and in strongly Catholic countries they began to 'conceal ... citizens already marginalized by a number of interrelated social phenomena: poverty, illegitimacy, sexual abuse, and infanticide.'[12] These 'houses of correction' expanded and could be found across Europe, America and Australia, where they did little to change their 'unforgiving principles.' 'By 1900 there were over three hundred such institutions in Victorian England and at least twenty north of the border in Scotland.'[13]

One explanation for the 'unforgiving principles' that were particularly inhumane in Ireland lies in the country's history. At the root is the relationship between the State and the Church. Unlike the UK, following the Reformation, the Church and the State in Ireland did not become separated and as a consequence the State saw fit, by the nineteenth century, to hand over the running of these

Birth mother, illegitimacy and adoption   49

asylums for disruptive women to the closed orders of nuns, where, 'out of reach and out of sight, the Movement became more inhumane and developed along more stringent lines.'[14] In theory, and as far as the State believed, the Magdalene Asylums were meant to be training schools for 'unmarried mothers, illegitimate and abandoned children, orphans, the sexually promiscuous, the socially transgressive, and often, those merely guilty of "being in the way".'[15] In fact many of these asylums had changed their name again and had become Magdalene Laundries, now being run on commercially lucrative lines. One result was that none of the inmates in a Magdalene Laundry had time for any education even though the State was paying the nuns to train these unfortunate people. The inmates worked long and exhausting hours, washing and folding sheets and other laundry work, and most of them were in a poor state of health. It is only from recent personal testimony and the Ryan Report of 2009 that we have learned what actual went on in these Laundries, and it would not be an exaggeration to say they were little short of prison camps.[16]

It took several years for the Ryan Report to be believed and it was only in 2013 that the State had to admit that it had tried to deny that they knew what was going on or had any responsibility for these Laundries.[17] The importance of personal testimonies to counteract the State denial cannot be exaggerated. They describe the cruel regimes that the nuns ran, and without these accounts the suffering might still be continuing and the inmates might still be incarcerated. What these testimonies have also revealed it that in some of the religious institutions illegitimate babies were being sold to wealthy families in the US. One notorious source of babies was the Sean Ross Abbey in Ireland that Martin Sixsmith (2009) wrote about in his book *Philomena*. The way this Abbey was run may have been unique but the period after the Second World War until the late sixties was when the 'trade' of illegitimate babies who had been born to young unmarried girls in Ireland was at its height.

It is not my intention to continue to depict the suffering these Magdalene Laundries perpetrated on many young girls as vivid descriptions of their torment can be found in many recent publications.[18] But the Magdalene Laundries did exemplify the continuing power of the Church and its belief that it was a mortal sin for a young girl to have sex outside marriage. And whether Protestant or Catholic, the Church's influence has continued to be felt in the 'rescue homes' for young unmarried mothers, run in the UK and the US, up until the 1970s.

How was it possible that these punitive 'rescue homes' endured into the last decades of the twentieth century? One way of understanding the enduring acceptance of the philosophy of these punitive institutional homes needs to be seen against the aftermath of the Second World War when civilian life was anxiously being restored. A social concern at this time was the need to reconstruct the idealised nuclear family that it was believed had existed before the war. Suddenly many women, who had worked in industry and munition factories and made an essential contribution to the war, found that they had to give up their work to the returning men and were expected to sink back into domesticity and child rearing, forgetting they had ever had an independent life. This ideal became

50   *Birth mother, illegitimacy and adoption*

popularised in feature films and glossy magazines in the 1950s. The propaganda of the magazines was that a woman's life was now fulfilled with all the latest shiny kitchen gadgets and her happiness was restored, in contrast to the war. For example, the well-known film of this period, *Brief Encounter* (1945), could be seen as a propaganda film about marital faithfulness. The incentive to commit adultery might have been a temptation in the war, but now it was the time to return to the safety of home and husband, however dull that might seem.[19]

But was everyone happy? And especially the daughters of these women? A recent documentary on Sylvia Plath, that included the writing of her novel the *Bell Jar* (1963), described the suffocation she felt in 1953 as she struggled to emerge from a society that wanted to keep her a smiling well-dressed virgin.[20] It was against the backdrop of this post-war society whether in the UK, the US or Ireland, that a young woman who had a sexual relationship outside marriage and became pregnant threatened the febrile hope of this new dawn. Feminism was in its early days and there was no legal abortion before 1967 or a contraceptive pill. Young girls would have received no sexual education either in the home or at school as it was believed that such knowledge might incite sexual desire. If a young girl did give into sexual desire and conceived a child out of wedlock the continuing solution was to tidy both mother and child away lest they brought social opprobrium to their family. The laudable hope of Lettice Fisher in the 1920s that there should be homes where young unmarried mothers and their babies could live and be supported had still not found either moral or economic support. Instead the familiar fate of the young pregnant girl was that she found herself in a punitive institution run by women who had little sympathy for her plight.

To give one example out of the many I could have chosen, Angela Brown offers a heart-rending account of the forced adoption of her son Paul in 1963.[21] She was turned out of her family home by her mother when she became pregnant after a one-night stand. It was feared she would bring the family into disrepute if she had an illegitimate child. Angela was fortunate that she found a young couple who employed her as a nanny because, as an unmarried pregnant woman, she lost her job. Two months before the baby was due, she signed into the Loreto Convent Mother and Baby Home in Essex run by Catholic nuns to have her illegitimate child. There she found herself treated with a total lack of compassion and had to work at least nine hours a day, with no rest and inadequate food as in the Magdalene Laundries. All the girls worked in the laundry, cleaned the home and church or looked after the babies in the nursery who were waiting to be adopted. Not surprisingly, the girls were exhausted by the time it came to give birth and Angela nearly died in childbirth. Angela was never allowed to forget the unforgivable sin she had committed and often found herself berated by the Reverend Mother. 'You dirty, dirty girl … All airs and graces and la-di-da ways you might have, but you're no better than a common hussy!' Angela was continually shocked by the way she was treated. She had been brought up as a Catholic and she could not believe that it was Christian to address her continually with contempt. '… Again and again, it hit me: how could they be so cruel to us, the women of God? It sometimes seemed like sport to them.'[22]

Birth mother, illegitimacy and adoption   51

It was expected that she would give up her son for adoption, indeed she had agreed to this before he was born. At the time of agreeing to the adoption she had no idea of how she would feel when her baby was born, and as a result she capitulated to the social and moral pressure that it would be better for her baby to have a proper home with a father and mother. What she had not expected was to feel overwhelmed by love for him when he was born and to be dominated by a wish to care for him. No-one had warned her that she might have such feelings and instead she was expected to look after him for just six weeks until the adoption papers came through, while at the same time she was not allowed to breast feed him. All the babies in the Loreto Convent were looked after by their mothers and were fed on a strict four hourly regime and never fed at night. The mothers were observed by the nuns at all times to prevent any lingering moments of loving attention that they might want to show their babies. The babies were left to cry if they were hungry or distressed as it was imperative that the four hourly regime was upheld. This schedule caused maximum suffering for both mother and baby, but it was likely deemed a necessary punishment for both of them.

The day came when Angela had to leave the home and take her baby to London to the offices of the Crusade of Rescue in Notting Hill Gate, where he was to be handed over to his adopting parents. The rest of Angela's autobiography charts the unforgettable experience of handing over her son and the searing grief that it caused her. Some years later she was fortunate to marry a man to whom she could tell her story and who supported her through all her suffering, not least her lengthy period of infertility. For many years they failed to conceive and there is research evidence to show that about forty per cent of mothers who gave up their child at birth can suffer subsequent infertility, though there are no biological reasons.[23] This is a finding that seems to contradict Fisher's research that suggested that a young mother whose baby was taken from them would often go out and get pregnant immediately. Perhaps all one can say is that a woman's fertility is deeply connected to her emotional state of mind and this becomes clear in the last chapter when I deal with reproductive technology.

In 1994 her son Paul, now called James, got in touch with the adoption agency, the Crusade of Rescue, to find out about his birth parents, and eventually Angela and her son did meet up. It was a restorative moment for Angela. She found out that James had had a loving and kind family but nevertheless he wrote to her that, '... there has always been a little insecurity surrounding me and I think this stems from not really knowing who I am or where I come from.'[24] Their reunion was very important for them both, but then things began to go slightly wrong. Angela's intense love and need to see him overwhelmed him and he had to point out that he had another family who took priority. This caused Angela to angrily cut herself off from him for several months. They did meet up again, but the book ends with Angela's comment, 'We are still feeling our way.'[25] And those words are echoed by many mothers who are reunited with their children. Many reunions are a healing experience but then begins another journey; the birth mother has to accept her child has had another mother and the adopted person comes up against the fantasied birth mother and her reality.

52 Birth mother, illegitimacy and adoption

Angela Brown's experience of giving up her son for adoption encapsulates many of the painful features for birth mothers as adoption developed after the First World War. Most of the mothers of the babies to be adopted were teenagers and so this meant that their parents still had legal responsibility for their welfare and could dictate the way the illegitimate baby was to be treated. As I have already suggested, the ethos of the time, after the Second World War and until the late 1960s, led most parents to insist their daughters give up their children as they feared the shame that would be brought to bear on the family if they acknowledged an illegitimate grandchild. Not only were the young girl's feelings totally ignored but it was assumed she would have no maternal feelings towards her baby when she or he was born and, therefore, she would feel no maternal grief at relinquishing her child. There was no socially acceptable space to mention the child again, either to her family or with her friends.

Without the personal memoirs of unmarried birth mothers, we would not have become aware that giving up one's baby at birth left a life-long grief. Universally, birth mothers testify to a feeling that half of their selves went missing when they handed over their baby and they were never the same again. 'I have lived with a broken heart since the day they took my daughter away,' one mother told me. Many became extremely depressed and they often behaved self-destructively. Some rushed into a bad marriage and immediately tried to have another baby in the hopes their grief could be assuaged by giving birth to another child. This confirmed the astute psychological point that Lettice Fisher made, nearly a hundred years ago, that if society deprives a young mother of her baby then she may go out and try to have another one to replace her lost child. It has been more convenient to ignore this observation.

The characterisation of the young unmarried mother that I have given draws upon middle-class families and their attitude to their daughters' unwanted pregnancies. In these cases, as we have seen, there was an expectation that an illegitimate baby should be conveniently placed out of sight through having the baby adopted. An attitude of shame surrounding illegitimacy was also to be found in working-class families, though the solution might be different. The popular novelist Catherine Cookson (1906–1998) came from an impoverished family in Tyne on Wear and she was led to believe that her grandmother was her mother and that her nineteen-year-old mother was an older sister. The alternative that the family faced was the terrifying Workhouse that loomed over the town. Everyone knew that if a child was placed there it would face a certain death and the young mother would be condemned for life. The solution was to hide the pregnancy within the family and Cookson's grandmother brought her up as her own. This has been historically a common form of *de facto* adoption and even today social workers may first approach family members to look after a child whose mother cannot care for him or her. But in the case of Cookson it failed to wipe out the shame she felt about her suspected illegitimacy. It hung over her all her life and her relationship with her natural mother remained distorted by suspicion.[26]

The accumulating evidence of the suffering of young mothers who were expected to give up their babies for adoption is confirmed in Ann Fessler's (2006) oral history, *The Girls who Went Away,* in which she interviewed over a hundred women '... about their relinquishment experience or their sentiments about adoption.'[27] One result of her research is that it is no longer possible to ignore the suffering that was caused to many birth mothers who were pressurised into giving up their baby for adoption. More generally it becomes clear that adoption has been predicated upon the anxieties of a society that did not want to be contaminated by unmarried mothers, and at the same time what was also being promoted was the belief that adoption was helping unmarried mothers because they did not want their children and certainly did not grieve their loss. This has been one of the important lies that birth mothers have had to contend with.

One example from Fessler involves a personal account from a professional psychologist called Judith. She felt she had been brainwashed into believing that if she did not agree to having her child adopted, she was cheating her baby of having a good life. With hindsight she reflected that no-one is ever in the position to know how a life might turn out or how well a birth mother or an adopting mother is going to manage. She was part of a culture that believed there was only one way of raising a child and that was the way of life exemplified by married white middle-class Americans. What was not acknowledged was that it was a culture that punished a vulnerable and dependent young girl. Judith was made to believe that she was not good enough to mother her own baby and she felt 'ashamed and desperate ... what was wrong with me? ... I really believed it would hurt my baby to be with me.' She later reflected that '... all the bullshit of a fancy house and degrees ... I don't think it makes a good mother, I don't think it makes a good father ... It feels like a real violation to me.'[28] It is hard not to conclude that forcing young girls to believe that they were not fit to be mothers was a form of emotional abuse. Fessler's oral history is a hard-hitting critique of the values of the early post-war years in the US that dealt with illegitimate babies, and Judith's feeling that the adoption process was a brain-washing of the birth mother's natural rights has found widespread support in the UK as well.

I am now going to consider the other side of the story which tells of the value of adoption and suggests that birth mothers do get over their grief and, in the end, they come to believe that the adoption was best for their child. One work that seems to summarise quite well the positive findings of mothers who give up their children for adoption is *The Adoption Triangle* (2005) by Triseliotis, Feast and Kyle. It offers a different perspective to the individual accounts from birth mothers who tend to be full of regret that they bowed to the social pressure to hand over their babies for adoption. The aim of this research was to reflect on the changes that had taken place since 1975 when adopted children were given the right to access their birth records and birth parents were allowed to leave their names on a register for their children. The question that was being asked was whether this more open approach to adoption had a better outcome for all concerned in contrast to the time when records were sealed.

54 *Birth mother, illegitimacy and adoption*

There is a caveat to these findings. The birth parents who contributed to this research were by now middle-aged and were part of the post-war generation. One question that such a survey raises is whether a written survey of elderly people is already out of date as the values of society have changed enormously in the last forty years. One critic wrote, '... inevitabl[e] limits' and the '... reliability and generalizability over time and place of adoption research' is problematic.[29] There is another difficulty; written surveys are necessarily constrained by the questions that are asked and the values of the researchers. This has led to the impression, in this report, that at times the answers seem as though the respondents were giving the answers that were expected.

In spite of these caveats there are nevertheless surprising similarities between this research and some of the personal accounts that birth mothers have given, namely they have all suffered as a consequence of giving their baby away. The survey is very large and contains research on all the members of the adoption triangle, but here I am only going to focus on the responses of birth mothers; this includes the birth mother's experience of giving up her baby, the account of her subsequent life and eventually her reunion with her grown-up child.

The study begins by asking ninety-three birth mothers about the historical conditions of forty to fifty years ago when the moral ethos was that an unwed mother should give up her child for adoption. A good summary of the responses was that the majority felt '... pressurized ... and bullied' into giving up their child because they '... had no choice.' There was no social security for unmarried mothers at that time and for most of them their own parents would not support them. There was one response that was common to them all. Each one said that '... ever since the parting I have lived with a feeling of loss and guilt.'[30] This experience of loss seems to exactly match the accounts that have been given in the published autobiographies of birth mothers, yet, the conclusions of this survey are very different. The research was focused on finding out if open adoption had lessened the sense of loss and guilt that these mothers suffered once the possibility of meeting their children was permissible. The memoirs of birth mothers have not been concerned with that question. They have been expressing their suffering and anger at a society that required them to relinquish their child. These subtle differences of intention leads inevitably to differences in conclusion.

As the research findings were sifted into some order, birth mothers were divided into two categories. There were those who were called 'sought' mothers, that is to say they waited until they were sought by their child, and as the term suggests, they were more passive and accepting of the facts of the matter. The other category was 'seeker' mothers who 'searched' for their child before the child sought them. 'Seeker' mothers tended to be angry about the adoption and subsequently suffered from depression or other mental problems; a fact that had tended to be ignored by doctors and health professionals. But, on the other hand, these 'seeker' mothers were more open about their suffering and were able to share their adoption experience with their subsequent partners. 'Sought' mothers tended to hide the birth of their illegitimate child from everyone, not least their partners.

The most arresting point that emerged from this survey was that, though all the ninety-three birth mothers never forgot the baby they gave up for adoption, seventy-nine per cent of them, when they were asked if adoption should be abolished, thought that it should not be, even though almost every mother had suffered. Many of the comments that were made were surprisingly anodyne, such as adoption was 'wonderful for unwanted children to have a chance in life' or, 'it brings so much happiness also to people who cannot have children.'[31] These altruistic conclusions have a strangely hollow ring to them, as though the responses to the question reflected an expected social opinion rather than a more personalised view that might have required further introspection. It might also be said that these mothers were defending themselves as a way of coping with their loss and their guilt.[32] In whatever way one might hear these responses, the survey found that the majority of mothers thought that adoption was a good thing for their babies, and only ten per cent thought 'if there was no adoption I would have brought up my child' and only eighteen percent thought adoption was 'nothing short of obscene.'[33] From this survey, should we perhaps conclude that those who write their memoirs about the enduring pain of being forced to relinquish their babies are the minority, the eighteen per cent?

All the mothers in the survey were 'absolutely over the moon'[34] when they met up with their children, though there were some anxious moments. The 'seeker' mothers who had already shared their experience with their partner, were not anxious about a meeting, whereas 'sought' mothers, who had tended to hide their experience from everyone, felt threatened when this hidden child was about to appear. Then an interesting twist emerges from the contact with a birth child: the 'sought' mothers tended to have a more comfortable relationship with their adopted child because they did not have any high expectations. By contrast the 'seeker' mothers, by definition, had always been more desperate to know about their child and consequently they could be experienced as too demanding and the adopted person would in some cases draw back. However, once a reunion had occurred, the majority of mothers felt less guilty, the stress of keeping the adoption secret was relieved and their depression was lifted. For '90 per cent of birth mothers, contact and reunion was a happy and satisfying experience' was the conclusion of this research.[35]

It seems clear from this survey that the opening up of the birth records for adopted children and birth mothers has made an important difference to all members of the adoption triangle: birth mother, adopted person and adoptive parents. This new openness may take some of the sting out of adoption and gradually adoption and illegitimacy will be seen as having no secret to hide, or shame to deny. But it must not be forgotten that this survey does show that society's punitive attitude towards illegitimacy caused deep suffering to these ninety-three mothers. They were expected to act against their deepest natural instinct to love and nurture their child in order that society's anxiety about sex outside marriage could be quietened. *The Adoption Triangle* fully acknowledges that birth parents have been assailed by feelings of 'loss, rejection, grief, sadness, guilt, fear and worry.'[36] But the research also shows that, in the cases where

56 *Birth mother, illegitimacy and adoption*

children have been adopted under the age of eighteen months and where contact and reunion with the birth mother has been achieved, there have been 'positive and reparative effects.'[37]

I did, however, find myself uneasy when the survey categorised the mothers into those who were 'seekers' and those who waited to be 'sought.' Once they are defined in this way it becomes very compelling to attribute characteristics to these mothers, in which 'seeker' mothers are seen as more troublesome whereas 'sought' mothers lie down quietly, as it were. I appreciate that any survey has the task of sorting out the evidence into a coherent argument, but the danger of categorising mothers in this way perpetuates a silent value judgement that has always accompanied unmarried mothers. For example, should we categorise the writers of memoirs about the adoption of their children as a minority who are angry and more likely to have a mental disturbance? Are they the ones who distort our views about adoption when in fact for the majority adoption is satisfactory? This would be an unfortunate conclusion because without the voices of the marginalised who have had the courage to write about perceived social injustice, little would have changed in the adoption process that I have been following.

In conclusion, my concern in this chapter has been to give an account historically of why birth mothers of illegitimate children have remained as shadows on the margin of adoption, unacknowledged and unwanted. Whether we look at personal memoirs or research accounts, we get a clearer picture of the way society has silenced the birth mother and denied her a voice until quite recently. This has been an abuse that has brought shame on the cultural and moral landscape of our society, whether we are on the side of adoption or against it. I think we can safely say that at last the existential agony for a birth mother who had to hand over her child to be mothered by another woman, and the existential longing by the adopted child to know the identity of its own mother, has been at last recognised by our society.

Notes

1 For instance, Gerhardt (2005), Schore (2002), Verrier (2009).
2 Triseliotis, Feast & Kyle (2005) p. xii
3 P. Thane & T. Evans (2012) p.208.
4 Robinson (2015) p. xiv.
5 ibid. p.44.
6 I shall not be dealing, in this chapter, with the more recent issue where birth mothers have their child taken away by social services because the child is not thought to be safe in her care. See Archer & Burnell (2003): 'Many birth parents understandably feel diminished and degraded by the experience of care proceedings and the permanent removal of their children, even if they have consented to this' (p. 208).
7 Quoted in McWhinnie (1967) p. 6.
8 McCarthy (2010) p.148.
9 ibid. p. 25.
10 ibid. pps. 10 and 29.
11 Smith (2007) pps. xvi–xvii. Also, Patrick & Barrett-Lee (2012), Fessler (2006).

Birth mother, illegitimacy and adoption 57

12 Smith (2007) p. xiii.
13 ibid. p.xv.
14 Robinson (2015) p. 11. Also, McCarthy (2010).
15 Finnegan (2001) p. 85. Also, McCarthy (2010).
16 Smith (2007) p.xiii.
17 Ryan Report (2009) Finnegan (2001) and many others.
18 Patrick & Barrett-Lee (2012), Sixsmith (2009), Smith (2007), O'Riordan & Leonard (2016), McCarthy (2010).
19 *Cosmopolitan* was a magazine founded as a family magazine in the US in 1886. A typical magazine of the 1950s would feature a smiling housewife showing off her new shiny kitchen. See also the film *Brief Encounter*, made in 1945 which repudiated adultery.
20 BBC Two documentary, *Sylvia Plath: Inside the Bell Jar*, 11.08.2018.
21 Patrick & Barrett-Lee (2012).
22 ibid. p.93.
23 Verrier (2009) p. 75.
24 Patrick & Barrett-Lee (2012) p. 228.
25 ibid. p.270.
26 Jones (1999)
27 Fessler (2006) p. 338.
28 ibid. pps. 149–150.
29 Treacher & Katz (2000) p. 228.
30 Triseliotis, Feast & Kyle (2005) p.52.
31 ibid. p. 90.
32 I am indebted to Val Parker for making this point.
33 ibid. p.73.
34 ibid. p. 73–76.
35 ibid. p. 95.
36 ibid. p.131.
37 ibid. p. 95.

References

C. Archer & A. Burnell (2003) *Trauma, Attachment and Family Permanence. Fear Can Stop You Loving*. London/New York: Jessica Kingsley Publishers.

BBC Four (2018) https://www.bbc.co.uk/programmes/bO9q9zgc.

D. Brodzinsky (1990) Surrendering an infant for adoption: The birthmother experience. In D.M. Brodzinsky & M.D. Schechter (eds) *The Psychology of Adoption*. Oxford: Oxford University Press.

A. Fessler (2006) *The Girls Who Went Away: The Hidden History of Women who Surrendered Children for Adoption in the Decades Before Roe v Wade*. London: Penguin Books.

F. Finnegan (2001) *Do Penance or Perish: A Study of Magdalene Asylums in Ireland*. Oxford: Oxford University Press.

S. Gerhardt (2005) *Why Love Matters*. London: Routledge.

K. Jones (1999) *Catherine Cookson. The Biography*. London: Constable.

R.L. McCarthy (2010) *Origins of the Magdalene Laundries: An Analytical History*. US/London: McFarland & Co, Inc., Publishers.

M. McWhinnie (1967) *Adopted Children. How They Grow Up: A Study of their Adjustment as Adults*. London/ New York: Routledge & Kegan Paul.

C. Newman (2018) *Bloody Brilliant Women. The Pioneers, Revolutionaries and Geniuses Your History Teacher Forgot to Mention*. London: William Collins.

58   *Birth mother, illegitimacy and adoption*

S. O'Riordan & S. Leonard (2016) *Whispering Hope*. London: Orion Publishing Group.

A. Patrick with L. Barrett-Lee (2012) *The Baby Laundry for Unmarried Mothers*. London: Simon & Schuster.

J. Robinson (2015) *In the Family Way. Illegitimacy Between the Great War and the Swinging Sixties*. London: Penguin Books.

J. Rowe (1991) Perspectives on adoption. In E.D. Hibbs (ed.) *Adoption: International Perspectives*. Madison: International University Press.

Ryan Report (2009) The Report of the Commission to Inquire into Child Abuse.

A. Schore (2002) Advances in neuropsychoanalysis, attachment theory, and trauma research: implications for self psychology. *Psychoanalytic Inquiry*. 22: 433–482.

M. Sixsmith (2009) *The Lost Child of Philomena Lee: A Mother, Her Son, and a Fifty-Year Search*. London: Pan Macmillan.

J.M. Smith (2007) *Ireland's Magdalene Laundries and the Nation's Architecture of Containment*. Indiana: University of Notre Dame.

P. Thane & T. Evans (2012) *Sinners? Scroungers? Saints? Unmarried Motherhood in Twentieth_Century England*. Oxford: Oxford University Press.

A. Treacher & I. Katz (2000) *The Dynamics of Adoption. Social & Personal Perspectives*. London: Jessica Kinglsley Publishers.

J. Triseliotis, J. Feast & F. Kyle (2005) *The Adoption Triangle Revisited: A Study of Adoption, Search and Reunion Experiences*. London: BAAF.

N. Verrier (2009) *The Primal Wound. Understanding the Adopted Child*. London: CoramBAAF.

5 Fathers and their illegitimate sons and daughters

In 1922 the child psychoanalyst Hermine Hug-Hellmuth (1871–1924), a member of the Vienna Psychoanalytic Society, pointed out that one of the profound difficulties that an illegitimate child faced was the absence of a father. 'These illegitimate boys and girls lack the early attachment to their fathers because it was destroyed by premature rejection.'[1] I think it would be true to say that Hug-Hellmuth was the first psychotherapist to recognise that an illegitimate child faced the lack of attachment to a father.

The absence of the father is further reflected in surveys on adoption that are described in terms of an adoption triangle that includes the birth mother, the child and the adopting parents. This has shifted slightly in a recent collection of essays from the Tavistock Clinic, *The Dynamics of Adoption* (2000), where the suggestion is that the triangle '... has become a circle'[2] that must include the social worker or the person dealing with the adoption procedures. Nevertheless, one is left with the impression that if adoption was not so painful, one might almost be led to believe that the adopted child had been immaculately conceived.

One obvious reason for the neglect of the father is that if the birth father had stood by the woman who was carrying his child, then there might have been less reason to put the child up for adoption. But their absence echoes more. Historically, birth fathers have been, for the most part, absent from the problems around adoption because as Hug-Hellmuth mentioned above, like the travelling salesman they have been able to disappear. They have not been required legally to sign their child's birth certificate and this has meant that there is seldom a record of their name. They have also been given a social dispensation for their behaviour, as the law stipulated that their illegitimate child was 'the child of nobody,' or more accurately the child of no man. This has allowed them to escape the economic burden of providing for their illegitimate child and they have certainly not experienced the same moral opprobrium of society as has the woman who bore their child.

Adopted children do have birth fathers and in some cases they want to know who their fathers are; at the same time, some fathers of illegitimate children are also beginning to emerge and they are daring to express their feelings about their children's adoption. They are asking to be recognised as having a part to play in the adoption process and they are challenging the popular assumption that they

60 *Fathers and their illegitimate children*

have no thoughts about their illegitimate child. What has been surprising to discover is that historically there have been a few fathers, who in spite of the love and care and acceptance that they have given to their illegitimate sons, find that the moral condemnation that their illegitimate sons have received has not been easily overthrown. Both father and son have suffered in equal measure to that of a woman and her illegitimate child. As an example of this powerful social condemnation of illegitimacy that men have suffered, I am going to begin with two privileged and well-educated fathers from the eighteenth century. They did not shirk their moral responsibility and they did recognise and accept their illegitimate sons with love and devotion; and furthermore, the birth of their child had a powerful impact upon them and the child remained an integral part of their emotional life, in spite of the subsequent events. What is tragic in these two cases is that, in spite of the loving devotion that these two fathers showed towards their illegitimate sons, the shadow of society's disapproval of illegitimacy was cast upon them all. No amount of money or social privilege could withstand the moral stranglehold of the Christian belief that children born outside marriage were in some way tainted, and the relationship between these two fathers and their sons was ultimately destroyed.

> ... nothing has ever hurt me so much and affected me with such keen Sensations, as to find my self deserted in my old Age by my only Son, and not only deserted, but to find him taking up Arms against me, in a Cause wherein my good Fame, Fortune and Life were at stake.[3]

These were the words Benjamin Franklin (1706–1790) wrote to his illegitimate son during the American War of Independence (1775–1783).[4] His son, William (1731–1762) was at the time Governor of the State of New Jersey, and continued to give allegiance to the British. This caused an irreparable conflict between father and son, not least because Benjamin Franklin had spent seven years in England trying to find a way of negotiating American independence from British rule. How did their relationship come to this destructive impasse? Their relationship began well, even though William was illegitimate and Franklin had little to do with William's mother. When Franklin did marry he brought William, as a small child, into the marriage with Deborah Read, but Deborah never liked him and when she at last had a daughter, William felt he was not wanted in the family. Benjamin Franklin never faulted in his interest and concern for his adored son and they remained intimate and the best of friends, travelling abroad together and discussing details of Benjamin's many interests. It was only at the time of the Civil War that the subterranean feelings occasioned by Williams's illegitimacy erupted between them.

It is not unusual for fathers and sons to battle and in some cases never see each other again. But there is an intensity of emotion in Benjamin's letter to William, quoted above, that suggests another internal drama was being played out between them. There is an intransigence on both sides that seems to have been fueled by the unspoken difficulty that both men faced about William's illegitimacy. From

Fathers and their illegitimate children 61

William's point of view, he had to mark out his independent worth, not least as a result of the social comments that had followed him all his life about his rumoured illegitimacy. He could not afford to be a challenging, innovative and revolutionary figure like his father. He needed, for his social, and we might add his psychological stability, to become deeply entrenched in the values of the rich and moneyed class of his time and in this way he would find acceptance. He did succeed in having a magnificent house and estate and becoming Governor of New Jersey. This was not the dream of his father for his son. Benjamin Franklin wanted a son who could be independent, not only legally independent of the British, but independent of the moral constraints of Puritan America. I am suggesting that both father and son were up against the intractability of William's illegitimacy, but both of them fought the moral condemnation of this fact in very different ways. Franklin believed that the moral disapproval could be overcome by mere force of will. William naturally, from his disadvantaged position, did not have the psychological strength to overthrow society's strictures. Tragically they were fighting with incommensurate weapons that left them bloodied and wounded and unreconciled. The love of a father for his illegitimate son could not overturn the values of the society they found themselves in.

To further illustrate the social and moral difficulties that fathers and their illegitimate sons have had to do battle with, I am going to take the case of the troubled life of Philip Stanhope (1732–1768) who was the illegitimate son of Lord Chesterfield (1694–1773). We know about the life of Philip through Chesterfield's *Letters to his Son* which are an extraordinary literary record of Chesterfield's dreams for his son. They were published in 1774 following Chesterfield's death in 1773.

Chesterfield was a Whig politician at the courts of George I (1660–1727) and George II (1683–1760). In 1728 he was sent by George II as Ambassador to the Hague where he had an affair in 1730 with a governess, Madelina Elizabeth du Bouchet, and she became pregnant. He brought Madelina to England when he returned and set her up in her own house with an entourage of servants, making ample provision for the birth of his son in 1732. The moment he saw his son he fell in love with him, yet in spite of all the well-known complications about inheritance and titles that Philip would suffer from being illegitimate, Chesterfield refused to marry Madelina. Ironically, in 1733 he married one of the illegitimate daughters of George I, Melusina von der Schulenburg; a marriage of convenience that was helped along by her wealth. They never had children.[5]

Philip was brought up with nannies and servants and tutors in his mother's house and every week he would be brought to Chesterfield House to be seen and talked to by his father. Chesterfield had educational plans to bring Philip up in such a manner that his illegitimacy would be tempered by a disciplined study that would iron out any unfortunate characteristics or social disabilities. A letter from Philip, when he is no more than five, complains 'you make me work like a galley slave.'[6] If it had not been clear from the start that Chesterfield loved his son, the arduous academic study that he put Philip through could be seen as the whimsical cruelty of a deluded man wishing to defy society's condemnation of illegitimacy;

62 *Fathers and their illegitimate children*

as it is, it stands as a tragic example of the fantasy of a father that the truth about the child's illegitimacy could be overthrown.

As Philip approached manhood he could not live up to his father's dreams. He was short and fat and he was shy and clumsy and certainly not the clever scheming diplomat who would adorn the finest courts in Europe. Philip survived the regime that his father put him through by going undercover and hiding himself. Ironically, in so doing he enacted the duplicitous life of the diplomat that his father had dreamed for him but not in the way his father had expected. Chesterfield over and over again wrote to Philip that in order to be successful he must '... get into the secrets of the court' by taking a mistress of a man in power.[7] Philip turned a deaf ear to his father and at sixteen he formed a lasting attachment to a sixteen-year-old Irish girl, Eugenia Peters. She was also illegitimate. They married secretly when Philip was in his early twenties and they went on to have two sons.

Chesterfield had written to Philip, '... whatever my success may be, my anxiety and my care can only be the effects of that tender affection which I have for you.'[8] Though that was undoubtedly true there was a sting in Chesterfield's attachment, for he also wrote, '... how proud I shall be of you ... as you may ... arriv[e] at perfection ... and with dread ... if you do not.'[9] Philip failed to be the perfect son of Chesterfield's dreams and condemned by his father he took a job in Germany as an envoy. In 1768, at the age of thirty-six, Philip died of 'dropsy' and it was only then that Chesterfield learned of the secret life of his illegitimate child.

In many ways Chesterfield's treatment of his son is so extraordinary that it is difficult to draw any conclusions. Few fathers go to such extremes and put their son through such a punishing schedule as they try to mould their child into an idealised image that will defy the constraints of society and its values. However, from the advantage point of the twenty-first century it is not difficult to imagine that Chesterfield's fathering of his illegitimate son was linked to his own unhappy childhood, in which his father loathed him, and called him 'an ignorant, worthless, amorous fop'[10] and added that he was no better than his maternal grandfather, Lord Halifax, a 'cunning, false, court knave.'[11] Perhaps the seeds of Chesterfield's dream of producing a perfect son grew from the contempt his father had visited upon him. The fantasy may have been that he [Chesterfield] could at least produce a son who would be worthy of his father [Chesterfield himself]. But he jeopardised this dream by not marrying his mistress and making his son legitimate and, in this way, he had defeated his project before he had even started. He knew his son could never inherit his title and he knew that illegitimacy even in the sophisticated Courts of Europe would always cause difficulties. He could not overthrow the stigma of his son's illegitimacy and like Franklin he became a disappointed and disillusioned father.

Fathers and their illegitimate daughters can have an equally turbulent time, with just as many distressing consequences as between fathers and their illegitimate sons. In contrast to the two accounts above, in which I chose two fathers who had battled to have the stigma of illegitimacy eradicated from their sons' history, I have chosen a fictional story about a father who is reluctant to

Fathers and their illegitimate children 63

acknowledge that he has an illegitimate daughter, and unsurprisingly this had equally tragic results. The work is Nathaniel Hawthorne's (1804–1864) *The Scarlet Letter.* What we do know about this novel, from Hawthorne's own admission, is that the underlying motive for writing this book was based upon his family history.

The story begins with Hester Prynne stepping out of prison with her baby daughter Pearl in her arms, and '... on the breast of her gown, in fine red cloth, surrounded with an elaborate embroidery and fantastic flourishes of gold thread, appeared the letter A.'[12] This emblem denoted her adultery and she was condemned to wear the gown for the rest of her life, lest she forget her unforgiveable sin.[13] Meanwhile Hester's lover and father of her daughter Pearl, the Reverend Arthur Dimmesdale, was standing in the crowd as she left prison. He looked on but he retreated from taking any responsibility for his child or for his mistress. In this painful tale Hawthorne was addressing the stifling attitude towards the sexuality of the Puritans in North America in the late seventeenth century. The Reverend Arthur Dimmesdale was not the travelling salesman who left an illegitimate child behind as he made off across the country-side, but he does represent a man who fathers an illegitimate child and is too frightened of the moral condemnation of a supposedly Christian society to publicly stand by this fact. The familiar result, as previous chapters have shown, was that his mistress was left to carry the legal and moral responsibility for their child and face a life of social exile as a 'fallen woman.'[14]

There is, however, something more that Hawthorne was bringing to our attention in this novella. In the portrait of Dimmesdale's illegitimate daughter Pearl, he described a child who longed to know who her father was and wanted him to acknowledge her. It has taken a long time to recognise that children may have an intuitive sense of their father's identity and where he might be concealed, in spite of being repeatedly denied the truth. Pearl tried to discover if she had a real father rather than a Father in Heaven, as her mother, Hester, told her. From the moment that Pearl first saw her father, when she and her mother left the prison, she was intuitively aware that he was connected to her. '... the poor baby ... directed its hitherto vacant gaze towards Mr Dimmesdale and held out its little arms, with half pleased, half plaintive murmur.'[15] Pearl's troubled and wayward behaviour throughout the story hinged upon the fact that however often she tried to get her mother to tell her who her father was Hester would not tell her. Pearl became maddened and Hester responded with exhausted irritation, crying out at one point, 'Though art not my child! Though art no Pearl of mine!'[16] It was only on his death bed that Dimmesdale acknowledged his daughter, 'My little Pearl ... dear little Pearl, wilt thou kiss me now? Thou wouldst not yonder in the forest! But now thou wilt? Pearl kissed his lips. A spell was broken.'[17]

The spell that was broken was the lie about Pearl's paternity; at the same time something more was resolved. Hawthorne had a profound understanding of the corrosive anger that Pearl faced day after day as she tried to discover who her father was. She was frustrated at every turn of her inquiry and was left in a fury in which she could trust no-one, not even her mother. It was only when her

64 *Fathers and their illegitimate children*

father did acknowledge her that she could turn her rage into ordinary human grief, and as Hawthorne wisely commentated, '… she could grow up amid human joy and sorrow, nor for ever do battle with the world, but be a woman in it.'[18] In other words, she could become an ordinary woman not a preternatural 'elfin child' who behaved as though she only had an airy connection with the world.[19] This tale is justly recognised as one of the finest novels of American literature. What makes it such a powerful tale about fathers and their illegitimate children is that Hawthorne asked the reader to recognise the torment that a child struggles with when it is lied to about its paternal origins.[20] What I have not considered is Hawthorne's understanding of Dimmesdale's dilemma as the father of an illegitimate child.

Here we enter into the worst excesses of the Puritan belief system that had deeply disturbed Hawthorne and his family. On his paternal side he came from Puritans who sailed from England in the mid-seventeenth century. As they gained status in their new homeland, they became involved in the Salem Witch Hunts. On his maternal side his family had also come from England in the seventeenth century and had been caught up in more complicated accusations of brother/sister incest. For Hawthorne, the stringent repression of sexual passion in his paternal family and supposedly licentious sexuality of his maternal ancestry ran their contradictory ways through his family history. This led Hawthorne to write that his ancestors disturbed his imagination and haunted him and left a 'deep stain' upon him. He found himself wondering how they had fared when they met their Maker and decided that one way to answer that question was to write about them and 'hereby take shame upon myself for their sakes, and pray that any curse incurred by them … may be now and henceforth removed.'[21] This is an interesting and original way of laying the ghosts of one's ancestors to rest.[22] Another aspect of Hawthorne's originality is that his story challenged the belief that fathers of illegitimate children do not care about them. Dimmesdale suffered daily for his rejection of Pearl. In the end it was his suffering that killed him and his death does help us to understand that many fathers are not immune to the conflict and distress that their illegitimate child will cause them, even if some, such as Dimmesdale, are too weak to accept the responsibility.

From these accounts of Franklin, Chesterfield and Hawthorne, they all in their different ways are helping us to understand that the father who has a child who is illegitimate can have many conflicting emotions and fantasies about the child. What they also help us to see is that a father's behaviour can cause the child much conflict. Pearl was denied knowledge about her father's identity and this left her angry and confused, Philip experienced the ideal that his father projected onto him as unmanageable, and William Franklin found himself expected to ignore the social pressures that condemned his illegitimacy. These examples are no more than an illustration of the way fathers and their illegitimate children can have a difficult relationship when a society is in thrall to puritanical beliefs about marriage and sexuality.

Illegitimacy has occurred throughout recorded history, but as has been suggested in previous chapters, it is over the last four hundred years in both the US and the UK that there has been an overriding condemnation of birth outside wedlock. In particular, it has been the young woman who has been left carrying the baby and been burdened by the moral condemnation of an outraged society, while for the most part the men vanished leaving a heavy footprint that has remained unrecorded. As a result, much less is known about the father of such a child and not surprisingly such a man has often found himself treated with dismissive contempt, whether in court or by the testimony of the woman carrying his child. Perhaps one of the most contemptuous expressions was voiced in recent research by one woman who described the father of her illegitimate child as 'a piss-weak turd.'[23]

Today, fathers are challenging the stereotype that they are irresponsible and uncaring, and they are beginning to give voice to the view that they have a place in their adopted child's history. This challenge needs to be seen alongside the more general change that has taken place over the way society, whether in the UK or the US, views illegitimacy. As has already been suggested in the previous chapter, in the UK since the 1970s and 80s adopted children are now allowed to see their original birth certificates and even though in most cases they search for the birth mother some are also wanting to know about their natural father. At the same time the voice of the mother who was pressurised into giving up her child for adoption has begun to speak out, and there are many heart-rending accounts of the suffering of such women, as we have already seen. Out of these two important cultural shifts research is beginning to emerge that suggests that fathers have very similar feelings to mothers when they give up their illegitimate child for adoption.[24] To date there have only been a few heart-felt autobiographies that fathers have written about the significance their unknown illegitimate child has had upon their lives.[25] These autobiographies hardly compete with the shelves of books that mothers have written about their agony, but nevertheless they are beginning to make a significant in-road into an emerging awareness that fathers also suffer when their child is adopted. Fathers are beginning to recognise that even if their child is given up at birth, the child stays in their mind and the loss of the child remains with them, unforgettably. One poetic description that has been given is that father and child are connected 'by invisible threads.'[26]

However, fathers are having a difficult time as they find themselves up against their history. As we have seen, for centuries their illegitimate child was called a *filius nullius,* a child of no father, and so legally fathers have never had to put their name to their child's birth certificate. The problem now is how can an adopted child find his father or a father find his adopted child while the father is still not expected to provide his name? The child has an almost impossible task if the father is unnamed. The father also finds that he has no way of finding where his child has gone, except if the birth mother will start the search. There has been an easing of this difficulty with the UK Adoption Contact Register that came into force in 1991. Now fathers can leave their name and address for their adopted child to find them. A similar register has been instituted in other parts of the world, such as in New Zealand where there has been a register since 1980.[27]

66 *Fathers and their illegitimate children*

To illustrate the complexity of the present situation for a father and his illegitimate child who has been adopted I am going to turn to two fathers who have written about their experiences. In the first case, Gary Clapton wrote his book, *Birth Fathers and Their Adoption Experiences* in 2003. What is significant about this book is that, as Clapton rightly claims, this '... is the first to be written about birth fathers and adoption.' And he states quite candidly that 'the book's origins lie in a mixture of professional and personal interest. In 1994 I met with my daughter whom I had last seen 25 years previously when she was a six-week-old baby, just prior to adoption.'[28] Clapton does not discuss the emotional impact this had upon him or his daughter but it does lead him to set up a research project to find out if other men who'd had an illegitimate child that was adopted were equally motivated to find their child. The project included 'in-depth interviews' with thirty men whose children had been adopted over twenty years before.[29]

What are the main discoveries of this research project? One salient feature is that the majority of these men suffered a 'grief reaction' following the adoption of their child.[30] They resorted to heavy drinking or promiscuity as they hoped to blot out the pain of the loss of their offspring. For some it felt like an experience of death without resolution because they knew the child was out there somewhere but were not able to know where their child was. For others they could feel that they had lost a part of themselves. This was made worse as neither the child nor the adoption could be mentioned because the fathers felt themselves to be tarnished by the same 'social stigma' as the mothers.[31] One question that is posed by the continuing grief that the father can suffer is whether it would be lessened if they were expected to play a more prominent part in the adoption process. At present a father can object to an adoption and this can extend the time of the adoption process, but in the end his opinion carries no legal weight in the final decision.[32]

A significant chapter in Clapton's book, that was called 'Life After Adoption,' illustrated one common feature. This was that 'the adoption of their child was unforgettable' for the majority of men. It was like 'the appearance of a ghost' for some, while for others 'there has never been a time when I was completely free.' These sentiments led Clapton to ask about society's concept of fatherhood. He suggested that it has been too narrowly defined as 'parenting' whereas in this research study he discovered that these men felt 'connected' to their child even in the cases where they had never even seen or held their child.[33] This then led to a further question about attachment. The suggestion was that these men were expressing 'affectional bonds' that linked them to their child even though they had not participated in a caretaker role.[34] In Clapton's words, '... a possible paternal process of early attachment suggest[s] that a bond felt by a father for a child can be formed without social interaction and sustained for years in the thoughts, emotions and psychology of the father.'[35] This is an important extension to the concept of attachment as it brings in the fathers in a meaningful way that stretches beyond the commonly accepted criterion of attachment being forged by one caretaker.

Fathers and their illegitimate children 67

Clapton's work raises other questions, such as the differences in the internal world of mothers and fathers. Do mothers hold more firmly to the internal image of their child than the father? And he wonders whether in some of the cases the father is in fact holding on to an image of the loss of the birth mother when he is overwhelmed by grief for his child. This is not a question he answers but it is explored in the next book by Gary Coles (2004). A final and more psychological problem that Clapton poses is about the earlier state of mind of the father who has an illegitimate child. For some of the men they had suffered an earlier parental loss or did not have a good model of fatherhood. There seemed to be a universal belief that a good father does not abandon his child whatever the circumstances, whereas the fathers in this research thought their failure was associated with an experience of not being 'adequately fathered' themselves in their early years.[36]

This psychological idea would link to the point that Coles made in his book, *Ever After* (2004) which I shall now consider. He questioned his inability to accept responsibility for his illegitimate child and concluded that it went back to his childhood. 'As a child I had not known what unconditional love was … Kay [the mother of his child] was the first person to appreciate me for who I was … Hers was the unconditional love that I had never received.'[37] In the delight of finding himself unconditionally loved by Kay when they met at university, the thought that there might be unintended consequences, such as a child if they had unprotected sex, did not enter his mind. Coles' account does give an insight into some of the complicated and unconscious motives that can lead unexpectedly to the fathering of a child. I need to emphasise here that I am not siding with the psychiatric view, popular in the 1940s and 50s, that it was the mentally disturbed or unbalanced who had illegitimate children, but Coles does make clear his emotional vulnerability and his need to search for love.[38]

The first half of Coles' book is a self-exploratory account of his fathering of his illegitimate son in 1966 when he was still in his late teens. It is a very personal account and some would say we should not generalise from it, nevertheless it does contain emotional descriptions that some later research corroborates.[39] When Coles fell into the warm and loving arms of Kay, they planned a relationship together for the rest of their lives. However, when Kay found that she was pregnant the relationship fell apart. She did not dare to tell her parents so Coles hoped that his father would financially support their relationship and the birth of their child. His father's response was that the family's reputation would be damaged, and Coles' future would be ruined. Coles could not discuss the problem with his mother, and he collapsed under his father's injunction. The lack of parental support and the perceived disgrace it would bring upon the family is a common feature that has led to the adoption of many children as we have seen in the previous chapter.[40] The result was that Coles rejected Kay who then had to disappear from the university and have their child secretly and away from her family. She had no other recourse than to give up their son, Peter, for adoption.

68   *Fathers and their illegitimate children*

Coles came to believe that his immaturity, the distant relationship he had with his father and his uncommunicative relationship with his mother were the ingredients that led to his inability to father his illegitimate child. But he hid this recognition from himself for twenty-five years. He married and had two children and, interestingly, he married a woman who herself had had an illegitimate child that had been given up for adoption. In spite of this mutual trauma they were unable to share their pain until Coles decided to find out what had happened to his son and Kay.

Coles could not search for his son without the help of Kay as his name had not been on the birth certificate. Meanwhile the laws in New Zealand where his son had been born were changing; Coles could put his name on the birth registration form and there was now an Adoption Information and Services Unit where he and Kay could leave their names and addresses so that they could be contacted by Peter if he so wished. What had also changed was that by 1985 in New Zealand children could legally search for their birth parents through an Adult Information Act.[41] The way had begun to open for adopted children and their natural parents to find each other.

Coles suffered a severe emotional blow when twice their son Peter (now called James) said he did not want to know anything about his original parents and he authorised a ten-year veto, when Kay and Coles left their respective addresses for contact. This veto is a legal feature in both Australia and New Zealand, and it prevented both of them from making any contact with him. But Coles was undeterred and believed that the veto had been encouraged by James' adopted mother, so he tried again, and though he eventually spoke to James and wrote to him, James again insisted he wanted nothing to do with Coles and another ten-year veto was put into place.[42] It was clear that James was very angry at the intrusion of his natural parents and he reserved especially angry feelings towards his father. In turn, Coles was angry at the law that allowed James to block him and he could do little more than acknowledge that 'I felt rejected by my son.'[43]

The first part of Coles' book is followed by two further sections in which he generalises from his own experience. He suggests that '... birth fathers ... have been little studied and are poorly understood' not least by themselves.[44] The first difficulty he encounters is that there has been a social embargo against men discussing their feelings about their illegitimate children. This has meant, from the point of view of research, that they are reluctant to put themselves forward.[45] The difference between Coles' research and that of others is that he is passionately informed by his own experience and so he is less willing to be deterred by the argument that his views may not be representative of others. His central argument is that a child who is given up for adoption experiences grief and loss that will eventually need to be faced; at the same time parents who give up their child experience guilt and shame that also must be acknowledged. It is only when these two wounds are identified within the internal world and not denied that healing can take place. This belief is reiterated from different angles throughout the remaining one hundred and fifty pages of the book while at the same time it is a message to his son James to whom the book is dedicated.

Research evidence suggests that there is only a small percentage of children who do not want to know about their ancestral past or meet their birth parents, and, sadly for Coles, James is one of them.[46] Coles is not deterred and ends the book in a way that can seem slightly patronising: 'People who refuse to meet the other are not in a position to offer healing or to be healed.' But he recovers from that position when he writes,. 'I trust James, in the not too distant future, acknowledges that he too suffered a loss when he was separated from his birth parents and realizes that Kay and I can aid his healing.'[47]

It is perhaps not surprising that given the passion with which Coles' book is written, he ends with more general questions about adoption and whether it has been a social experiment that has run its course, '... adoption no longer serves any overriding social purpose which outweighs its negative aspects.'[48] What is fueling his argument is his belief that '... adoption does not create families. It destroys them, and the consequences are loss and grief. That an adoption occurs in the first instance means that there has been a family breakdown.'[49] What is true is that adoption has been a legal fiction from the point of view of genealogy. Adopted children are given a new identity that is derived from their adoptive parents and they have been expected to believe that they are not descended from their natural parents. As we have already seen, the legal right an adopted child now has, in some parts of the world, is that it can request its birth certificate and this has challenged the false assumption that its biological parents are its adopted parents.

Coles, and others, want more openness in the hope that it will lessen the inevitable loss and grief of both birth parents and their child. The suggestion is that there should be 'open adoption' in which birth parents, their child and the adoptive parents should be allowed contact.[50] In New Zealand there has been a discussion as to whether adoption should be seen in terms of 'enduring guardianship.'[51] This would mean that an adopted child always maintained its original identity. In Australia something similar is being discussed. Adopted children should be provided with a 'permanent care option' while maintaining their legal status with their birth family.[52] This solution is particularly pertinent where there is a diminishing number of children that are being given up for adoption.[53]

We are left with several questions when it comes to birth fathers and their illegitimate children. Should adoption be abolished, as Coles advocates, or at least should fathers be encouraged to sign their child's birth certificate so that they could be found? Should fathers be helped to recognise that the birth of their child will remain in their psyche, like a ghost, for the rest of their lives even if they never see him or her? One group of researchers who might equivocate that we can generalise from Coles' and Clapton's personal experiences are Triseliotis, Feast & Kyle (2005) whose work *The Adoption Triangle* I have already considered in the context of birth mothers. They have a detailed section on birth fathers, that I shall briefly consider.

The most arresting aspect about this research is that, despite the very similar emotional reactions of the fifteen fathers they interviewed to those of Clapton

70   *Fathers and their illegitimate children*

and Coles, the conclusions they come to are very different. Their overall research project is to find out whether the more open adoption that is happening today across many parts of the world has had a damaging effect upon the adoption process. And their clear answer is that openness has been a good thing, and that all members of the triangle find greater emotional resolution with eighty per cent of those involved in adoption satisfied by the result. The fact that they only had fifteen fathers who were willing to complete the survey meant that the researchers were unwilling to make any safe generalisations about fathers and their illegitimate children. For my part I believe that these fifteen fathers make an interesting contribution to this research survey by confirming that they share the same emotional suffering as described by Coles and Clapton. Fathers of illegitimate children are not indifferent, yet while these researchers are unwilling to generalise from the fifteen fathers who responded, this survey on birth fathers has the effect of leaving them on the periphery and that is a place where they have always resided.

I want to suggest that in spite of Triseliotis, Feast & Kyle's caution, these fifteen fathers can be seen as making a substantial contribution to our psychological understanding of the emotions that birth fathers do feel towards their illegitimate children. To take one example this research found that the majority of these men had been in stable relationships with the women who then had their children, and this counteracted the popular view that they were feckless young men having a one-night stand. In spite of these men being in stable relationships with the girl they loved, the majority agreed that they were not ready or too immature to take on the responsibility of fatherhood. So, when their parents condemned them for having an illegitimate child, they felt compelled to do what their parents told them to do because '... in those days you had to do as your parents said.'[54] This last sentence is a reminder that the social attitude towards illegitimacy after the last war and up until the mid-seventies was very punitive, whether you were a father or a mother of the putative child. It also illustrates the way our beliefs are irremediably influenced by the social pressures of the time.

All the fathers in Triseliotis, Feast & Kyle's survey were left with a feeling of being powerless and helpless over the adoption and this left them with an overriding sense of depression, sadness, grief and anger. Some went out and got drunk, others turned their back on the whole affair and led a wayward life for some time afterwards. Others felt it had affected all future relationships and, in the end, all regretted the adoption. Again, this matched Coles' personal view that the adoption had not only affected his relationship with his wife, but he came to recognise that the adoption needed to be faced. As we have already seen, Coles was desperate to meet up with his son, and the research of Triseliotis, Feast & Kyle found that fathers who had met up with their children were overwhelmingly delighted and not only did they feel '... their life had been enhanced as a result of contact' but they felt better able to cope '... with past feelings of loss, guilt and worry connected with the adoption decision and the parting with the child.'[55]

We see that the research of Triseliotis, Feast & Kyle and Coles' findings are very similar when it comes to the emotions that birth fathers felt following the

Fathers and their illegitimate children 71

adoption of their children. Yet Triseliotis, Feast & Kyle are much more cautious regarding the status of their findings about birth fathers: 'Even though the findings mostly confirm what birth mothers had to say on the same issues, nevertheless they need to be treated with great caution.' They then go on and say, 'The experiences of these fathers were real for them but they cannot be generalized' because it was 'too small a number [fifteen fathers] for reliable analysis.'[56] I do not want to get into an epistemological debate about the nature of our psychological knowledge and how it is acquired. Instead I want to reiterate my view, that I have been suggesting throughout this book so far, that the prejudice that society has placed upon birth mothers, adoptees and birth fathers has only begun to be counteracted by the personal accounts that fathers such as Coles and Clapton have given. It is when such individuals dare to speak out about the injustice they have felt, and when they begin to voice the unsayable, that society gains some psychological understanding of their suffering and hopefully some change can begin to take place.

In this chapter I have been describing an important cultural shift that has taken place as fathers of illegitimate children are beginning to recognise that they play a part in what has up until now been delimited as an 'adoption triangle.' An 'adoption circle' may be a better description, in which fathers' feelings about their illegitimate children have a place. Clapton and Coles are good examples of fathers' contribution to the circle, even if we might not agree that adoption is an unnatural social experiment that should be abolished.

I have no doubt that Coles' emotionally searing account will resonate with some of those men who have not explored this painful area. Hopefully it will also encourage birth fathers to recognise that they have feelings that are powerful and enduring and begin to talk about them. If we are prepared to take the research of Triseliotis, Feast & Kyle at face value, that is to say to take on board that 'the experiences of these fathers were real for them,' then their research confirms much of the work that was done by Clapton and Coles. On the other hand, the research of Triseliotis, Feast & Kyle is keen to emphasise that adoption works well for the majority, and this contradicts the personal views of Clapton and Coles, who are against adoption. I was left wondering whether Triseliotis, Feast & Kyle had underplayed the fears, worries and losses that adoption imposes on fathers in their enthusiasm to evaluate adoption positively. There were, after all, over a quarter of adopted children who had not been happy with their adoption.[57] So I want to end this chapter with a point that was well expressed by Howe, Sawbridge & Hinings (1992): 'Adoption is only to be viewed as a reasonable course of action under circumstances which may themselves be unreasonable.'[58] It is this view, in all its complexity, that some birth fathers are beginning to explore.

Notes

1 Maclean & Rappen (1991) p. 51.
2 Prynn (2000) p. 67
3 Lopez & Herbert (1975) pps. 257–258.

72 *Fathers and their illegitimate children*

4 'A letter was found written in 1763 by the son of one of Franklin's close friends "…'tis generally known here his birth is illegitimate and his Mother not in good Circumstances … some small Provision is made by him for her but her being not of the most agreeable Women prevents particular Notice being shown, or the Father and Son acknowledging any Connection with her.'" Lopez & Herbert. (1975) p. 23.

5 Shellabarger (1951).

6 ibid. p. 315.

7 ibid. pps. 323–324.

8 ibid. p. 332.

9 ibid. p. 332.

10 ibid. p. 336.

11 ibid. p. 336

12 Hawthorne (1850) pps. 75–80 (1970).

13 In the UK in the nineteenth century women with illegitimate children who were forced to find a roof over their head in a Workhouse were made to wear a grey gown with a yellow stripe across it, known as a 'Badge of Shame.' Hamblin (1977).

14 Hawthorne (1850) p. 94.

15 ibid. p. 121.

16 ibid. p. 120.

17 ibid. p. 268.

18 ibid. p. 226.

19 In Thomas Connolly's (1970) Introduction to the Penguin edition of *The Scarlet Letter* he suggests that the A that Hester Prynne wears on her breast represents for Pearl her missing father. p. 18.

20 Hawthorne (1850) pps. 41–42.

21 ibid.

22 Loewald (1980) 'Those who know ghosts tell us that they long to be released from their ghost life and laid to rest as ancestors.' p. 249.

23 Quoted in Howe (1992) p. 56.

24 Clapton (2003), Triseliotis, Feast & Kyle (2005).

25 Coles (2004).

26 ibid. p. 76.

27 Clapton (2003), Coles (2004).

28 Clapton (2003) pps. 11–12.

29 ibid. p. 14

30 ibid. p. 116.

31 ibid. p. 119.

32 In the DoH (2013) guidelines to adoption the father is not referred to, p. 21.

33 Clapton (2003) pps. 125–155.

34 Ainsworth (1991) pps. 37–38.

35 Clapton (2003) p. 186.

36 ibid. p. 197.

37 Coles (2004) p. 68.

38 Howe (1992) takes issue with the idea that these young people are socially deviant.

39 See Triseliotis, Feast & Kyle (2005).

40 ibid.

41 In the UK this had been possible from 1975.

42 In the UK in 2002 a similar veto was introduced into the Adoption Contact Register. Triseliotis, Feast & Kyle (2005) p. 15.

43 Coles (2004) p. 59.

44 ibid. pps. 85–89.

45 In their study on the perspectives on birth fathers Triseliotis, Feast & Kyle (2005) not only have a very small number but less than half of the men who were approached were willing to participate. p. 315.

Fathers and their illegitimate children 73

46 ibid. p. 187. Four per cent of illegitimate children did not want to know their birth parents.
47 Coles (2004) p. 230.
48 ibid. p. 237.
49 ibid. p. 233. See an interesting comment on the particular Western culture of putting babies up for adoption is in Susan Wadia-Ells' book *The Adoption Reader* (1995). She asked a group of birth mothers to contribute to a book she was editing on the experience of placing a child up for adoption. One writer, Kathleen Scully Davis, described the enraged feelings of the Mexican father of her illegitimate child: 'Angelo had no clear idea of why, if I wasn't going to keep the child, I wouldn't let him keep it. Who ever heard of giving away babies? In the Mexican community there is *always* a place for a baby ... Everyone in his family, especially his mother, would take care of the child.' p. 20.
50 ibid. p. 234.
51 ibid. p. 234.
52 ibid. p. 235.
53 For instance, in Australia, about 10,000 children were given up for adoption in the seventies, and 178 in the nineties, Coles (2004) p. 235. In the UK, 16,164 children were given up for adoption in 1968. In 1985 there were 4,189 and less than half of those were babies under one year. Howe (1992) p. 3.
54 Triseliotis, Feast & Kyle (2005) p. 319.
55 ibid. pps. 329–331.
56 ibid. p. 315.
57 About thirty-two per cent had described their experience of adoption as unsatisfactory. Triseliotis, Feast & Kyle (2005). p. 298.
58 Howe, Sawbridge & Hinings (1992) p. 18.

References

M. Ainsworth (1991) Attachments and other affectional bonds across the life cycle. In C. Parkes, J. Stevenson-Hinde & P. Marris (eds) *Attachment Across the Life Cycle.* London/New York: Routledge.

C. Archer & A. Burnell (2003) *Trauma, Attachment and Family Permanence: Fear Can Stop You Learning.* London/ New York: Jessica Kingsley Publishers.

P. D. S. Chesterfield (1774) *Letters Written by Lord Chesterfield to his Son.* London: Classic Reprint Series (2018).

G. Clapton (2003) *Birth Fathers and their Adoption Experiences.* Philadelphia/London: Jessica Kingsley Publishers.

G. Coles (2004) *Ever After: Fathers and the Impact of Adoption.* South Australia: Clova Publications.

DoH (2013) Adoption: Statutory Guidance. www.gov.uk. A. Hamblin (1977) *The Other Side of Adoption: Natural Mothers and their Adoptees Tell Their Own Story.* Surrey: Jigsaw Publications.

N. Hawthorne (1850/1970) *The Scarlet Letter and Selected Tales.* T. E. Connolly (ed.) London: Penguin Books.

D. Howe & J. Feast (2000) *Adoption, Search & Reunion.* London: The Children's Society.

D. Howe, P. Sawbridge & D. Hinings (1992). *Half a Million Women: Mothers Who Lose Their Children by Adoption.* London: Penguin Books.

H. Loewald (1980). *Papers on Psychoanalysis.* New Haven, CT: Yale University Press.

C-A Lopez & E.W. Herbert (1975) *The Private Franklin. The Man and his Family.* New York: W.W. Norton & Co.

74   *Fathers and their illegitimate children*

G. MacLean & U. Rappen (1991) *Hermine Hug-Hellmuth: Her Life and Work*. London: Routledge.

B. Prynn (2000) Adoption from a social worker's point of view. In A. Treacher & I. Katz (eds) *The Dynamics of Adoption. Social & Personal Perspectives*. London/Philadephia: Jessica Kingsley Publishers.

S. Shellabarger (1951) *Lord Chesterfield and His World*. Boston: Little, Brown & Company.

J. Triseliotis, J. Feast & F. Kyle (2005) *The Adoption Triangle Revisited*. London: B.A.A.F.

S. Wadia-Ells (1995) *The Adoption Reader: Birth Mothers, Adoptive Mothers and Adoptive Daughters Tell Their Story*. California: Seal Press.

6 Foster carers

I began the last chapter by suggesting that the concept of the adoption triangle could be more accurately replaced by the adoption circle that included the father. In this chapter I want to add another crucial figure into this circle, namely the foster mother or carer. The foster carer is called upon at the moment when a child is taken into care and may look after the child for a year or two before an adoption has been put legally into place. It is not surprising therefore that the foster carer may well be the first remembered person in an adopted child's life, but as I have discovered she is also an often forgotten and disregarded anchor in everyone else's mind

In Chapter One I took the case of the mythical Pythia in Euripides' play *Ion* and suggested she was an emblem of the unsung hero of foster-parenting. She had brought up Ion from birth, when Apollo had snatched him from the cave where his mother Creusa had left him. Her *de facto* care of him meant that there was no social expectation that she must keep Ion at an emotional distance from her. Instead, as any woman who looks after a new-born baby for any length of time, she grew to love him and cared well for him, and he in return called her mother in name even if not mother by birth. What was important about Pythia's foster care was that she had also held his identity in mind with the tokens that Creusa had left in his cradle. It was these tokens that held such symbolic importance not only for the forward thrust of the play but also for Ion's discovery of his origins and Creusa's re-finding of him. Pythia played the selfless role of a loving mother while at the same time guarding the tokens of love that connected him to his birth mother. Such a foster mother may be no more than a mythical Greek hero, but her tale helps us to imagine the powerful emotional experiences that are entailed in being a foster mother and to appreciate the selfless contribution that foster caring has often made in the history of child-care.

However, there has been another shocking side to the history of foster mothers. In 1858 Sir Joseph Bazalgette laid down the new sewage system in London. The work required that the Thames should be drained and at the bottom of the river they found 'the bodies of two hundred and eighty murdered babies.'[1] A little later in 1870, the bodies of 276 babies who were under one week old were found in Brixton and Peckham and a Mrs Waters was hanged for her wilful neglect of babies who were 'farmed out' into her care.[2] One result of these gruesome

76 Foster carers

findings was that new legislation, the Infant Life Protection Bill of 1871, was brought in as an attempt to save unwanted babies from an early death by requiring that foster mothers should be registered and inspected and that the number of babies they could look after was to be regulated. But judging from the case of Mrs Dyer in 1896, who 'was caught disposing of babies entrusted to her care by strangling them and throwing them into the Thames'[3] unwanted babies were still coming to an untimely end more than thirty years later. The social problem of how to care for the illegitimate baby when the unmarried mother had no economic support was of enormous complexity, as we have already seen in Chapter Two, and by the nineteenth century the type of foster care that was available was failing to ease the problem.

These two examples, of the mythical Pythia and the all too real Mrs Waters and Mrs Dyer, show how foster parents have played a significant part in the history of infant care, for good and for ill. As I have tried to pick my way through the history of foster caring, one of the most arresting features has been the way that the importance of foster care has been little regarded and foster parents are described as no more than 'a port in a storm' while a better arrangement is made for the child to be adopted.[4] How has this come about? There was a well-known case of *R. v. Nash* in 1883 that cut to the heart of the dilemma about the role of fostering and established that foster care could be disregarded when considering what was best for the child.[5] The case was important because the mother was given, for the first time, natural rights over her child even if she or he was born out of wedlock. This legal ruling has had positive repercussions for mothers ever since. But in its wake the case has led to foster parents being placed at the bottom of the list of valued child-care.

When Rose Carey was fourteen in 1875 she was seduced and became pregnant and was turned out of her home by her father. When she had her illegitimate daughter in 1876 she found a working-class couple, Mr and Mrs Nash, who agreed to care for her child for a weekly sum of money. Rose Carey could not continue the payment for long as she became ill and was hospitalised. The Nashes continued to look after Carey's daughter without payment and naturally grew fond of her. Four years later Carey fell on better times and became 'the kept mistress of a gentleman.' She wanted her child back but the Nashes felt that Carey's child was their own and they refused to let her go. There followed a year of litigation as the battle for the care of this child was waged in Court and then the Appeal Court. The contradictory judgements of several judges led in the end to a finding that '... There is in such a case a sort of blood relationship, which though not legal, [Carey's daughter was illegitimate] gives the natural relations a right to custody of the child.'[6]

We have already seen that when Justice Blackwood pointed out that an illegitimate child was a *filius nullius,* the mother was deemed to have custodial responsibility for her child, though she had no legal rights. Now this judgement was going further as it was stated that 'the affection of the mother must be taken into account in considering what is for the benefit of the child.' This might be seen as heralding a new understanding of the emotional ties between mothers and their children, but in this case the benefit for Carey's daughter was not straightforward. The judgement was that Carey's daughter was to be sent to her aunt, whom she did not know, because presumably Carey did not want the care of her daughter, though this is not specified. The reasoning behind the idea that this would be of 'benefit' to Carey's daughter was that she would become more respectable, or as Sir Charles Bowen ruled, 'When we consider what is for the child's benefit, the scale is turned by on respectability of the persons with whom it is to be placed.'[7] 'Respectability' was seen as of greater value than the stable working-class home that the Nashes had provided for Carey's daughter. One can hear echoes of this judgement to this day.

The result of this ruling was, as already stated, indicative of a change for the better in the attitude towards illegitimacy, and the natural rights of any mother who had a child out of wedlock were upheld and she could become a legal parent. But it has led to foster parents finding themselves in an ambiguous place in the care system in which they have no rights or voice. They are expected to provide temporary care that can end at any time and the emotional burden this puts upon them is not considered to be of account. In this particular case, it must have caused great suffering to Carey's daughter and her foster family. Overnight, as it were, the life of the Nashes and Carey's daughter was brought to an end without warning.

Several Children's Acts followed on from the *R v. Nash* ruling with the overall intention of supporting mothers and their babies. Today, if a child has to be taken away from his or her parents, the aim of social services is that this should only be a temporary measure. The underlying goal must be to restore the child to the mother or the family eventually.[8] This idea has had the unfortunate tendency to re-enforce the impossible position of foster care and foster parents are now exhorted to 'avoid alienating their foster children's affections from their families of origin.'[9] This may sound admirable in intention as far as the natural family is concerned but it does not take into account that it is an almost inhuman task for foster parents. How can they avoid feeling affection for the child they look after, especially if the care has continued for several years?

This situation becomes particularly acute when foster parents take on new-born infants who are under state care and protection. Such babies may have been born to parents who already have a history of violence or abuse against their previous children or who may have drug or alcohol problems. They are placed temporarily into foster care while social workers decide whether the infant can be returned to the family or whether he or she should be adopted. This period of care can often be lengthy as the parents need to agree to adoption and they can hesitate for months or years, or refuse all together.[10] Unsurprisingly, in such cases a strong attachment will be formed between an infant and the foster carers and inevitably the child will come to believe that the foster carers are the real parents. When this relationship comes to an end both parties will suffer and in the words of one foster carer, 'We lost a child to adoption very dear to our hearts ... and have been grieving for this child, therefore leaving me depressed on occasions and feeling whether it was all worthwhile.'[11] Another foster mother said 'The children we'd

78 *Foster carers*

had for nearly three years were moved on and I'd become particularly attached and they to us... And I've come to the point where I just can't do it again. That was one of my lows. I felt emotionally drained.'[12] These are heart-rending accounts of the task that foster carers are expected to surmount. How can foster carers 'avoid alienating the affections' of these children, especially if child has never known its original family? It surely flies in the face of the natural affection that will inevitably grow between a loving caretaker and a child. Yet there continues a silent devaluation of the human concern of foster parents as can be seen in the fact that 'foster parents,' are now called 'foster carers' and the impermanence of foster care is underlined.[13]

Another impossible difficulty for foster carers is the conflict that their care creates with adoption, if foster care continues for any length of time. There is substantial evidence that adoption is the best solution for children who have to be taken into care. Children need a permanent home but foster care, by the very way it has been designed, is not built to provide that. So, at the very outset foster care will create unintended psychological problems of broken attachments for any child who is fostered over several years. A recent case will illustrate this problem. Marie was a young unmarried eighteen-year-old girl who had her baby in a Mother and Baby Home. She'd had a very fractured childhood and she was in and out of care herself having experienced little adequate mothering. She stayed with her baby in the mother and baby unit as the social workers tried to help her learn how to mother her baby. After three months it was decided she was not able to look after her child safely and so he was put into foster care. This lasted a few months. The reason this came to an end is not known but he was placed with another foster carer. He was with this second foster mother for nine months and was finally adopted at aged fifteen months, by which time he had lost his mother and two foster carers.

This child has been adopted by a loving couple and adjusted well but he can have frightening and violent meltdowns.[14] The adopting parents did appreciate the early attachment that their son had made to his second foster mother and they recognised the importance of the foster mother's love for the boy. The adopting parents and foster carer took a little time in which the foster mother helped the child to trust his adopting parents, and this went someway to soften the pain of loss that the boy felt. Overall, however, research reveals that some of the most vulnerable children are the ones who are expected to be the most resilient to the experience of multiple care givers, even though it flies in the face of the need of permanent attachment for such children.

It is hard not to think that foster care has become the 'ugly sister' to the Cinderella of adoption even though foster care is an 'intrinsic' and necessary part of the care system.[15] One research group found a subtle stigmatisation of foster care, as though it was not 'normal.'[16] While another quoted a foster carer who said, 'Sometimes I feel you are at the bottom of the pile. Everyone's views – child/parent/social worker – seem to come first.'[17] This feeling of being at the bottom of the pile has been confirmed in much research. 'Foster carers are second class citizens,' one foster carer commented, while another said 'Foster carers are unimportant and their views ignored.'[18]

Foster carers 79

It is not only the work of therapists working with attachment theory at such places as the Tavistock Clinic who have emphasised the need for permanence for children in care.[19] This has been well confirmed in the research by Sinclair et al. (2005). They show that the best outcome for a child who has to be taken away from its family lies with the first foster family who take the child in. Yet as we have already seen, the present social system that endeavours to place children into adoption means that 'the emotional capital accumulated through the relationships between foster carers and children' is squandered.[20] One reason for this situation is that foster care has no legal foundation. This predicament has echoes of the difficulties that *de facto* adoption had before the Adoption Act of 1926, in which adopting parents had no legal rights over the children they adopted. Now we find that the delegated responsibility that foster carers are given limits the decisions they may make over the children they look after. They may be overruled by social services and find, for instance, that they have to ask permission from social services if the child wants a sleep over.[21]

To add to their difficulties, foster carers can feel they are 'living in limbo ... filled with unbearable uncertainty' from one day to the next.[22] They can never be sure when their child might be taken from them, as the underlying philosophy of foster care is that it should be seen ' ... as a means to an end rather than a placement of choice.'[23] What started off as a good solution to the immediate needs of children who had to be taken into care, has had a disruptive effect on the psychological development of the child. This was not what was intended but all the evidence shows that foster care runs counter to a child's need for an enduring and secure relationship. It creates a 'limbo placement' that is not in the child's best interest.[24]

One good description of the 'limbo' nature of foster care, is to be found in the memoirs of Allan Jenkins (2017) where in his experience foster care was little more than a 'holding pen' in which one was waiting for ' ... a dread visit from the social worker, who might pass you along, around or back.'[25] His memoirs begin in the early sixties when Allan was put into a Barnardo Home in infancy by his disappearing mother. He had an older half-brother, Christopher, and they were fostered when Allan was five and Christopher was seven by a couple, Lilian and Dudley, who were middle-aged and unable to have children. Allan and Christopher spent several years living in the country in Devon and Allan has many nostalgic memories of country life that led him eventually to find solace and meaning in gardening and writing about it. The foster parents offered them a certain peace and security that allowed both boys to find a way of healing some of their wounds and they seemed to be doing well enough. But trouble broke out as they approached adolescence and it became clear that they were no longer the dream sons of their foster parents. When Allan was fourteen and at boarding school he was waiting to be collected by Dudley for the Christmas holidays, but Dudley never arrived. Instead a social worker picked him up and told him that his foster parents found he was 'too much trouble, they are too old ... They didn't sign up for problems, puberty, illicit sex.' And Allan was signed back into the city's care.[26] He was made homeless, destitute and never saw Dudley again.

80   *Foster carers*

I think Allan's painful memoirs contribute to a more general debate about foster care and adoption. He wrote, 'I was proud to bear the mark of foster child but adoption is another level of belonging, gossamer close to never having to worry about being sent back, no longer on sufferance.'[27] This gossamer thread of longing to be in a permanent family besets children in care, and foster caring can be seen to undermine this elemental need because it is conceived as temporary. Allan discovered that Lilian and Dudley did consider adopting him and Christopher. One factor that may have persuaded them against adoption was economic. Allan found many letters that Dudley had written to social services over the years when Allan was in his care, asking for money for clothes and any extras the boys might need and it seems that Dudley was reluctant to spend his own money on them, even though he was not poor. This made Allan aware of the painful fact that Dudley was always calculating the cost of the care of his two foster children.

The fact that foster care is paid work may be one good explanation as to why it is seen as temporary by the state. It is undoubtedly true that the fee is an important factor in the decision that a foster carer makes in taking on the work. However, in a recent report forty-five per cent think the money they get is inadequate.[28] But in spite of the dissatisfaction that foster carers express about the amount that they are paid, the money plays a significant part in why they choose to become a foster carer in the first place. In adopting families, by contrast, there is no financial transaction from the state and it is assumed that adopters are able to provide care because they have greater financial resources. One can see that from the point of view of the state, adoption is financially preferable to paid foster care and this economic fact must play a part in social workers preferring adoption over foster care. However, while social workers may be striving to place a child into adoption, what bars them from considering foster carers as potential adopters is that many foster carers do not want to adopt the child as they would have to forgo the financial support. 'It is frequently only the need for a boarding out allowance which prevents legal adoption [by foster carers].'[29]

The nature of foster care has changed since Allan and his brother were fostered in the sixties. Now a child of five may be thought to be too old to be adopted and will be termed as having 'special needs' or being 'hard to place.' Such children may have had several foster placements and will have been emotionally fractured by their earlier experiences. In cases where adoption is not possible, the foster carers may find they are being lent on to provide a quasi-adoptive and more permanent home and suddenly, overnight as it were, they become valued 'long term foster carers'[30]. The concept of 'long term foster carer' seems to contain a silent hope that such 'a foster home ... might become an adoption home,'[31] but this hope is for the most part an illusion, not least because of another confusion that long-term foster carers face, as is well illustrated in the following case of eleven-year-old Adam.

Adam had been brought up from birth by his grandmother. At a certain time, and this is not specified in the report, the grandmother asked social services to take him into care and left the area. Adam was put into foster care and his grandmother would make irregular calls to him and promise visits that she failed to keep. When visits were arranged with the grandmother a pattern began to emerge: after about four days she would feel she could not cope with him and he would be returned to his foster home. Here was a situation where, on the one hand, the grandmother avowed her love for Adam while, on the other, she rejected him because of his bad behaviour. Understandably, Adam was troubled by his grandmother's erratic behaviour which sent him 'beserk,' but social services and the foster carer were caught up in an impossible situation.[32] The long-term goal of the social worker was to facilitate Adam's eventual return to his family and his foster carer was expected to look after him when needed while remaining at an emotional distance. This situation was clearly not in the best interests of anyone, least of all Adam or his foster carer. Adam could never be sure where his home lay and his foster mother who gave him 'consistent care ... and is very fond of him and committed to him' could never know how long he would remain with her. What upheld this impossible situation was the legal rights of the grandmother who could insist she wanted him returned to her, but could expect to return him to his foster carers when he was too difficult for her to manage.[33] It seems from this example that 'long term fostering' needs to be more securely based.

There is another difficulty that arises with long-term quasi-adoptive foster care when the young person reaches sixteen to eighteen. He or she may have been with foster carers for several years but when they reach this age, they are expected to leave their foster home and the money the foster carers received comes to an end. The state does provide for other accommodation for the young adolescent but in many cases he or she is too immature to manage independence. It is at this moment that it becomes painfully clear that there is an emotional cost that the young person has to pay because of the impermanence of long-term foster care. Some foster carers may be relieved that their work has come to an end, but there are many others who feel that at sixteen or eighteen a young person still needs a home. The research evidence of Sinclair et al. (2005) suggests that unless these fostered children get into training or university they do not flourish when they leave foster care and find themselves on their own. One child reported, 'my foster carers are the only family I had coz I haven't a family that cares about me ... now I am alone ... I was unhappy because I've moved around too much and every time I settled in somewhere I had to move again.'[34] Most young adolescents still need the support and concern of parents as they take the next step towards independence. This leads Sinclair et al. (2005) to suggest that foster carers should be supported financially for as long as it takes to get their child well established in an independent life. The idea that financial support should be given to foster carers of young people beyond the age of eighteen is supported by the statistical figures that suggest a quarter of all young people in custody had been in care that was no longer available.[35] In other words these adolescents were expected to leave their carers before they were emotionally able to look after themselves.[36]

82 *Foster carers*

I now want to give some flavour to the incredibly difficult, complex and often painful work that long-term foster carers are doing when they take on and offer a home for some of the nation's least favoured and hard to place children. Robin Solomon (2018) ran a group for foster carers, who were in difficulties and at the end of their tether. The idea behind the group was that if the carers could understand the reason for the way their unmanageable children were behaving they might be helped and the foster caring might be less in danger of breaking down. In the beginning it was a tumultuous experience for everyone as the distraught foster carers acted out the destructive projections that they were containing from their disturbed children. They behaved towards Solomon as though they were the delinquent and uncaring children they were looking after, and in the early days of the group there was '… chaos, the selfish presentation of some of the members … echoing the experience of the beginnings of the new placement.' Solomon reeled back despondent and exhausted by the impact of the group and tried to understand what was going on. In their turn the foster carers were full of grievance about Solomon's ineptitude. Solomon came later to see that the group's reaction to her reflected the foster children's reaction to their new foster home. She also came to understand something of the tumultuous feelings that these foster carers must have felt when their 'foster children … burst … into their homes, ignoring or conversely grabbing the carer's attention, imposing their own social rules … often full of grievance.' The conclusion, as the group came to an end, was that foster carers of 'hard to place' children needed support. With the help of the group they were better able to hold and understand 'the grief and disturbance of the children' and there was less danger that the care would break down and less likelihood that the children would be rejected and sent to yet another foster home.[37]

As I end this chapter on foster care, I want to suggest that there has been a significant re-evaluation of the work of foster carers. This has been partly fueled by the shortage of foster carers. Until quite recently foster carers tended to be a married working-class couple where the man went out to work and the wife stayed at home to look after the children. As more women are going out into full-time work and changes in the way family life is structured are taking place, there are fewer people who want to take on such arduous work. This has led to questions being asked of foster carers about their experience and the ways in which they would like to see changes. A particularly good summary was given about what needed to change if more foster carers were to be recruited, in Sinclair, Gibbs & Wilson (2004). One idea was that foster carers should be paid a salary with a pension. This could mean that they had some legal protection, especially in cases where they had been accused of abusing their foster children, or at times when parents demanded that their children should be returned. If their work was salaried, not only would they find that they were regularly paid but a salary would cover the cost of the destruction that many disturbed children perpetrate on the homes of foster carers. It might also mean that they could expect to be better informed about the children they were being asked to look after and given better support.

Another contribution to the re-evaluation of foster carers is the research by Boswell & Cudmore (2018). They take a more psychological direction and draw attention to the importance of foster carers in the emotional life of the children they look after. They do not question the assumption that it is in the best interest of the child to move from foster care into adoption but what they point out is that foster carers and the children they care for both face a loss when the child is adopted or returned to its family. They suggest that there has been a collective 'blind spot' in recognising this attachment loss which in turn can further the child's fear that it is un-loveable.[38]

Boswell & Cudmore offer eight recommendations to mitigate this 'blind spot'; the most important of which is that the break from the foster carer should be taken slowly and that continuing contact should be maintained for some time between adopters and foster carers, not least because 'One of the most distressing aspects of being in the care system is the experience of broken attachments, leaving children with an underlying sense of impermanence and low self-esteem.'[39] What they also show is that the broken attachments that foster children experience are two-way and the foster carers experience the loss of their child as well. When they were asked what they felt on relinquishing their child, a typical answer was, 'I don't think that they [the social workers and prospective adopters] realise you've had her from a baby, and you end up loving them ... You raise them like yours, you care for them as your own kids.'[40]

I hope it has become clear that I believe the work that foster carers are doing is heroic. It never ceases to be impressive that they are prepared to offer themselves as parents in this way. For many they hold on to the belief that their care does make a long-term difference to the child. Their philosophy could be characterised by the following words: 'The world may be different because I was important in the life of a child.'[41] While I am sure that in some cases this is true, I think that Sinclair, Gibbs & Wilson (2004) are right to point out that there needs to be 'a change of assumptions about foster care.'[42] At the moment foster carers are taking on work that differs from the expectation of adoption. They are taking on by choice the care of some of society's most vulnerable children and their altruistic work and their status as quasi adopters is providing an alternative form of parenting. There needs to be new legislation that gives foster carers some of the security of adoption while demarcating that what they offer is different. What might this mean? One interesting piece of research has suggested that foster carers might need to be more stringently assessed for it was discovered that foster carers who were securely attached were much more likely to be successful in caring for highly disturbed children.[43] If foster carers were then provided with more psychological training and theoretical understanding of the problems that beset insecurely attached children, this would lessen the number of breakdowns between foster carers and their difficult children.[44] This more intensive training would shift the assumptions about foster carers; they would be seen as registered professionals and they could expect to be rewarded and protected. In this way the assumption that foster care is not 'normal' would be cast in a new light.[45] I want to give the last word to Dr

84 *Foster carers*

John Macleod, who in a recent letter to *The Guardian*, wrote: 'foster families need generosity and love but also fair pay.' By this he meant that foster families, like himself and his wife, should have proper employment rights, training in 'skills to foster' and at least a minimum wage. Macleod acknowledges that to implement these changes would be expensive, but this needs to '.... be offset by better lives for the cohort of young people who currently leave care destined to make up around half of the prison population.'[46]

Notes

1 K. Adie (2000). p. 310.
2 I. Pinchbeck & M. Hewitt (1973) pps. 613–615.
3 ibid p. 597.
4 *The Shorter Oxford Dictionary* (1973).
5 P. Coles (2015)
6 I. Sinclair, I. Gibbs & K. Wilson (2004) p. 127.
7 J. Teichman, (1982) pps 67-69.
8 M. Steele (2006).
9 G. Schofield, M. Beek. K. Sargent with J. Thoburn (2000).
10 I. Sinclair, I. Gibbs & K. Wilson, (2004) p. 9.
11 G. Schofield, M. Beek., K. Sargent with J. Thoburn (2000) p. 3.
12 'For birth families, having a child in care was not a desirable situation... child adopted would have been so very much worse.' In I. Sinclair, I. Gibbs & K. Wilson (2004) p. 287.
13 I. Sinclair, I. Gibbs & K. Wilson (2004) pps. 68–69.
14 G. Schofield, M. Beek., K. Sargent with J. Thoburn. (2000) p. 87.
15 Personal communication.
16 I. Sinclair, C. Baker, K. Wilson & I Gibbs (2005) p. 7.
17 ibid. p.167.
18 I. Sinclair, I. Gibbs & K. Wilson (2004) p.71.
19 ibid. p. 98.
20 J. Kendrick, C. Lindsey., L. Tollemache (2006).
21 I. Sinclair, C. Baker, K. Wilson & I Gibbs (2005) p. 40.
22 B. Tizard (1977) p. 10.
23 L. Emmanuel (2006) p. 253.
24 J. Rowe & L. Lambert (1973) p. 16.
25 I. Sinclair, C. Baker, K. Wilson & I Gibbs. (2005) p. 11.
26 A. Jenkins (2017) p. 5.
27 ibid. p. 60.
28 ibid. p. 53.
29 I. Sinclair, I. Gibbs & K. Wilson, (2004) p. 28.
30 J. Rowe & L. Lambert (1973) p. 15.
31 ibid. p. 15.
32 J. Rowe & L. Lambert (1973) p. 17.
33 G. Schofield, M. Beek., K. Sargent with J. Thoburn (2000) pps. 272–273.
34 I. Sinclair, C. Baker, K. Wilson & I Gibbs. (2005) p. 29.
35 fullfact.org.the guardian.com
36 P. Solomon (2018). See also, BAAF. (2006) & (2008).
37 'More than 65,000 children are being fostered and a further 6,500 foster families are needed in the next six months.' (*Guardian*. 9.10. 2019)
38 S. Boswell & L. Cudmore (2018) p. 89. I need to thank Dorothy Judd for pointing out their research work.
39 ibid. p. 92.

Foster carers   85

40   cited in J. Andrews (2006) p. 273.
41   I. Sinclair, I. Gibbs & K. Wilson (2004) p. 146.
42   ibid.
43   M. Steele (2005).
44   ibid.
45   I. Sinclair, I. Gibbs & K. Wilson (2004) in particular pps. 105–125 on formal support.
46   *Guardian* letters 26.10.2019.

References

K. Adie (2000) *Nobody's Child*. London: Hodder & Stoughton.
J. Andrews (2006) In J. Kendrick, C. Lindsey & L. Tollemache (eds) *Creating New Families: Therapeutic Approaches to Fostering, Adoption and Kinship Care*. London: Karnac.
BAAF (2006) *Managing Difficult Behaviour: A Handbook for Foster Carers of the Under 12s*. London: BAAF.
BAAF (2008) *The Foster Carer's Handbook: For Carers of Children 11 years and Under*. London: BAAF.
S. Boswell & L. Cudmore (2018) Identifying 'blind spots' when moving children from foster care into adoption. In M. Bower & R. Solomon (eds) *What Social Workers Need to Know*. London/New York: Routledge.
P. Coles (2015) *The Shadow of the Second Mother: Nurses and Nannies in Theories of Infant Development*. London/New York: Routledge.
L. Emmanuel (2006) The contribution of organizational dynamics to the triple deprivation of looked-after children. In J. Kendrick, C. Lindsey & L. Tollemache (eds) *Creating New Families: Therapeutic Approaches to Fostering, Adoption and Kinship Care*. London: Karnac.
A. Jenkins (2017) *Plot 29: A Memoir*. London: 4th Estate.
J. Kendrick, C. Lindsey & L. Tollemache (eds) *Creating New Families: Therapeutic Approaches to Fostering, Adoption and Kinship Care*. London: Karnac.
J. Rowe & L. Lambert (1973) *Children Who Wait*. London: A.B.A.A.
G. Schofield, M. Beek, K. Sargent with J. Thoburn (2000) *Growing Up in Foster Care*. London: BAAF.
I. Sinclair, C. Baker, K. Wilson & I. Gibbs (2005) *Foster Children: Where They Go and How They Get On*. London: Jessica Kingsley Publishers.
I. Sinclair, I. Gibbs & K. Wilson (2004) *Foster Carers: Why They Stay and Why They Leave*. London: Jessica Kingsley Publishers.
R. Solomon (2018) In M. Bower & R. Solomon (eds) *What Social Workers Need to Know*. London/New York: Routledge.
M. Steele (2006) The 'added value' of attachment theory and research for clinical work in adoption and foster care. In J. Kendrick, C. Lindsey & L. Tollemache (eds) *Creating New Families: Therapeutic Approaches to Fostering, Adoption and Kinship Care*. London: Karnac.
J. Teichman (1982) *Illegitimacy: An Examination of Bastardy*. Ithaca, New York: Cornell University Press.
The Shorter Oxford Dictionary (1973) Oxford: Oxford University Press.
B. Tizard (1977) *Adoption: A Second Chance*. London: Open Books.

7 The adopted child

Historically the fortunes of the adopted child, as we have already seen, have been complex and interwoven with cultural traditions, social and religious values, and not least the entrenched belief that if the child was born out of wedlock it was in all probability carrying its parents' faulty genes or 'bad blood.' Since the Second World War this perception has shifted and by the 1970s there was a noticeable rise of concern for the adopted child. New questions began to be asked. How successful has adoption been? What do adopted children feel? And alongside these far-reaching questions there was a debate about whether the secrecy surrounding birth records was in the child's best interest. In this chapter I shall consider some of the earliest research findings about the adopted child in which the efficacy of sealed records became a central issue. I shall follow this by looking at the conflict that closed records created for the adopted adult. In my conclusion, I shall suggest that there still remains much to be debated about the psychological journey of the adopted child.

One of the earliest research findings that helped to open up questions about adoption procedures was a study of the life history of adopted people. This was undertaken by Mary McWhinnie (1967) between 1954 and 1956 who asked a straightforward question that had been unthinkable until then.[1] How successful was adoption for all those who were involved? This was an investigation that challenged the belief that legal adoption was the perfect solution to the social problem of unwanted children. But McWhinnie was undeterred and as a social worker she was in a good position to have access to adoption records. She was shocked to discover that there was 'no well-defined policy for adoption placements, and secondly, ... [no] ... indication of how successful adoptions were on the whole, and where they are not successful why this is so.'[2] She thought it was imperative to answer these two questions in the light of Bowlby's book *Maternal Care and Mental Health* (1952) in which he had stated that

> It is urgently necessary in many countries to make studies of what in fact happens to the illegitimate child of today – how many achieve a satisfactory home life with their mothers or immediate relatives, how many eke out their existence in foster-homes or institutions, and how many are adopted and what is the outcome.[3]

The adopted child 87

McWhinnie's research sample was drawn from people who had been born in Scotland and they were aged between twenty and sixty.[4] One of the most distressing conclusions she came to was that twenty-one adoptees out of the sample of fifty-eight were still struggling with deep emotional problems. This was a severe challenge to adoption at the time. Several reasons were suggested for the difficulties these adopted children had faced but the most far-reaching of her findings was that their problems were linked to the emotional capacity of the adopting mother. McWhinnie found that the securely attached mother had a more securely attached adopted child, whereas a mother who had health problems, whether psychological or physical, was the least able to form a strong attachment to her adopted child. In other words, the current adoption procedures had not considered the mental or physical state of the adopting mother and there was little recognition by social workers that adoption difficulties might follow. This was a revolutionary idea at the time but it has gradually been recognised as an important contributory factor to unsuccessful adoptions; today a thorough assessment of adopters and foster carers is commonly in place to find out how securely they are attached.[5] McWhinnie's research also supported another of Bowlby's findings that the child fared better the younger they were adopted. She found that the most successful adoptions were with children under the age of a year who had not experienced repeated broken attachments.

One of the ghosts that still lingered around the adopted child at the time of the research was the unconscious cultural stigma of being born to an unmarried mother. This would often reveal itself during the turbulent moments of adolescence when some adopting parents would round on the child and say such things as, 'you are a slut like your mother' or 'your mother was no better than a prostitute.' Such phrases could not only have a long-lasting effect upon the child's self-esteem but would help to confirm in the child's mind that she or he was different from its adopting family, which of course was true. Unsurprisingly, McWhinnie's research indicated that a new brush was needed to sweep away the unconscious prejudices that still attached to the stigma of illegitimacy. She believed that this could be done by ceasing to pretend that the adopting family was the same as a natural family. This obviously meant that the child's birth records needed to be open and available; in this way everyone could see the true nature of the situation and any damaging epithets that might be thrown at the child in moments of exasperation and stress could be challenged. Even more importantly she went on to state, it was every child's legal right to have 'ready access to factual information about their biological parents.'[6] And that wise comment helped to bring about lasting change.

At the same time as McWhinnie was publishing her research in the mid-sixties there was another important contribution to the debate about secrecy and birth records. This was the work of David Kirk in the US. He wrote two challenging books: *Shared Fate* in 1964 that was followed twenty-one years later with *Adoptive Kinship* in 1985. As a sociologist he had a different angle of vision about sealed birth records. He saw the sealed records as perpetuating a deception about kinship. 'When a person cannot legally obtain basic documents relating to

88 The adopted child

his or her own life, then that person does not have the basic rights and duties of adults as that term is defined in society.'[7] This led him to argue that the adoption of someone else's child posed new kinship structures that are different from biological kinship structures. A 'hoax' was being perpetuated by adoption societies who encouraged adopting parents to believe that there was no difference between the adopted child and the biological child. 'The definition of adoptive kinship as the equivalent of consanguineal kinship is false and misleading' and 'adoption has been officially obscured as a social fact' by 'sealed records of birth and adoption.'[8] This frank confrontation with the anxiety about the adopted child has had a very significant impact on adoption procedures and beliefs ever since. At the same time, it faced the adopting family with a paradox. It was a 'family' but not a 'nuclear family.'[9] What makes Kirk's argument come alive is that he and his wife adopted four children, so he wrote from his own experience and confronted many of the awkward questions his children asked, not least questions about incest. Could his daughter marry her brother because there was no blood relationship? At the time, in theory she could. And this fact in itself added important weight to his argument that the non-consanguineal kinship structures of adoption needed to be recognised. Kirk's two books were important milestones that started to point the way to a recognition that society should face the fact that there was a difference between an adopted child and a biological child and this should be recognised rather than hidden in secret records. The limitation of his research was that something was still missing, namely the voice of the adopted child.

If we return to the UK and McWhinnie's research in the sixties, it took several more years, until 1975 in fact, for every adopted child to have the legal right to see its birth record. In the US this is still a disputed right in most states.[10] Furthermore, it was not until 1989 that the child's rights were endorsed by the UN Convention on the Rights of the Child. But then a new anxiety arose. As we have seen McWhinnie had challenged the idea that the sealed record was in the best needs of the child.[11] Her view was partly due to an anomaly that had occurred in the adoption procedures; most adopting parents were being counselled to inform their child that it was adopted and it was encouraged that this should be done at an early age. The problem was that while the birth records were still sealed there was little that adopting parents could tell their adopted child, and the child naturally had many anxious fantasies about why their birth mother had given him or her up. It was becoming clear that adopting parents needed to know more about their child's background, especially when it came to health issues, and adoptees were beginning to ask more detailed questions about where they had come from. This general need for change was echoed in the Houghton Committee Report of 1970, that stated that a child needs to know about its origins 'for the proper development of a sense of identity and in order for his adoptive parents to have a fuller understanding of him.'[12]

The next research helped to inform the Houghton Report. In 1973 Triseliotis published a book called *In Search of Origins*. He questioned, between 1969 and 1970, seventy adoptees who, like McWhinnie's group, had been brought up in Scotland. He was not questioning the success of adoption, indeed all his research is

The adopted child 89

based on his belief that adoption is a good thing.[12] He was pursuing a more psychologically laden question. Why were some adoptees driven to search for their original parents whereas others might want to know about their ancestry but were not concerned to meet up with their biological parents? In other words, though there seemed to be a universal wish amongst adoptees to have their birth records opened, a distinction could be made between those who felt compelled to know their original parents from those who were not particularly interested.[13] The conclusion Triseliotis came to was that the searchers who wanted to meet up with their biological parents were the ones who were most disaffected by their adoption experience, 'The ones who were mainly satisfied with their adoptive home life were looking for information that would help them to complete themselves, while the more disillusioned ones were hoping for nourishment from mainly the mother.'[14] The implication of this conclusion was that if your adoption had been less than satisfactory you would be more likely to want to meet up with your original parents.

This was not the conclusion that many adoptees wanted to hear, nor was it the conclusion of other researchers such as Schechter & Bertocci (1990) who wrote, 'When the individual is disconnected from her biological family of origin, important aspects of the past and future are obscured.'[15]Verrier (1993) emphasised this even more strongly when she wrote, 'Although the idea of searching to reconnect with the biological mother is filled with conflict and anxiety, it should not be regarded as pathological. It should, in fact, be regarded as healthy.'[16] Taking a more middle of the road position, Howe & Feast (2000) suggested that 'Searching … can either be seen as a normal part of development or as an adverse response to adoption.'[17] Whatever the psychological truth of this debate, one finds that most adoptees believed that it was not their neurosis or unhappiness with their adopting family that propelled them to search for their original parents but a more profound existential contradiction that is inherent in adoption. How can they integrate the conflict of having two different heritages if they do not know their origins? A further contribution to this difficulty was that many adoptees were outraged and had felt that they had been lied to about their origins if their adopted parents had refused to answer their questions. Indeed Triseliotis (1973) would seem to support their distress because he believed that our self-perception '… is partly based on what our parents and ancestors have been, going back many generations.'[18]

Triseliotis' research findings that those who want to meet up with their natural parents are more disillusioned and unhappy with their adoption has caused further contention, not least because it is not clear that non-searchers are more psychologically contented with their adoption than those who search. There is some qualified evidence, suggested by Howe & Feast (2000), that 'non-searchers' anxiety about upsetting their adoptive parents is sufficiently strong to suppress the desire to search; [and] non-searchers have stronger fears about what a search may unearth.'[19] So this debate illustrates well the way that researchers cast their own shadow upon the way they interpret the evidence and we need to bear this in mind when we try and understand the subtle undercurrents that have rippled through the adoption process.

90   The adopted child

It was becoming apparent by the late seventies that there was an unmistakable groundswell of angry adult adoptees who could no longer be ignored. They gave voice to their dissatisfaction, at not being allowed to know about their origins by publishing their memoirs and, gradually, they achieved world-wide recognition. The best known accounts written by adoptees came from the US where sealed records were kept tightly shut.[20] One of the first to give voice to her concerns was the civil-rights pioneer Jean Paton (1908–2002) who, in 1968, described her bewildering adoptive journey in *The Orphan Voyage*. This opened up a new world of exploration about the experience and the psychological impact of being adopted. There followed another important memoir, *The Search for Anna Fisher* (1973) by Florence Fisher who travelled the world to find out who the child called Anna Fisher was. This name had been written upon a piece of paper she had found in her adopted mother's desk. When she discovered it her mother snatched it out of her hand and refused to answer any questions about who Anna Fisher might be. It was of course Fisher herself. She then undertook a brave but troubling journey to find her biological mother and father. She succeeded, in spite of the records being sealed, but when she met her biological mother, her mother initially denied she was the woman that Fisher was looking for. Their meeting was not a healing experience for either of them, and they were unable to make a relationship. By contrast her later meeting with her father was joyous and long lasting. What impelled Fisher to continue her twenty-year search for her birth parents was that she knew she had been lied to by her adoptive mother and she believed that above all else she had a right to know who she was. This very personal voyage helped to change public opinion and to establish that the adopted child has a legal right to know of its parentage.

There followed another important memoir, *Twice Born,* by Betty Lifton in 1975. This autobiography challenged more directly Triseliotis' view that an adopted child who insists on searching for its birth parents is more likely to have had an unhappy adoption experience and have mental health difficulties. This book also challenged the psychoanalytic view of the time that the searcher must be neurotic if it cannot accept that its adoptive mother is its real mother. When Lifton was seven her mother told that she had been adopted but she was expected to never mention this fact to her father, for he wanted her to believe he was her true father. She kept that secret until the day he died but it left her very uneasy. She loved her mother and was happy enough, but throughout her childhood she had felt disquieted in a way that had no words. When she was older she found an explanation for this feeling: 'I was born into a society [that] prophesied that I would bring disgrace to my [birth] mother, kill her reputation, destroy her chances for a good bourgeois life.' She had silently internalised this moral belief and it had left her confused about her identity. 'Looking into the mirror my eyes searched for clues.'[21] She could find no answer. When she grew into adulthood and was writing her first book, she experienced her lack of identity in a graphic way. 'I could find no voice to speak through, no style that seemed natural ... I was a shadowy, unsubstantial person, floating, not skating, through each experience.'[22]

The adopted child   91

She married the well-known psychiatrist, Robert Lifton, and he encouraged her to explore her feeling of being a shadow of her real self by confronting the meaning of her adoption. Robert Lifton was at that time training to become a psychoanalyst and knew the psychoanalytic world in Boston. Through his contacts it was arranged that Lifton should meet with Helene Deutsch (1884–1982), who had been in analysis with Freud. Deutsch's response to Lifton's desire to find out about her mother was to suggest that her wish was neurotic, and she needed an analysis to help her give up this desire to know about her past, adding 'The biological mother is unimportant in a case like this. The only reason you want to find her is that you did not have a good relationship with your adoptive one.'[23] Happily, for those who have taken heart from Lifton's defiance, she continued her search for her parents and challenged the legal opposition that she encountered.

Lifton managed eventually, and with much skill, to get around the legal prohibitions that were imposed upon her and one consequence was that she showed up the weakness of the closed system and demonstrated the way it could be short circuited. It also meant that she did find her parents. One result was that societies for adoptees, such as ALMA – the Adoptees' Liberty Movement Association – or Orphan Voyage, or Reunion Registers sprang up all over the US, and some states began uneasily to open up limited files on adoption, though the US is still dragging its feet behind Europe. The change of attitude towards sealed records that has taken place can in large part be attributed to the moral outrage of adopted people, such as Jean Paton, Florence Fisher and Betty Lifton.[24] These authors have helped to make clear that concealing an adopted child's origins is contravening its human rights. But perhaps more importantly they have helped to open the door on adoption and its meaning to adoptees with questions such as, 'how is one's identity formed?' and 'does it develop within the matrix of one's adopted family?' or 'are there inherited physical and psychological characteristics that contribute to the building blocks of one's sense of self?' These problems are more open to debate and reach back into the old 'nature and nurture' argument, though it has now become a discussion about genetic inheritance and its impact upon the psychological model of attachment theory.

There are many things to be said about Lifton's book. It has been helpful in confronting what Freud called the 'family romance,' which suggested that many children, as they face their ambivalent feelings towards their parents, invent a family romance that their 'real' parents are far superior and they have merely been adopted. The configuration of the 'family romance' for adopted children is necessarily different to the one Freud had in mind, because indeed they do have two sets of parents. All adopted children have the more difficult task of integrating not only the love and hate that they feel towards their adopted parents but they have to find a way of accommodating their progenitors as well, such that one set of parents does not become the depository of anger and disappointment while the other ones become idealised.

This difficulty can be played out when adopted adults meet up with their birth parents. The myriad fantasies that each will have held about their original family will be met by a reality that is necessarily different, and a lot of psychic work will

92   *The adopted child*

have to be done to find a satisfactory resolution on both sides. In many instances the dream of reuniting in perfect oneness with the original mother is shattered. The birth mother is often a quite vulnerable woman. In Lifton's case her mother was a very unsure and unhappy woman who had hidden her daughter's birth. She was too frightened to admit Lifton's birth to her son and family so Lifton found herself in a limbo where she was both accepted by her mother but hidden from the wider family. In the case of Fisher, mentioned earlier, who eventually tracked down her mother, she was confronted by a woman who said 'I'm not the person you are looking for,' even when all the evidence was in front of her.[25] One reason for these painful encounters in the seventies and eighties was that a child born out of wedlock was still seen as a badge of shame, as we have seen over and over again, and as a result the searching adult often found its birth mother wanted them to remain hidden. The new dawn of the opening up of birth records was leading to unexpected difficulties.

It is easy to see, with hindsight, that the legalised adoption procedures, whether in the UK in 1926 or the US in 1851, that concealed the child's origins were a violation of the child's human rights. It was as Kirk (1985) said a 'hoax' to uphold the cultural wish that the adopted child should be believed to be identical to the biological child. We can feel outraged that a child should be lied to about its parents, as today we have a stronger belief that our identity is forged on the anvil of generational history; the colour of our eyes, our height and the texture of our hair are all features that we inherit from our parents and research reveals that there is an almost universal desire for an adopted child to know what its birth parents look like. Sealed records have meant that adopted children do not have the privilege of celebrating their genetic inheritance. To add a little levity to this difficult debate, there was a much-ridiculed anecdote in my family. My grandmother and my mother's nanny were overheard to be arguing about the back of my sister's neck. Whose neck had she inherited? This was an argument that could only be possible in a family of known grandparents, and though it is in many ways a hilarious incident it also serves to highlight the uneven ground that adopted children experience. There is no-one to argue as to the looks the child has inherited, even if it is only the back of the neck!

It is also hard not to feel that there has been a tendency to see adopted children as disposable property. It is not unusual to find even to this day that adoptive mothers may be asked how much their baby cost. This attitude highlights the painful fact that throughout history a child's emotional needs have not received much attention until quite recently. This is not to say that all children have been unwanted, but it is to contend that it was only in the twentieth century that there was a significant shift of interest in the emotional and psychological life of the child.[26] This new attitude can be seen in the growth of Child Guidance Clinics, and in the published work of many remarkable child therapists from Hug-Hellmuth (1920) and Klein (1921) onwards. But an interest in the mind of the adopted child has lagged at least forty years behind.[27] If one thinks about why this has been the case, it becomes clear that the model of the nuclear family has not been wide enough to include the complex emotional experiences of adopted children.

The adopted child brings another life into the adopting family and has had other attachments, however fleeting, and these attachments add other structures to the inner and outer world of the child. 'Adoption ... spans the inner and outer worlds in particularly complicated ways. ... the internal worlds of the birth family ... the themes of parental sexuality ... the professional networks ... the legal system ... cultural values and beliefs, ideology; and even myth.'[28]

I find myself at this stage wondering why is it so painful to study the adoption literature? Shouldn't we all be rejoicing that adoption is the perfect solution for children who cannot be looked after by their own family? They have a chance of family life and loving care. And here I find there is a territory within the heart of adoption that we prefer to leave out. The adopted person's journey is so painful to hear because we have to face the fact that the adopted child, however successful the adoption may be, is a child who has suffered trauma and grief; in the words of Winterson (2011) 'there is an absence, a void, a question mark at the very beginning of our lives.'[29] It is this ineradicable and bodily experience of loss that distinguishes all adopted children from stepchildren or children who are never separated from their family; this is not to say that children from intact families never suffer or become depressed or have psychological difficulties but it is to say that there is a distinguishable emotional experience of having been given up for adoption that leaves a life-long mark whatever the age of separation and however loving the new mother may be.[30] Even a child who has suffered extreme abuse and cruelty from its family will often say 'I want my Mum!' to its adopted mother.

The idea that a baby adopted at birth suffers from an inexpressible grief has been argued in Nancy Verrier's (1993) book *The Primal Wound*. We have already seen in the work of Triseliotis (1973) that he believed that '... adoption is felt as a form of abandonment or rejection irrespective of the quality of the other experiences.'[31] Verrier goes further. She believes that what makes adoption so painful is that it creates a psychic trauma if a mother and baby are separated at birth; there will follow an existential crisis in the body of the infant that feels like an experience of death. The suggestion is that a natural bond with the mother will have grown in utero that links the unborn infant to the smell and the feel and the sound of the mother, heart-beat to heart-beat, or as Schore describes it, 'right brain to right brain.'[32] This bond needs to be distinguished from the attachment that develops over time with the mother or caretaker. Verrier believes that if the infant is adopted at birth the natural bond is severed and however hard the adopting mother tries she can never replace the birth mother. This is the trauma that the adopted child and its adopting mother have to find a way of facing and understanding; that is not to say that a good enough attachment cannot be forged but that moments of psychic collapse can occur, nevertheless, in the life of the adopted child. Rustin (1990) described this most eloquently when she wrote,

> Even in the most favourable circumstances, there has been an experience of moving from one mode of being mothered to another. This may be felt at quite a primitive level – smells and shape of mother's body are different, the

94   *The adopted child*

way of being held, fed, put to bed will all be a little different ... Even for a small baby, this transition in primary care is deeply registered, even though it is not understood.[33]

Verrier's book was based upon her own experience of adopting a three-day-old daughter, in 1969, and much has changed since then with the appreciation of Bowlby's attachment theory to the problems of adoption. At the same time there is substantial research evidence that an adopted child does manage the grief of being separated from its mother and adopted children do flourish. But what remains important in Verrier's work is the fact that the ghosts of the lost parents loom in the psyche of the adopted child even though there are many different ways of managing this loss. However, Verrier's idea of the primal wound has not found universal acceptance and she has been challenged by women who believe her view stigmatises adoptive mothers as 'un-natural.' For instance, one group of researchers accept that there is a primal loss that both an adoptive mother and child suffer, but believe that adoption can create 'resilience and recovery from loss as it is loss itself.'[34] While this is an important recognition that loss can be faced and give strength, it misses the psychological point that any child who is separated from its birth mother, at whatever age and whatever the experience, suffers. And the loss of this primary bond becomes increasingly important when considering the adoption of older children who are named 'hard to place,' as we shall see in a later chapter. So, in spite of the social and psychological changes that have taken place since Verrier wrote her book, the concept of the primal wound is as relevant to adoption today as it was in the 1960s and needs to be understood by all adopting parents, though it should not be used as a weapon to devalue adoptive parents but more as a support to help them negotiate their difficult and sometimes heart-breaking work.

As an example of the expression of the primal wound, Verrier discovered that if her daughter cried at night she could not comfort her. Her daughter would turn away from her, as though she was trying to tell Verrier that her arms were not the right ones, she needed her birth mother's arms. Verrier came slowly and painfully to understand that her daughter was grieving the loss of her biological mother and was not rejecting Verrier when she refused to be comforted. This is a familiar scenario that adopting mothers and foster carers encounter with adopted children of any age. What has only quite recently been recognised is that adopting parents need help to understand that their rejecting child is grieving and therefore their seeming hostility is rooted in traumatic loss.

As I come to the end of this chapter, I am going to turn to three examples of the adoption experience from the point of view of the adopted child. In the first example I have chosen triplets whose mother died at their birth in 1932. They were adopted, but at that time there was no language or even the idea that they had suffered a trauma, so their experience helps to highlight the change in social and psychological beliefs when contrasted with the other two examples of children who were born thirty years later. In 2003 Hunter Davies wrote about these triplets in a book called *Relative Strangers*. [35] Davies keeps himself to the

The adopted child   95

factual surface as he interviews the triplets, yet their responses do reflect the ethos of the 1930s, when the adoption of children was heralded as a perfect solution for all concerned.

The triplets were born in a Workhouse because it was '... the only hospital that would take ... [their mother] in without charging her.'[36] In other words, their parents were poor farm labourers with few resources. Their widowed father already had six other children and could not look after three delicate children, who were not expected to live. They remained in the Workhouse until they were taken on by the National Adoption Society. The triplets, two girls and a boy, were non-identical and were separately adopted and by the time they were four they were all settled with good adopting parents. One girl was adopted at eight months by a divorced mother with two of her own children, the second girl was two when she was adopted by a middle-class family who could not have children and had already adopted another child. The boy was not adopted until he was three and a half and again by a couple who could not have children. He remained their only child. Two of the triplets were never told they were adopted and believed their adopted parents were their real ones until they reached adulthood; the one who was told she was adopted and a triplet was never interested in knowing about her siblings or her family.

One of the things that is noteworthy about the accounts that the triplets gave to Davies is that they were all very happy in their adopted homes, and even the boy, David, who was not adopted until he was nearly four, seemed to have fitted into his new family seamlessly. Not one of them looked into the mirror and agonised over their origins or questioned their self-identity when they were adolescent, and when in adulthood they learned they were adopted they all expressed a total lack of any curiosity about finding out about their origins. In Triseliotis' view they were all 'non-searchers' who had been happy with their upbringing. I would want to add that their lack of curiosity also reflected the culture of the time in which the inward search for your feelings was neither rewarded nor respected and if you were not told you were adopted, there was no reason to question your origins.

This unquestioning attitude is in marked contrast to the twenty-first century culture of curiosity where investigation into one's social origins has become acceptable and fashionable. *Who Do You Think You Are?* is a popular television programme that carries the implication that if you do not know your heritage you cannot know who you really are. This concern did not affect the triplets until the wife of one triplet, David, encouraged him, or should we say 'allowed' him, to think about his origins and gradually the family history unfurled. Sixty-nine years after they had been separated the triplets met up, to the satisfaction of them all. Reading this account of the triplets' lives, following the death of their mother, gives the impression that their adoption gave them an untrammelled emotional life and this in turn reflected the belief in the satisfactory solution that held adoption in place at the time.

The cultural embargo on adopted children being curious about their origins has not always been as happy as that, and I have interviewed people who were adopted in the 1930s and 40s who have emphatically held on to their 'non-

96 *The adopted child*

searching' position as though they were defending themselves from something unthinkable. They do not want to know who their parents were and they do not believe that knowing about them could make any worthwhile contribution to their present life. What has happened more recently is that some of these 'non-searchers' find themselves being challenged by their children who are asking questions such as 'Who were my grandparents?' The children of non-searchers are prepared to investigate their parents' origins and to demand answers. This naturally brings up anxieties in the non-searchers as they face pressure from the outside that threatens their inner world. The experience of the triplets could be reassuring to these non-searchers. They can see that the triplets were delighted to discover all their siblings and this in turn helps to reinforce the idea that the truth about one's origins is not necessarily destructive.

My next example raises the issue that knowing about one's origins is not in all cases simple. The scarcity of children to adopt in the late twentieth century and the twenty-first century has meant that increasing numbers of couples have turned to inter-racial and inter-country adoption and taken on children who not only do not look like them, but have a very different cultural heritage. This presents all members of the adoption process with new difficulties that have become clearer as such adoptees have begun to voice their experiences. I am going to use as my text 'Living in Half Tones' written by an adoptee, Me-K Ando, who was Korean and adopted into the US by a Japanese mother and a Swedish-German father.[37]

One of the painful observations that Me-K Ando makes at the beginning of her article addresses a fundamental question: 'How could this white man and this Asian woman have conceived me?' The question about one's conception is one that all children have to ponder but, in this case, it was made more acute because Me-K Ando's parents could not possibly have conceived her. 'People look at me, and don't know what to think.' And she did not know what to think either. Me-K Ando came to believe that her identity was a construction, 'a manufactured identity' of '... who I would become,' built up, in part, because she looked different to her parents. We have already seen that many adopted children have been dismayed at not looking like their adopted parents, but for a child who has racial characteristics that are different from their adopted parents the problem becomes more acute. Me-K Ando's identity confusion was further symbolised by the different names that she had been given. Again, this is something that most adopted children experience, but in her case it expressed an existential crisis that was compounded by language. When she was adopted she was called Karen, to reflect her new US identity, Hiroko to reflect her Japanese mother's origins, and Mackenheim which was her father's family name. She'd had another name when she was adopted from an orphanage in Korea, Baik Me Kyung, not a name that would trip easily off American tongues. *Baik,* meant 'white' in Korean and this name was associated with the English woman called June White, who ran the orphanage where Me-K Ando lived. Me Kyung was added 'because it was a "pretty" name.' Me-K Ando's different names reflected her orphaned state. There was no record of her original name because she was picked up in the streets of Chechon at a year old by a social worker, who said her mother had died and no-one knew where her father was.

The adoption journey that Me-K Ando travelled was extremely painful to hear. In her conscious memory her Japanese mother was her mother and her Swedish-German father was her father, but she nevertheless experienced deep confusion. 'I looked at my mother but did not really see her. I could only see my father's pale skin and blue eyes, light brown hair. He represented what I was to become.' This was a dream she could of course never fulfil, and she became more and more distant from him as she believed she disappointed him. With her mother it was slightly different; Me-K Ando's identity confusion did ameliorate as she grew up and she could be thankful that she and her mother shared at least an Asian background.

She decided to return to Korea and find June White, the woman who ran the orphanage where she had been placed, hoping to find out more about her birth mother. As is common with many adopted children, Me-K Ando imagined that June White, her remembered 'caretaker' mother, had been a kind and loving person who would be pleased to see her again. The truth was that White was not interested in her and could not find any details about her mother except she had died, which was why Me-K Ando was brought to the orphanage. Me-K Ando's disappointment was compounded when White said to her 'I remember that you just clung to me when you got here. You know how you can just tell sometimes when babies are insecure. You were really scared, and wouldn't let go of me. That's why we tried to get you adopted straight away.' Me-K Ando felt with this remark that White had put a knife into her. The searing account of the little love she had received as a motherless baby was difficult to bear and it was made more difficult because Me-K Ando did not want her Japanese mother, who had accompanied her on this visit to Korea, to see the extent of her anguish as her fantasies about her early life were shattered.

Much research, such as that of Triseliotis (1973), discussed earlier in the chapter, has shown how difficult it has been for adopting mothers to accept their adopted child's past attachments. Adopting mothers have held a hope that they and their baby can start anew, and this has meant that many have not wanted to know about their child's birth mother. This seems to have been the case with Me-K Ando's Japanese mother. '... don't cry. It won't help, you know' was her attempt to console Me-K Ando. Mourning and grief were not to be part of the adoption journey that Me-K Ando and her adopted parents travelled, and Me-K Ando felt obliged to respond accordingly: 'I tightened my entire body to control the heaves that threatened to overtake me.' She ends her reflections on the difficulty of being an adopted Korean child in the US with an inward exhortation not to cry because crying 'symbolized chaos to me, a tangible loss of control. I didn't want to be out of control, at the orphanage, with my [Japanese] mother. I managed to hold back all my tears.' At the end of her account of her adoption journey Me-K Ando reflected 'I must release myself in order to achieve some kind of meaningful closure'; and here she seems to be saying she has still to learn to cry, and mourn her losses.

My third and final example helps us to understand the inner life of the adopted child in fine detail and at the same time brings together many of the issues raised

98 *The adopted child*

in this chapter. I have also chosen it because it is the best account I have read of the paradox that every adopted child has to negotiate, that of being given away by its living mother and then of becoming attached to another mother. 'She was my mother. She wasn't my mother.'[38] This experience is psychologically different from being an orphan or a stepchild as the adopted child's journey involves two competing claims to a life fully lived. I think this will become clear when I consider the autobiography of Jeanette Winterson's (2011) *Why Be Happy When You Could Be Normal?*. Winterson was adopted at six weeks old in 1959.

It is clear from the beginning that Winterson's adoption is not a happy one. Winterson and her adoptive mother get off to a bad start. Winterson cries for the first two years of her life and her mother believes 'The Devil led us to the wrong crib.'[39] One significant change that has taken place since 1959 when Winterson's adoption took place is that Mrs Winterson would not be acceptable as an adoptive mother today. She was a 'flamboyant depressive; a woman who kept a revolver in the duster drawer and the bullets in a tin of Pledge' who also had multiple health issues, 'a prolapse, a thyroid condition, an enlarged heart, an ulcerated leg that never healed, and two sets of false teeth – matt for everyday, and a pearlised set for "best".'[40] She weighed twenty stone.

Mrs Winterson had encased herself in the armour of the Pentecostal Church while preparing herself for the Apocalypse, but paradoxically Mrs Winterson's obsession with preparing herself for death brought some rewards to Jeanette's bleak and unloved life. Jeanette became enamoured with the language of the St James translation of the Bible that Mrs Winterson read to her every day. 'I especially like the "quick and the dead" – you really get a feel of the difference if you live in a house with mice and mousetraps.'[41]

It was Jeanette's love of language, learned from Mrs Winterson's reading of the Bible, that gave her the creative energy to find 'a language tough enough to say how it is.'[42] And in finding a language that was tough enough 'to say how it is,' Jeanette's autobiography reaches beyond the personal and illuminates some of the universal features of adoption. An adopted baby is a 'broken-hearted baby,'[43] echoing the same words as Verrier. This broken heart leads to anger and the acting out of 'what it feels like to be one who doesn't belong.'[44] This behaviour can easily bewilder and anger all those who are around but, what has not been recognised until quite recently, is that the anger is quickly followed by despair in the adopted child: 'I don't know why I don't please ...'[45] And perhaps more importantly, Winterson adds, 'All adopted children blame themselves,' and this is an inevitable characteristic that all adopted children feel.[46]

There were uniquely horrifying features about Winterson's experience with her adoptive mother, where she was locked into the coal cellar or put out of the house all night to sleep on the front door step, and in early adolescence she was put through an exorcism. Happily, most adopted children are not treated in this way. But Winterson did display difficulties that many adopted children experience, notably a problem in understanding what she was meant to learn at school. She expressed her intellectual confusion in this way: '... adoption drops you into the story after it has started. It's like reading a book with the first few pages missing.

The adopted child 99

It's like arriving after curtain up. The feeling that something is missing never, ever leaves you – and it can't, and it shouldn't, because something is missing.[47] This inability to thrive at school is familiar in many adopted children because there is often a lack of recognition that 'something is missing' in an adopted child's life. They are distracted by their confusion or 'broken heart.' But when this is acknowledged, both at home and at school, the intellectual difficulties can begin to dissolve and a child's inherent intelligence can begin to grow.

Winterson's unhappy childhood did lead her to a serious suicidal breakdown after her success with her first semi-autobiographical novel, *Oranges Are Not the Only Fruit* (1985). Her fame had not given her the love she needed to heal. She had internalised a pattern of behaviour, that she had experienced with Mrs Winterson, of pushing away friends and being left desolate because she was again on the outside. Inexorably she was led back into the unhealed trauma of being given up by her mother when she was six weeks old, and who, she learned, had breast-fed her throughout this period. Here she discovered her violent destructive rage as well as the desperate infant inwardly calling 'Mummy Mummy.'[48] She had the strength to hold on through this phase of madness and found a way of working with her own mind's 'brokeness' by writing a children's story that helped to contain her. I don't want to suggest that all adopted children are prone to a suicidal breakdown, but Winterson's breakdown did lead her to the farthest reaches of her mind where she discovered rage and despair and a difficulty in letting herself be loved. These are the emotions that are embedded in the unconscious mind of the adopted child, but if they are recognised and spoken about by all those concerned then they have a better chance of healing.

The end of Winterson's autobiography brings her to a meeting with her birth mother, and in its description, we get a fuller picture of the paradoxical position that adopted adults face when they meet their infant image in the eyes of their birth mother. Mother and daughter were delighted to meet each other, and Winterson recognised there were similarities between them. 'Yes we are alike. The optimism, the self reliance. The ease we have in our own bodies.'[49] She also heard that her mother had really loved her and had not wanted to give her up. Then the question arose, how could Winterson reconcile what she had become now, Oxford educated, in contrast to '... a big noisy family who go ballroom dancing and live forever'?[50] A painful cultural distance yawned, 'I feel proud – of them, of me, of our past, our heritage. And I feel very sad. I shouldn't be the only one to have been educated. Everyone is intelligent.'[51] This recognition was followed by another and more complicated understanding that, in spite of her traumatic upbringing, 'Mrs W gave me ... a dark gift but not a useless one.' Winterson was straddled between two competing emotional loyalties, to her birth mother and to Mrs Winterson who was 'monstrous and impossible ... but how absolutely right for someone like me.'[52] On the third meeting with her mother, Winterson had a row in which she expressed her anger with her mother for abandoning her and through this she was led to recognise that Mrs Winterson had at least been there for her. At the end she acknowledges that 'I have to hold these things together and feel them both/all.'[53]

100 *The adopted child*

I began this chapter with the question that McWhinnie asked in 1954: what is the experience for an adopted child? I have ended with one unique and vivid account, written sixty years later, that helps to answer some of those questions. Adoption is a good solution for those children who cannot be looked after by their original families, but nevertheless adoption does involve heart-break and existential doubt; why me? what have I done wrong? And this is often followed by anger and despair. These are universal emotional responses that naturally follow. The contribution that Winterson's autobiography has made to the adoption literature is that she makes it clear that there are creative ways of dealing with this difficult beginning if you can find 'a language tough enough to say how it is' and a capacity 'to hold these things together.'

Notes

1 McWhinnie (1967) pps. 1–35. I want to thank John Mason for sending me McWhinnie's obituary that in turn led me to her work.
2 ibid. p. 24.
3 Bowlby (1952) p. 100.
4 McWhinnie (1967) p. 31.
5 See Oppenheim & Goldsmith (2007). In particular Steele et al. (pps. 58–90) who emphasised the significance of attachment facilitating behaviours in adopting parents for successful adoption, and Dozier et al. who recommended the increased training in attachment theory for foster carers. (pps. 90–109).
6 McWhinnie (1967) p. 268.
7 Kirk (1985) p. 121.
8 ibid p. 160.
9 ibid. p. 158.
10 Howe & Feast (2000) p. 84.
11 In Scotland the birth records had been available since 1930 to any child over the age of twelve. Goldstein, Freud & Solnit (1973).
12 Triseliotis & Russell (1984), Triseliotis, Feast & Kyle (2005).
13 Triseliotis (1973) p. 3.
14 Triseliotis (1973) p. 159.
15 Schechter & Bertocci (1990) p. 84.
16 Verrier (1993) p.21.
17 Howe & Feast (2000) p. 17.
18 Triseliotis (1973) p. 166.
19 However Howe & Feast (2000) do also suggest that 'Non-searchers do think about issues of identity and worth but do not experience any great pressure or need to address them: their experience is one of feeing highly integrated into the life of their adoptive family about which they feel very positive.' (pps. 179–180)
20 There have been fewer publications in the UK about the experience of being adopted, and perhaps two of the best known are Kate Adie's (2006) autobiography, *Nobody's Child* and Jeanette Winterson's (2011) *Why Be Happy When You Could Be Normal?*
21 Lifton (1975) p.3.
22 ibid p.78.
23 ibid p.99.
24 Wayne-Carp (1998) adds another contribution. He suggests that the media attention of the Watergate Scandal of 1974, and the later TV film of Alex Haley's *Roots* in 1977, were crucial in bringing about changes in liberalising adoption practice in the US. The authorities were no longer believed to uphold the truth.

The adopted child   101

25 Fisher (1973) p. 205.
26 See Pinchbeck & Hewitt (1969/1973) on the changing face of child care.
27 The Child and Family Department of the Tavistock Clinic set up the Fostering and Adoption Team in 1983. Kendrick, Lindsey & Tollemarche (2006). See also the setting up of the Post-Adoption Centre in 1986. Archer & Burnell (2003). More recently, the work of Rustin (1999) and Music (2019) has increased the understanding of the child's internal world as a result of early trauma.
28 Hindle & Shulman (2008) p.1.
29 Winterson (2011) p. 5.
30 When I was writing *The Second Mother* (2015) I was considering children who were brought up by nannies and suggesting that when their nannies left, the child lived with un-mourned melancholia. I was particularly influenced by the work of M. Suchet (2007).
31 Triseliotis (1973) p. 155.
32 Schore (1994, 2002).
33 Rustin (1990) p.3.
34 Smith, Surrey & Watkins (2006) p. 156.
35 Davies (2003).
36 ibid p.10.
37 Wadia-Ellls (1995) pps. 179-.189. I am not annotating every quotation with the page number as it is a short essay. On more detailed inter-country adoption see also I A C. China, Intercountry Adoption Centre, www.icacentre.org.uk.
38 Winterson (2011) p. 99.
39 ibid. p.1.
40 ibid. p.1.
41 ibid. p. 28.
42 ibid. p. 40.
43 ibid. p. 20.
44 ibid. p. 7.
45 ibid. p. 113.
46 ibid. p. 39
47 ibid. p. 5.
48 ibid. p. 162.
49 ibid. p.216.
50 ibid. p. 217.
51 ibid. p. 218.
52 ibid. p. 214.
53 ibid. p. 229.

Bibliography

K. Adie (2005) *Nobody's Child*. London: Hodder & Stoughton.
C. Archer & A. Burnell (2003) *Trauma, Attachment and Family Permanence: Fear Can Stop You Loving*. London/New York: Jessica Kingsley Publishers.
J. Bowlby (1952) *Maternal Care & Mental Health*. 2nd ed.World Health Organisation. no.2.
P. Coles (2015) *The Shadow of the Second Mother: Nurses and Nannies in Theories of Infant Development*. London/New York: Routledge.
H. Davies (2003) *Relative Strangers. A History of Adoption and a Tale of Triplets*. London: Time Warner Books.
A. Fisher (1973) *The Search for Anna Fisher*. New York: Arthur Fields Books.
S. Freud (1909) *Family Romances*. S.E.9. 235–245.

102   *The adopted child*

R. Goldberg (2000) Clinical work with adults who have been adopted. In A. Treacher & I. Katz (eds) *The Dynamics of Adoption: Social and Personal Perspectives*. London/Philadephia: Jessica Kingsley Publishers.

J. Goldstein, A. Freud & A.J. Solnit (1973) *Beyond the Best Interests of The Child*. New York: The Free Press.

D. Hindle & G. Shulman (2008) *The Emotional Experience of Adoption; A Psychoanalytic Perspective*. London/New York: Routledge.

D. Howe & J. Feast (2000) *Adoption, Search & Reunion: A Long Term Experience of Adopted Adults*. London: The Children's Society.

H. Hug-Hellmuth (1920) Child psychology & education. *International Journal of Psychoanalysis*. 1. 316–318.

D. Hughes (2016) *Trauma*. London: CoramBAAF.

J. Kendrick, C.Lindsey & L. Tollemache (2006) *Creating New Families. Therapeutic Approaches to Fostering, Adoption and Kinship Care*. London:Karnac Books.

H.D. Kirk (1985) *Adoptive Kinship: A Modern Institution in Need of Reform*. US/Canada: Ben-Simon Publications.

M. Klein (1921/1975) The development of the child. In *Love, Guilt and Reparation and Other Works 1921–1945*. New York:Delta Books, pps. 1–54.

B. Lifton (1975) *Twice Born: Memoirs of an Adopted Daughter*. New York: McGraw Hill.

G. MacLean & U. Rappen (1991) *Hermine Hug-Helmuth*. New York/London: Routledge.

M. McWhinnie (1967) *Adopted Children How They Grow Up*. London: Routledge & Kegan Paul.

G. Music (2019) *Nurturing Children. From Trauma to Growth Using Attachment Theory, Psychoanalysis and Neurobiology*. London/New York. Routledge.

D. Oppenheim & D.F.Goldsmith (2007) (eds) *Attachment Theory in Clinical Work with Children: Bridging the Gap between Research & Practice*. New York:The Guildford Press.

J. Paton (1968) *Orphan Voyage*. New York: Vantage Press.

I. Pinchbeck & M. Hewitt (1969/1973) *Children in English Society*. Vols 1 and 2. London: Routledge & Kegan Paul.

M. Rustin (1990) quoted In A. Treacher & I. Katz (eds) *The Dynamics of Adoption: Social and Personal Perspectives*. London/Philadephia: Jessica Kingsley Publishers.

M. Rustin (1999/2008) Multiple families in mind. In D. Hindle & G. Shulman, *The Emotional Experience of Adoption; A Psychoanalytic Perspective*. London/New York: Routledge.

M. Schecter & D. Bertocci (1990) The meaning of the search. In D.M. Brodzinsky & M.D. Schecter (eds) *The Psychology of Adoption*. Oxford:Oxford University Press.

A. Schore (1994) *Affect Regulation and the Origin of Self*. New Jersey: Lawrence Erlbaum Associates.

A. Schore (2002) Advances in neuropsychoanalysis, attachment theory, and trauma research: implications for self psychology. *Psychoanalytic Inquiry*. 22. 433–484.

B. Smith, J.L. Surrey & M. Watkins (2006) 'Real mothers': Adoptive mothers resisting marginalisation and recreating motherhood. In K. Wegar (ed.) *Adoptive Families in a Diverse Society*. New Jersey/London: Rutgers University Press.

M. Suchet (2007) Unravelling whiteness. *Psychoanalytic Dialogues*. 17. 667–886.

C. Thomas & V. Beckford with N. Lowe & M. Murch (1999) *Adopted Children Speaking*. London: BAAF.

J. Triseliotis (1973) *In Search of Origins. The Experiences of adopted people*. London/Boston: Routledge & Kegan Paul.

The adopted child 103

J. Triseliotis (2000) Identity formation and the adopted person revisited. In A. Treacher & I. Katz (eds) *The Dynamics of Adoption: Social and Personal Perspectives*. London/ Philadephia: Jessica Kingsley Publishers.

J. Triselotis, J. Feast & F. Kyle (2005) *The Adoption Triangle Revisted*. London: BAAF.

J. Triseliotis & J. Russell (1984) *Hard to Place: The Outcome of Adoption and Residential Care*. London: Gower.

N.W. Verrier (1993) *The Primal Wound: Understanding the Adopted Child*. London: CoramBAAF.

S. Wadia-Ells (ed.) (1995) *The Adoption Reader. Birth Mothers, Adoptive Mothers and Adopted Daughters Tell Their Stories*. California: Seal Press.

E. Wayne Carp (1998) *Family Matters. Secrecy & Disclosure in the History of Adoption*. Massachusetts/London: Harvard University Press.

J. Winterson (2011) *Why Be Happy When You Can Be Normal?*London: Jonathan Cape.

8   Adopting parents today

In the last three chapters I have considered birth mothers, birth fathers and the adopted child. In this chapter I shall look at the fourth point of the adoption quadrangle: the adopting parents. I have decided to limit my discussion to adopting parents who take on what are called 'hard to place' children; that is to say children who are at least one year old and are usually older.[1] They will have been taken away from their parents by social services and will have been fostered and in care before they are adopted. I shall also include the adoption of another group of children who are taken away by social services from their parents at birth because their parents are addicted to drugs or alcohol. I am not looking at inter-country adoptions where it is still possible to adopt a baby at birth.[2] The difficulties that these older children are presenting to their adopting families, lead me in the second half of the chapter to discuss the work of a post-adoption service, Family Futures, that is providing a much-needed multi-disciplined approach for adopting parents and their disruptive children.[3]

Before I give some examples of the problems that adopting parents and these older children can experience, it is important to remember that today there are fewer new-born babies that are available for adoption because an unmarried mother with an illegitimate child is no longer seen as a threat to the moral foundation of our society, and so her child does not need to be found another 'respectable' family. Today, adoptive parents who are desperate for a child will find the majority of children who are available for adoption are not only over a year old but are also more troubled. The early days of adoption when it was possible to go to a Mother and Baby Home, choose a baby and take it home a few weeks later have passed and instead, that relatively simple transaction has been replaced by lengthy bureaucratic procedures.

While I said that for the most part the only children that are available for adoption are older, there are some babies, as I have already mentioned, who can be adopted because they have been taken away at birth from their parents who have alcohol or drug problems. Nevertheless, these are not easy or straightforward adoptions. These babies may be suffering from foetal alcoholic syndrome and this can leave lasting damage to their brain. As one psychiatrist has written, such a new-born infant

Adopting parents today   105

like any addict deprived of his substance, must go through withdrawal. This is a terrible thing to watch, as the helpless new born twitches uncontrollably and cries out in pain. Nothing can stop this pain – neither feeding nor cuddling – so even if the mother could care for the child, there would be next to nothing she could do.[4]

Once the baby has stabilised she or he may appear as quite normal and the neurological damage done to their brain in the womb may not appear for a few years. When symptoms do emerge the parents may then find themselves with a child whom they cannot control and as difficult to manage as any troubled child who was adopted when older.

The problem of how to help the adopting parents of all these damaged children has brought about some innovative changes in therapeutic thinking and is leading to an acknowledgement, as Music (2019) writes, that 'We are on the cusp of a paradigm shift in therapeutic work, one requiring an integration of multiple orientations, from neurobiology, attachment theory, psychoanalysis, systemic thinking and more.'[5] This multi-disciplined approach has been found to be essential if adopting parents and these traumatised children are to be helped. The basis of this therapeutic thinking is Bowlby's psychobiological attachment theory that has included the interview schedules of Ainsworth (1978.1991) and Main (1985) ,[6] as well as the insights of neuroscience on the development of the infant brain.[7] The theory suggests that there are four types of attachment behaviour that have been observed between mothers and their babies: secure attachment, avoidant attachment, resistant or ambivalent attachment and a category of disorganised/disorientated attachment that was added later. The disorganised/disorientated attachment was a response that had puzzled observers. In 1991 Main wrote, 'parental behaviour associated with the "D" category [the disorganised/disorientated] is not yet known.'[8] However, Ainsworth and Eichenberg's (1991) research suggested that this Category D attachment was linked to an infant who had been frightened by the mother's response, and in turn the mother with a disordered infant had had a parent who had frightened her as a child.[9] It was becoming clear, as Bowlby said, if '... we postulate the presence within the organism of an attachment behavioural system regarded as a product of evolution and as having protection as its biological function, many of the puzzles ... are found to be soluble.'[10] Bowlby's insights about the importance for the infant to feel safely protected from the moment of birth have opened new doors onto the understanding of the long-lasting effect of trauma on the development of the infant mind if this biological function is impaired or missing.[11] At the same time the theory suggests that if a secure attachment is established the baby will be able, over time, to modulate her or his emotions. If all goes well, by the time the child has reached three or four years old he or she will have begun to internalise a model of relationships that includes the development of a capacity to think and also to make narrative connections.[12]

106 *Adopting parents today*

The neuroscience of the brain has made perhaps the most significant contribution to attachment theory.[13] In 1991, Schore began his prolific research into the neurological basis of attachment and quite crucial in this work has been the understanding of the way the infant brain and body thrives if it is well-nurtured by a sensitive caregiver. Without this sensitive synchronising of 'right brain to right brain' of mother and child, the infant becomes stressed and this sets in motion chemical reactions in the body and the brain of the child that can deform the growth of the neural pathways and compromise the health and the emotional life of the child. However, though it may sound quite idyllic that the 'right brain to right brain' of mother and baby are in perfect synchrony with each other, there are also moments when they are out of sync.[14] The crucial observation about these times, when mother and baby are out of sync, is that not only are they inevitable but they are also necessary. It is the failure of harmony and the reparation of these moments that over time leads to the creation of secure attachment. For the insecurely attached child these moments of reparation are missing.

The infant brain shows a bottom-up growth, from the primitive reptilian part of the brain in the brain stem, to the mid-brain or limbic system where the amygdala lies, to finally the orbito- frontal cortex, where the right side of the brain via the growth of the corpus callosum joins up with the left side of the brain. Early damage to the development of the neurological pathways in the brain, through neglect or abuse, can devastate the brain's capacity to grow and change, and, as Music (2016) pertinently commented, 'Once the experience is burnt into the circuits of the amygdala it is there forever.'[15] It has been found that the size of the corpus callosum, that links the higher functions of the brain on the left side with the earlier right side of the brain, is smaller in the brains of traumatised children, leading to their intellectual impairment.[16]

There are other bodily difficulties that an infant can suffer. I have already suggested that an infant's brain can be damaged if the mother drinks alcohol or takes drugs during pregnancy; there is now further research evidence that an infant in utero can be affected if the mother is traumatised or stressed herself. This can create higher cortisol levels in her infant that in turn may lead to attachment difficulties when the child is born.[17] Overall, it is safe to say that due to the research that is being done in neuroscience on the developing infant brain and body, it has been found that raised cortisol levels are associated with the troubling disorganised attachment disorder, Category D, that is now being associated with borderline personality disorder.[18] Many of the older children who are adopted may have this disorder, and this can lead not only to the difficulties that adopting parents have to face, but also to the painful fact that these damaged children are always on high alert, whether it is to respond with a fight/flight reaction, or whether it is to shut down and dissociate from the circumstances they find themselves in.[19]

If we turn now to the present-day adoption procedures, it is important to keep in mind the research evidence of early infant attachment. A change following the Children Act of 1989 saw a radical shift in the philosophy of adoption as it

Adopting parents today 107

moved from 'the perfect baby for the perfect family' towards a belief that there should be 'a family for every child, not a child for a childless family.'[20] In order to achieve this goal it was recommended that in the first place, if a child had to be removed from its family, social workers should do all they could to facilitate the return of the child to its original family. While the rehabilitation of the child back into its family must seem the most ethical way of thinking about families in crisis, this has proved to be more fraught with difficulties than was expected. For instance, there have been many cases where the contact with the birth family can have unfortunate consequences on the child's mental health. As Burnell (2003) commented, 'Working with many families where children have had direct or indirect contact, [with their dysfunctional birth families] ... direct contact represents contamination and retraumatisation.'[21] Then there have been the economic difficulties that have been exacerbated by the last ten years of austerity. A recent article in *The Guardian* (2019) was headed, 'The Children Act. Has this far-reaching law stood the test of time for families?' One answer from a respondent to that question, Ruth Scotten, who is both a social worker and adoptive parent, seems especially pertinent:

> The idea of putting children at the heart of legislation was good in theory but I don't think it has been executed particularly well. My view is that children aren't heard and they are not always at the centre of things. This is due to a lack of resources to effectively implement the act.[22]

The Children Act of 1989 may have been admirable in its conception, but it has thrown up unforeseen difficulties.

To return to the cases where there has been a failure to rehabilitate a child back into the original family, inevitably there will follow a lengthy assessment by social workers of prospective adopting parents. At the same time there will necessarily be discussions with the birth parents about releasing their child for adoption. In some cases birth parents can end up in court disputing the proposal to have their child adopted. Therefore, it is not unusual to find that two or three years will have passed before an adoption is finalised.[23] One unintended consequence of this new approach of trying to rehabilitate birth families and their troubled children has meant that many children in fact suffer more when it fails. They can be shuttled between social care and rehabilitation and experience several disruptive years before they find a permanent placement. Inevitably, this will compound their attachment fears and will augment their distrust of close relationships. At the same time, the dreams of the adopting parents of creating a 'normal' happy family will be subtly eroded. It is not unusual to find that by the time adopting parents have had a child placed in their care they will say, 'You are so blinkered. You think it is going to work. You pour your love into these children and they are going to love you back without any problem.'[24]

Another way of looking at the increasingly fraught experience of parents and their late adopted child is to realise that the Children Act of 1989 was founded on economic considerations. The act dovetailed in very nicely with Government

108 *Adopting parents today*

concerns about the cost of institutional care or the fostering of children. It was clear that adoption was cheaper and a better way of providing 'family life' for children in care. What was not taken into account was that the new thinking about adoption entailed lengthy bureaucratic procedures that are not in the best interests of the child. Ironically, the economic argument that it was cheaper to have a child adopted, could be substantiated by Bowlby's attachment research in the 1950s on the damaging effect of institutional care. So, while there have been good psychological, ethical and economic reasons for taking children out of institutional care and placing them in adoption, what has got lost is the damaging effect that lengthy bureaucratic procedures can have on these children. A child who is potentially adoptable may have had many years of uneven care and this increases the emotional difficulties for all concerned.[25]

When the Children Act of 1989 was finalised, the ethical, social and economic changes in the philosophy of adoption had already been finding support in the development of psychoanalytic thinking that had been taking place. One book, written in 1973 by Goldstein, Freud & Solnit, was called *Beyond the Best Interest of the Child* and it had an influence on the thinking behind the act. The authors began by postulating the concept of the 'psychological parent,' in contrast to the 'biological parent.' The 'psychological parent' was the person who looked after the child from birth and who became the important attachment figure, yet they were not endorsing Bowlby's attachment theory. What they were offering was a challenge to the belief in the sanctity of blood kinship. They suggested that '... the physical realities of conception and birth are not the cause of emotional attachment.'[26] And so paradoxically this view paved the way to greater confidence that adoption could succeed because there was no good psychological reason to uphold the sanctity of the tie between mother and baby.

It was only thirty years later that the dispute between biological kinship and psychological parenting becomes a contentious issue. As we have seen in Chapter Six, by the late 1970s there were beginning to emerge some adopted children whose biological history had been hidden from them and they were demanding their rights to information about their parentage. Betty Lifton challenged the psychoanalyst Helene Deutsch, who claimed that Lifton's biological parents were unimportant; and in 2009 Verrier's concept of the 'primal wound' challenged the idea that there is no emotional attachment of the baby to the birth mother. Nevertheless, at the time when Goldstein, Freud & Solnit wrote their book, the concept of the 'psychological parent' helped to uphold the promise that an adoption could provide a good alternative for a child who could not live with his or her birth parents. This has proved to be the case and there has been little dispute that adoption has been highly successful, especially in those cases where the child is under a year old.

Adoption has only become more problematic once the idea of late adoption became imaginable and more troubled children were considered adoptable. An important influence on the idea that late adoption could be successful came from the US and, in particular, the work of the psychiatrist Foster Cline (1992). He furthered the understanding of the attachment difficulties of disorganised/

Adopting parents today 109

disorientated children, termed Category D, mentioned previously. In his book *Hope for High Risk and Rage Filled Children,* he was influenced by Bowlby's attachment theory, and went one step further. He termed these troubled children as suffering from 'reactive attachment disorder.'[27] This added a new dimension to the understanding of these children, and eventually this led to them being categorised as suffering from borderline personality disorder. But in 1992 Cline was postulating no more than that children were suffering from 'reactive attachment disorder,' and if they were to be successfully adopted, they needed to be treated with a new technique by confronting, head on, their troubled behaviour. For instance, therapists and adopting parents should confront these children with a benign paradoxical injunction, such as telling the child to see if it could scream louder, when it was in meltdown. The idea behind such a technique was Cline's belief that it helped the child quite quickly face its anger and fears and learn that their rage did not damage the therapist or the adopting parents. This is a technique that has not found support in the UK but, nevertheless, Cline's work helped to show that Bowlby's attachment theory could be applied to tackling the problems of attachment disorder in the late adoption of disturbed children. In the words of Archer (2003) 'With the innovation of late-placement adoptions, permanency planning and open adoption in the 1990's, it was American therapeutic practice that led the way, providing much needed hope for families with "high-risk children".'[28]

This brief account of the changing 'patterns of adoption' describes a picture that is beginning to emerge; adopting parents have to expect that their dreams of creating a 'normal' family will not be the reality and, amongst their many difficulties, they may have to face critical value judgements from the authorities if their child is seen to be troublesome.[29] For example, Leichtman who wrote the introduction to Kimble Loux's (1997) exploration of her adoption difficulties, *The Limits of Hope,* that I will later go on and explore, suggested that there is a deeply held conviction by society and many social workers, that a child in an '… unconditionally loving environment[s] provided by "good" adoptive families will eventually neutralize the legacy of past abuse and neglect.'[30] This belief is soon shattered when adopting parents find that unconditional love is not enough and instead they have an angry child who is disruptive and unable to settle into family life. Often adopting parents have feared to ask for help lest their child would be taken away by the authorities because of their conviction that they have failed to love the child well enough. As one adopting parent said, 'You're very conscious of putting on a good front and initially don't want to ask for help because it would seem like a bit of a failure.'[31] It is not hard to imagine the escalating difficulties that can get perpetuated by this vicious circle of false beliefs.

Alongside the mistaken belief that there is a magic wand of 'unconditional love' that can be waved and all will be well, there is a further undermining factor that adopters of these late placed children often have to face. They find that they are 'ill-prepared and out of their depth.'[32] It is not unusual to find similar accounts to the following description from a desperate adopting parent: 'She would scream and scream and throw herself down on the floor and she'd

110 *Adopting parents today*

keep that up for ages, sometimes several hours, when she was inconsolable. It was incredibly difficult.'[33] Or, 'The past four years with this traumatized child have been an escalating, passion-filled war of attrition, for which absolutely nothing had prepared us,' wrote another distraught adopting parent.[34] The behaviour of these traumatised children is a common reaction to their disrupted early life, and in many cases the social workers have not provided enough detail on the child's earlier experiences which inevitably adds to the adopting parents' problems.

If one imagines the heart break of the little girl who 'screamed inconsolably' or the boy who gave his parents 'four years of hell,' it is hard not to agree with van der Kolk (2014) who wrote, 'After forty years ... I regularly hear myself saying ... how could parents inflict such torture and terror on their own child.'[35] We want to believe that families are 'safe havens in a heartless world' and adoption has been believed to offer such a solution when families fail.[36] But adopting parents today, who take on these raging children, are, in many cases, taking on children whose attachments have been devastated. They can of course make a difference to the internal map of these children over time and there is reassuring research evidence that suggests many adopters and their children are satisfied by the outcome in the end.[37] But on the evidence of van der Kolk (2014), adopting parents cannot 'fill up the holes of early deprivation.' The adopting parent will always be the 'wrong person, at the wrong time, in the wrong place.'[38] This is a tough belief to embrace and adopting parents need all the help they can get as they face the limits of hope. One of the striking things that I have found over and over again, as I have read accounts given by adopting parents of their troubling children, is that they had no idea of what they were getting into or the nature of their child's difficulties. On top of this they found that there was inadequate support and limited access to the necessary professional knowledge of how to manage their child. Adopting parents need to know that they have taken on a terrified child who will need a lot of help before it can mobilise more modulated defenses, and their task is to be more than a 'good enough' parent; they have to be a 'super' parent that provides their child first of all with a feeling of safety.

I am now going to move into some case material to illustrate the problems that some adopting parents can face. In the first case, the difficulties an adopting mother had with her child reached into the adopting mother's own early life. As has already been suggested, it has been increasingly recognised that an insecurely attached adopting mother can have profound difficulties if her adopted child provokes her own disrupted attachments.[39] In this case Cynthia, the adopting mother, had had an alcoholic father who abused all his children and an alcoholic mother who could not protect them. When Cynthia was adolescent her parents divorced and Cynthia married quite young. She had one daughter but following a further complicated pregnancy, which left her infertile, she and her husband decided to adopt another daughter, Luisa, when their own daughter was four. There is no mention of how old Luisa was when she was adopted.

Adopting parents today 111

Sometime later, Cynthia needed help with her adopted daughter, following the break-up of her marriage. She entered therapy and her therapist came to understand that Cynthia's difficulties with her adopted and adolescent daughter stemmed not only from Luisa's early experiences but also from Cynthia's own unresolved relationship patterns. The most prominent difficulty was Cynthia's rage against Luisa when her needy behaviour triggered Cynthia's fear of being humiliated and shamed. It was this unregulated aggression in Cynthia that would sweep her away and that made for such a difficult relationship with her adopted daughter. Luisa was a constant reminder to Cynthia of her own beliefs that she was the faulty one, the one who was not good enough. In the words of Cynthia's therapist, 'Because Cynthia is so avoidant of her own needs for comfort and safety, as they leave her vulnerable to fear and humiliation, she often misses Luisa's cues and fails to see her as a separate person with needs and feelings of her own.'[40]

This case illustrates the way that adopted children, who have suffered traumatic separation from their earliest caretaker, need robust and confident parents if they are to find a way of managing well enough their physical and psychic responses to people and the world around them. They need parents who can hold on to their own belief that they are 'good enough' even when their child continually confronts them with rage and criticism and violent acting out. Cynthia and Luisa's troubled relationship illustrates how the difficult behaviour of an adopted child can become dangerously disordered if it triggers maladaptive behaviour in the adoptive mother. They are a good example of why both need outside help if such an adoption is to succeed well; and the case is a reminder that some adopting mothers, who may have had a troubling early life, can find it difficult to form a secure attachment with their adopted child.[41]

I am now going to turn to another case that comes at adoption from a very different angle. In this case the adopting parents are already successful parents of three natural children and decide to take on two hard to place children, because they have a social conscience and are aware that there are a lot of unwanted children in care. It is a personal account of the trials that Ann Kimble Loux, an adopting mother, went through, and she called her book *The Limits of Hope* (1997). In 1974, Kimble Loux and her husband, Mark, adopted two sisters of three and four.[42] This was in the US and there are of course some differences in procedure in the adoption of older children in the UK. But, nevertheless, this case serves to highlight the difficulties that most adopting parents of children who have been traumatised have had to face. At the same time this book is a reminder of the welcome changes that have taken place, over the last thirty years, as the effect of infant trauma on later development has become increasingly refined, both in the US and the UK.[43]

When Kimble Loux and her husband adopted Margey and Dawn they already had three young children of their own, and with hindsight this created an unexpected difficulty for these two adopted sisters. These children had known little about family life and they were expected to fit into the life of three children who were older, secure and more competent than them. One result was that

112 *Adopting parents today*

their behaviour was inevitably measured against their siblings' behaviour. This was the first difficulty that no-one had recognised. The eldest, Margey, was restless and withdrawn; she could not engage in eye to eye contact and could not bear to be touched. By contrast Dawn was over friendly and would go to anyone who would touch her and put her on their knee. She was described as 'sweet and cute.'[44] They had come directly from foster care and had no conscious memory of their mother. The first nightmare that Kimble Loux and her family faced were meal times. The two sisters gulped down food and drink and never seemed to be satisfied, eating twice as much as the other children. By the second week Kimble Loux and her husband could see that there was something seriously wrong with these children, but they had been given no information. It needs to be remembered that this adoption took place in 1974, before there was a legal obligation to provide as much information as was known. The girls' behaviour made the parents increasingly angry and they had serious thoughts about giving them up. To add to the confusion, when the social worker who had arranged the adoption was consulted, she could offer no understanding of the girls' behaviour and instead gave them reassurance. 'You have a beautiful family. You're making such a good home for these girls. God is going to reward you. He will give you strength.'[45]

The only information they were provided with was that Margey and Dawn had been in and out of foster care all their lives and at three months Dawn had been hospitalised for malnutrition. They were also told the parents had been alcoholic and Margey had been found with bruises on her head, but that was the extent of the knowledge they were given. There was no-one they could consult to help them understand the distressing and exhausting behaviour of their two daughters who stole food, clothes and toys and were unable to play and were disappointingly unlovable. School became a nightmare as none of the teachers had been trained to understand the disruptive behaviour of traumatised children, and the children found themselves without friends and shunned and teased by other students.

The parents struggled on and at six months they formally adopted the girls, but in their hearts they felt that 'so much of the joy as parents' had been taken away.[46] Their difficulties left them feeling more and more isolated and this was compounded by the lack of support or psychological understanding from social services or psychiatry. Kimble Loux was left feeling 'voiceless and helpless' and guilty that she could not love these two girls as she did her three other children.[47] She had been given no realistic expectation of what the children could achieve and one result was that she expected that the two girls could give up their anti-social behaviour if they tried hard enough. In other words, she saw their disruptive behaviour as a failure of will or intention. But there was something else that no-one had warned her about, and that was that these children had needs that they seemed never to be able to meet: 'Dawn's seemingly endless emotional needs frightened Mark and me.' [48]

The one thing that the adoption services had warned Kimble Loux about was the difficulty they might encounter when the girls reached adolescence. And this was when chaos broke out. Almost overnight when Margey reached twelve, she

Adopting parents today 113

became obsessed with her looks and repudiated her real athletic gifts which had done much to restore her sense of worth and pride. She failed at her schoolwork, deliberately changed her grades, and she stole clothes and make-up from school friends and Kimble Loux. When she was confronted with her delinquent behaviour, she asserted that 'her grades were not anyone's business but her own' and this included her lying and stealing; 'I don't care about anyone but me.'[49] Dawn, less angry but nevertheless following devotedly in her sister's footsteps, said 'I want to go somewhere where I can't be hurt.'[50]

The physical and emotional energy that always accompanies this adolescent period of growth, broke through the defenses that the two sisters had built up to protect themseves from their suffering. Their earlier traumas could no longer be contained and they raged. Margey cut herself off from all dependent attachments, and Dawn yearned nostalgically towards a dream that somewhere with the right person she would feel safe. By this time Kimble Loux was at the end of her tether, as she was also dealing with three other adolescent children, and her own work as a lecturer at university. When the idea of sending Margey to a boarding school was suggested it seemed like an answer from heaven: 'Just the thought made me feel as if rocks were falling off my shoulders.'[51] But being sent away spelt even greater disaster for Margey. She felt she had been 'shipped out yet again,'[52] and she turned the full force of her despairing rage on to Kimble Loux: 'If I'm a bad daughter, you're a bad mother,' she yelled.[53]

Margey's life then careered into ever more self-destructive behaviour. She was uncontrollable and ran away from two boarding schools and, when she was arrested, she ended up in a juvenile detention centre and then a psychiatric hospital. It was when Margey was in the hospital that her psychiatrist demanded that he should be given access to her early life history, which was supposedly sealed. There, for the first time, Kimble Loux learned of Margey's early suffering. When Margey was about two she was discovered to have three broken ribs and a fractured skull with bruises around her head and face. There was also evidence that she had probably been sexually abused. Not surprisingly, she was diagnosed with borderline personality disorder by the psychiatrist, and Kimble Loux was advised that it would no longer be possible for Margey to live at home. However, there was no suitable safe institution where damaged adolescent children could go and tragically Margey's life spiralled downward into drugs, unsafe relationships and finally prostitution and life in and out of jail.

When Margey and Kimble Loux reached this pit of darkness, Margey was given some therapy in the psychiatric hospital and some glimmer of understanding between the two of them broke through from time to time; not least because as Kimble Loux said, 'The longer Margey lived away from home the easier it was to feel sympathy.'[54] This was clearly true for Margey as well who was able to write an insightful letter to her mother in which she acknowledged that she often felt that

You don't seem to really care about what's going on with me and that hurts my feelings and makes me feel insulted ... and when I feel hurt I get mad,

114 *Adopting parents today*

real mad, and makes me mean and want to lash out at you. But then every time that happens I get depressed later and feel like the biggest fuck up and I begin to hate myself for the things that I've done.'[55]

There are few more eloquent descriptions of Margey's mental state than her own understanding of the disrupting emotions that overwhelmed her and made her life so difficult. It also beautifully captures the vicious circle that entangled both mother and daughter.

The difficulties with Dawn were less dramatic and less heart-rending for both parents because they were less entangled. Dawn was more upfront: 'How come you guys never accepted me for what I am?' she would reiterate over and over again, and Kimble Loux's response would be, 'You remember I promised you over and over again we'd get along better if you quit doing just three things – lying, stealing, disobeying.'[56] They could be said to be on different tracks, with Dawn longing to feel confidently accepted whatever she did and her mother believing that with a little effort Dawn could give up her difficult behaviour if she so wished and then they would get on. Dawn did not stir up Kimble Loux's visceral rage as Margey had and so they always remained more distant. Dawn, like Margey, left home early and married and had a child by the time she was nineteen. Her behaviour was much less self-destructive than Margey and she was able to sustain a relationship with her husband.

It was only when Dawn had her first son that some new medical knowledge about Dawn became available and helped to explain why Kimble Loux had found her behaviour so difficult to understand. Dawn's son, Billie Ray, failed to thrive, and it was easy to attribute his problems to Dawn's difficulties in mothering him. Social services stepped in and he was taken to a specialist medical centre. There he was diagnosed with a genetic disorder known as Williams Syndrome. The features of this disorder are numerous and lead to physical features such as a small elfin appearance, low intelligence but a happy-go-lucky personality that forgets and forgives. It is carried through the maternal line. When Kimble Loux researched into this genetic disorder, she discovered that many of the difficulties that she experienced with Dawn could be explained by this syndrome: 'Feeding difficulties, ... incessant chatter ... over friendly with strangers ... no interest in playing and interacting with peers ... frequently demands attention... easily upset by criticism ... concentration difficulties ... impulsive.'[57] While it was undeniable that Dawn had had a very disrupted early life, and a disorganised attachment would readily explain her difficulties, in the light of her diagnosis of a genetic disorder, the attachment disorder clearly does not explain everything about Dawn and Kimble Loux's difficulties in relating. Dawn's genetic disorder played a large part in her behaviour. What this case serves to highlight is that severe attachment disorder can be exacerbated by a genetic disorder, and this in turn would suggest how important a thorough medical examination needs to be in the case of troubled children as it might lead to fewer breakdowns as noted above.

Kimble Loux's challenging book ends on a realistic note. She eventually developed an ongoing and accepting relationship with both her daughters that

Adopting parents today 115

seems to serve them well enough by keeping them apart. 'Margey knows ... I will not bail her out of jail' and with Dawn, she writes, 'the miles between us contribute toward all these improvements in my relationship ...'[58] She then writes an Afterword that makes an important contribution to the debate about how to manage late placement children. She suggests that the marketing of these children in magazines and TV programmes gives a false promise to kind-hearted couples who are stirred by this type of advertisement. It is inappropriate that, '... families fortunate enough to be intact are being asked to solve social problems without the extensive expertise and support such undertakings require.'[59] This leads to the sensible recommendation that there should be more expert advice on the hazards that occur in adolescence for these children, not least because Kimble Loux came to understand that the two girls 'were much more focused on their sexuality as a potential solution' than her own three children.[60] The idea of a damaged child seeking sexual relations not for pleasure but as a solution to their existential crisis is an important explanation for the connection between adolescent pregnancy and child deprivation. Adopting parents need to be aware that this desperate way of searching for love and attention that their adolescent daughters might pursue has little to do with sexual desire.

Kimble Loux makes another important recommendation that there should be frequent respite care, either in the form of camps, or alternative homes or even institutions. In this way, there would be no drastic separations, such as sending Margey to boarding school, which felt like the ultimate abandonment. Finally, prospective adoptive parents should be well versed in theories about attachment and well informed about the possibility that 'there will never be any guarantee that children who do not trust will change their minds.'[61] They also need to face that loving an unloving child puts one to the limits of what is possible. At the time of writing this book in 1997, Kimble Loux quotes that '25% percent of at-risk adoptions are terminated' and she contends that many others would be hard pressed to say they had had a successful adoption.[62] This raises the difficult question that in some cases 'terminating the arrangement' might be in the best interests of everyone. What needs to be considered is that there may be children who are so seriously troubled that the best environment is an institution because 'families were too intimate, too intrusive, too demanding.'[63]

Following this sombre yet realistic account of one family's experience of adopting two traumatised children I am now going to turn to the work of a post-adoption organisation called Family Futures, and in particular their book, *Trauma, Attachment and Family Permanence* (2003). The provision they offer is a creative way forward for adopting parents who are having difficulty in bringing up children who have suffered early abuse, and their work also provides a helpful comment on the type of difficulties that Kimble Loux described. One of the greatest stumbling blocks Kimble Loux faced was that the adoption agencies seemed unable to countenance that her children had difficulties and she became increasingly isolated as she believed her problems could never be spoken about because they were her fault. The philosophy of Family Futures challenges the assumption that adoption difficulties need to be hidden. They believe that the adoption of

116   *Adopting parents today*

children who have been maltreated needs to be openly talked about and faced or these children will make impossible demands upon the adopting parents. This is what Family Futures sets out to provide.

Before Family Futures was founded in 1998 several post-adoption societies had been created in the UK in the 1980s, such as Adoption UK, NPN (Natural Parents Network) and PAC (Post-Adoption Centre), as a response to the reluctance of social services to acknowledge the problems that adopting parents can face. All these different organisations contributed to a change in thinking about the adoption of older and more troubled children. In the case of Alan Burnell, the editor of *Trauma, Attachment and Family Permanence*, he had been the director of the Post-Adoption Centre (PAC) established in 1986 before he moved to Family Futures. He had a co-editor, Caroline Archer, who had been helped by him when he was still working at PAC. She had been having difficulty with her four adopted children but had been very nervous when she approached PAC because 'we had been hurt, and made to feel culpable for our children's on going struggles.' Contrary to her anxieties she had found that Burnell and his co-workers 'opened up a new world to us: a world within which we had choices over the help we received for our family and where what we, as parents, thought and felt was truly valued.'[64] It was from this mutually rewarding experience at the Post-Adoption Centre that Burnell and Archer agreed to co-edit the book on Family Futures together.

The children who are brought in desperation by their exhausted and despairing parents to Family Futures, or who are referred by local authorities, are children who have suffered early developmental trauma and they are 'stuck' emotionally, doomed to act out, over and over again, their experiences in the hands of adults who had terrorised them. An example of the work of Family Futures is described in the case of two children, Jenny and Marty. Unlike Kimble Loux's two children, Jenny and Marty are not actual children, but two 'composite' portraits of children whom the centre has treated. Nevertheless, there are important similarities between Kimble Loux and her children and the 'composite' portraits of Jenny aged nine and Marty aged eight and their parents. The significant difference is that Kimble Loux and her husband fought in the dark with little help whereas these children, Jenny and Marty and their parents, were helped to understand why they were all in such a state of distress.

When a family is referred to Family Futures, the whole family, mother, father and children, are assessed, using insights from 'individual, couple and family work.'[65] Following the assessment, the whole family are invited to the centre for intensive therapy. The children are each given an individual therapist, and the parents have a different one. At the end of a day of therapy the whole family joins together for family therapy, in which there is open discussion, and at this point, the children's therapists may bring back into the group information they have been given by the children. The overall aim of the work is to shift the disruptive attachments of the children that make everyone's life so impossibly difficult. One of the best ways to engage the whole family initially is through active therapy. This means that at the end of a day of therapy everyone plays a group

Adopting parents today   117

game; they may have to get around an obstacle course, or they will be asked to paint a large picture together, and the hope is that through such playful interaction the children will gradually learn that it is safe to begin to trust that their parents will look after them properly.

It is an exhausting experience to read of the work, which in itself gives some measure of the depth of involvement of all members in the group. By the end of two or three days of intensive therapy the 'composite' family will have learned more about why they are all suffering so acutely. The adopting family will be given an opportunity to face again their disappointment that they were never able to have their own biological children. They will also be helped to accept their feelings of rejection and failure that they are not able to satisfactorily parent the children they have agreed to adopt. The more painful task that the whole family will have to face is the cruelty the children have suffered at the hands of their birth parents. Family Futures insist that all the details of the children's past history must be available, and that it must be shared with the adopting parents. When it comes to the children, they need to know about the reality of what they have suffered but this needs to be taken more gradually. As is already too familiar, the adopting parents are seldom given the full account of why the children have had to be taken into care and this leaves the parents fumbling in the dark. The philosophy of Family Futures is predicated upon the expectation that by revealing the extent of the physical and the psychological damage to the children, both the parents and the children will find a better way of dealing with the past.

In the case of the children who need to face their past trauma, it is assumed that an older child such as Jenny, will have vivid memories of her mother and an idealised longing for her to come and save her from her present family that she hates. Over time, and perhaps with a meeting with her mother, she is helped to realise that this is an unrealistic expectation, as she witnesses her mother's inadequacy. Alongside a possible meeting with her mother, Jenny will be helped to face the extent of the traumas she experienced, such as sexual abuse, and how her present behaviour is a response to her traumas. The hope is that eventually she will come to feel that her behaviour is no longer a necessary defense in the present circumstances, and that she will have a more coherent understanding of her past history, often termed 'narrative history.' In the case of the younger child, Marty, who will not have such an available conscious memory, he will be helped by gradually being told the extent of the brutality he faced. Over time, and with a lot of holding and soothing he may come to feel that his excessive temper tantrums are not necessary. His behaviour may change as he realises that his rage was his way of defending himself against his vulnerability and hopefully he may begin to allow his parents to protect him and 'baby' him. Jenny's journey will be more difficult.

What is impressive about the account of this intensive all-day therapy is that a family, who came with little hope that they could continue to all live together, leave with a life-changing experience that lightens their steps. There are still years of hard work ahead, but there is hope that they will all find a way of managing better as they are offered extensive help over the next two years at the very least.

118 *Adopting parents today*

The fictional parents in the presented case are better able to 're-parent' their children after the intensive week. They are encouraged by the team to allow the children to regress, while at the same time they are counselled to continue with play and physical contact. In this way they can all begin to have a few good times together and these can become the building blocks of greater harmony. It is to be hoped that during the two or three days of intensive therapy that the children's gradual knowledge and acceptance of their past history will help them to face the false hope that they will be able to return to their original family. They will confront the reality that they do have 'good enough' parents in the present, even though they would have wished their lives could have been different. Family Futures also offers an important therapeutic intervention by making an educational therapist available to help the children and their school to understand the difficulties that everyone is facing.

After writing *Trauma, Attachment and Family Permanence*, members of the therapeutic team went on to do research into the efficacy of their work with impressive results, even though the sample was quite small because the number of assessment tools used increased the statistical significance.[66] The therapy, that is called Neuro-Physiological Psychotherapy (NPP), is based on a sequentially structured plan that draws on the understanding of the early years of infant brain development. Fundamental to the work is the research evidence from neuroscience. As we have already seen, neuroscience has shown that early trauma effects the development of the primitive brain and as a result it leads to emotional and physiological dis-regulation in the child that leads to fight/flight or dissociation. These are reactive responses and Family Futures are finding ways to reduce this physiological reaction. The therapy begins with providing sensorimotor experiences through art and drama and play, as such activities all use bodily experience primarily. Once these first steps have been initiated, the child begins to have bodily experiences of pleasure and fun and this gradually builds up a capacity to trust and include others; this in turn initiates the next step towards attachment to the parent and therapist. Once positive attachment responses have been mobilised this allows the child to start to be able, with help, to regulate his or her emotions and this ushers in the growth of the mid-brain or limbic system. Over time and through the slow steps of the developmental sequence from bodily states to attachment, the cortical brain, that bridges the right side of the brain with the left, develops and this allows the child to begin to have a coherent story of her or his life, including a past or 'narrative' history.

The idea that therapeutic help for these traumatised children needs to be planned sequentially on the basis of the brain development is an innovative approach that is achieving success. In one of their research papers the troubled behaviour of the children, who had received therapy from Family Futures, had changed and endured over time. Perhaps even more importantly, none of these children 'had received a formal caution, charge or conviction, compared to 33.3% of the control group.'[67] This in itself is an impressive result and needs to be taken into account when costing the provision of Family Futures type therapy against the cost of criminal proceedings for the 33.3 per cent of children

Adopting parents today 119

who had had no help.[68] The therapy provided is of course expensive because they have found that the best therapeutic help is to provide is a 'wrap-around multi-disciplinary, brain-based, development and attachment focused intervention'[69] This requires a group of highly skilled therapists from the separate disciplines of art, drama, individual, family and educational therapy, all working together to provide containment and insight into the difficulties of the whole family. Furthermore, Family Futures needs in most cases to be relied upon over several years and be available at short notice, though the intensive phase of therapy only lasts for two or three days. All the research evidence that they have provided suggests that this multi-disciplined approach is changing the lives of traumatised children and their stressed parents and bringing about long-lasting benefits to all concerned. It surely behoves the Government to consider the long-term financial benefit of this type of mental health provision and recognise that it helps these children so they do not end up as casualties within the prison system or mental health system, costing the Government far more. One challenging issue that has arisen from the Family Futures research is the suggestion that 'a functional MRI study may provide more definitive evidence about the nature of the neuro-physiological change' they are helping to bring about.[70] But as they say, that is for the future.

In conclusion, I want to return to a comment made by Kimble Loux. She wrote that it is inappropriate that, '… families fortunate enough to be intact are being asked to solve social problems without the extensive expertise and support such undertakings require.'[71] As has been suggested throughout this chapter, adopting parents today face a very different task in comparison to those in the past who were able to choose a baby born out of wedlock of a few weeks old. They are performing an invaluable service to our society by providing a home to some of our most deprived and damaged children. They will be discovering that the family of their dreams may never be fulfilled and they may be feeling they are a failure. But they are not, they are heroes as they face their disappointment and the rage of their distressed children. They need all the help that society can give them as they struggle to ameliorate the neurological and emotional damage that has been done to their children. In the words of Burnell (2003) what is needed is that there should be 'Increasing realistic awareness within the community, developing broader social responsibility, and providing this precious population of caregivers with more systematic and coherent information and resources.'[72]

Notes

1 Briggs (2003) p.26. I have to thank Kate Springford for putting me in touch with Adrian Briggs who directed me to this work.
2 See in particular, Overseas Adoption Helpline, www.oah.org.uk, for a good description of the process. There is a brief description of an inter-country adoption in Chapter Seven.
3 Archer & Burnell (2003).
4 Cline (1996) p. 59.
5 Music (2019). p. 2.

120   *Adopting parents today*

6 Ainsworth, Blehar, Waters & Wall (1978), Ainsworth & Eichenberg (1991) Main, Kaplan & Cassidy (1985).
7 Bowlby (1969, 1973, 1980), Schore (2002).
8 Main, Kaplan & Cassidy (1985) p. 140.
9 Ainsworth & Eichenberg (1991) p. 180.
10 Bowlby (1980) p. 293.
11 for example, Beebe & Lachmann (1997), Krystal (1997), Laub & Auerhahn (1993), van der Kolk & van der Kolk (1987).
12 Ainsworth & Eicheberg (1991) made an interesting philosophical point that a securely attached child can be distinguished by the capacity 'to think about thinking.' p. 128.
13 Liotti (1992, 1999), Panksepp (1998), Porges (1997), Siegel (1999), Solms (1996) Trevarthen (1993) to name but a few.
14 Schore (2002) '… in these exchanges of affect synchrony, as mother and infant match each other's biological rhythms, each recreates an inner psychophysiological state similar to the partner's … These mutually attuned synchronized interactions are fundamental to the healthy affective development of the infant.' p. 441.
15 Music (2019) p. 49. See also Archer & Burnell (2003) 'Associations [have been found] between elevated cortisol levels and attachment disorganisation in infancy. Areas of the developing brain that may be affected by excess corticosteroids include fronto-temporal areas, including mentalising deficits … and the hippocampus system.' p. 132–133.
16 Music (2019).
17 Fisk (2000) 'demonstrated that an 18-week foetus reacts to uterine distress with increased secretion of the stress hormone cortisol.' Quoted in Archer (2003) p. 81.
18 Cline (1997), Schore (2002).
19 Porges (1997).
20 Howe (1998). see also Department of Education, *Adoption: A Vision for Change*, March 2016.
21 Burnell (2003) p. 204.
22 *The Guardian* (13.11.2019) p. 44.
23 On average it took twenty-seven months for an adoption to be finalised. The figures were given for 2014–2015.
24 Selwyn, Sturgess, Quinton & Baxter (2006) p. 84.
25 ibid.
26 Goldstein, Freud & Solnit (1973)
27 Cline (1992) p. 59.
28 Archer (2003) p. 63.
29 Selwyn, Sturgess, Quinton & Baxter (2006).
30 Leichtman in Kimble Loux (1997) p. ix.
31 Selwyn, Sturgess, Quinton & Baxter (2006) p. 127.
32 ibid. p. 92.
33 ibid.
34 Greenmile (2003) p. 113.
35 van der Kolk (2014) p. 132
36 ibid p. 31
37 Selwyn, Sturgess, Quinton & Baxter (2006), Howe (1998).
38 van der Kolk (2014) p. 286.
39 Howe (1998). 'Recent research in developmental psychology is recognising that the way parents have dealt with and continue to deal with their own childhood experiences affects the way they parent their own children.' p. 200. See also Steele, Kanuik, Hodges, Hillman & Henderson (2003).
40 Slade (2007) p. 247.
41 Steele, Kanuik, Hodges, Hillman & Henderson (2003).

Adopting parents today 121

42 Kimble Loux (1997).
43 A survey of 1165 placements made by the UK voluntary agencies between 1980 and 1985 concluded that one in five broke down within five years of placement. This was even greater with children who were adopted between nine and eleven, in which forty per cent were disrupted. Thoburn (1991), Rowe (1991). Selwyn, Sturgess Quinton & Baxter (2006) suggest a third of late adoptions are disrupted.
44 Kimble Loux (1997) p.5.
45 ibid. p.11.
46 ibid. p.23.
47 ibid. p.25.
48 ibid. p.37.
49 ibid. pps.45–46.
50 ibid. p.49.
51 ibid. p.52.
52 ibid. p.63.
53 ibid. p.72.
54 ibid. p.79.
55 ibid. p.111.
56 ibid. p.189.
57 ibid. p.239.
58 ibid. p.258.
59 ibid. p.260.
60 ibid. p.114.
61 ibid. p.262.
62 ibid. p.263. Music (2019): 'In recent years we have rethought trauma and developed new clinical approaches … New understandings of trauma explain why it can be vital to … build positive, safety-based feeling states.' pps. 117–121.
63 Kimble Loux (1997) pps. 264–265.
64 Archer & Burnell (2003) p. 15.
65 ibid. p. 82.
66 McCullough & Mathura (2019). See also Vaughan, McCullough & Burnell (2016) and McCullough, Gordon-Jones, Last, Vaughan & Burnell (2016).
67 McCullough & Mathura (2019) pps. 13–14.
68 There is research evidence from the US, Teplin et al. (2002) that '… people with childhood histories of trauma make up almost the entire criminal justice system in the USA.' Quoted in de Zulueta (2006) p. 4. Also van der Kolk (2014): '70% of prisoners in California spent time in foster care while growing up.' p. 168. Also, many of the children who come to Family Futures have been turned down for help by CAMHS services who continue to disinvest in the mental health provision for children and families who do not meet their referral criteria. Vaughan, McCullough & Burnell (2016).
69 Vaughan, McCullough & Burnell (2016) p. 1.
70 McCullough & Mathura (2019) p.14.
71 Kimble Loux (1997) p. 260.
72 Archer & Burnell (2003) p.60. See also the research commissioned by the DoH on *Supporting Adoption: Reframing the Approach*, Lowe, Murch, Borkowski, Weaver, Beckford with Thomas (1999). '… there is a growing realisation that, at least with regard to older children, there can be no question of the authorities washing their hands of the matter once the adoption order is made.' p. 10.There is also the suggestion that the Government is recognising the adoption of older children, can result in child to parent violence (CPV). 'It's the new big thing in adoption and even the Government is throwing money at it by making grants to adoption Support organisations.' Coogan (2014).

References

M. Ainsworth, M. Blehar, E. Waters & S. Wall (1978) *Patterns of Attachment: A Psychological Study of the Strange Situation.* Hillsdale, New Jersey: Lawrence Eribaum Associates.

M. Ainsworth & C. Eichenberg (1991) Effects of infant-mother attachment of mother's unresolved loss of an attachment figure, or other traumatic experience. In P. Marris (ed.) *Attachment Across the Life Cycle.* London: Routledge.

C. Archer (2003) Weft and warp: Developmental impact of trauma and implications for healing. In C. Archer & A. Burnell (eds) *Trauma, Attachment and Family Permanence.* New York/London: Jessica Kingsley Publishers.

C. Archer & A. Burnell (2003) (eds) *Trauma, Attachment and Family Permanence.* New York/London: Jessica Kingsley Publishers.

B. Beebe & F. Lachmann (1994) Representations and internalization in infancy: Three Principles of Salience. *Psychoanalytic Psychology.* 11. 127–165.

J. Bowlby (1953) *Child Care and the Growth of Love.* London: Penguin Books.

J. Bowlby (1969) *Attachment and Loss. Vol 1. Attachment.* New York: Basic Books.

J. Bowlby (1973) *Attachment and Loss. Vol 2. Separation: Anxiety and Anger.* New York: Basic Books.

J. Bowlby (1980) *Attachment and Loss. Vol 3. Loss.* New York: Basic Books.

A. Briggs (2003) Adoption and permanence today: A discussion. In C. Archer & A. Burnell (eds) *Trauma, Attachment and Family Permanence.* New York/London: Jessica Kingsley Publishers.

A. Burnell (2003) Setting up the loom: Attachment theory revisited. In C. Archer & A. Burnell (eds) *Trauma, Attachment and Family Permanence.* New York/London: Jessica Kingsley Publishers.

F. W. Cline (1992) *Hope for High Risk and Rage Filled Children.* Evergreen, Colorado: EC Publications.

F.W. Cline (1996) *Uncontrollable Kids: From Heartbreak to Hope.* Golden, Colorado: The Love and Logic Press Inc.

D. Coogan (2014) Responding to child-to-parent violence: Innovative practices in child and mental health. *Health Social Work.* 39. 2.

C.R. Daniels (2006) *The Science and Politics of Male Reproduction.* Oxford/New York: Oxford University Press.

F. de Zulueta (2006) Inducing traumatic attachment in adults with a history of child abuse: forensic applications. *British Journal of Forensic Practice.* 8. 3. 4–16.

DoH (2001) *National Adoption Standards for England.* London: DoH.

N. Fisk (2006) Does a foetus feel pain? *The Times.* 28. 03. 2000.

J. Goldstein, A. Freud & A.J. Solnit (1973) *Beyond the Best Interests of the Child.* London/New York: The Free Press.

L. Greenmile (2003). 'A Hard day's night': A parent's perspective. . In C. Archer & A. Burnell (eds) *Trauma, Attachment and Family Permanence.* New York/London: Jessica Kingsley Publishers.

D. Howe (1998) *Patterns of Adoption.* Oxford: Blackwell Science.

A. Kimble Loux (1997) *The Limits of Hope: An Adoptive Mother's Story.* Charlottesville/London: University Press of Virginia.

H. Krystal (1997) Desomatization and the consequences of infantile psychic trauma. *Psychoanalytic Inquiry.* 17. 126–150.

D. Laub & N. Auerhahn. (1993) Knowing and not knowing massive psychic trauma: Forms of traumatic memory. *International Journal of Psychoanalysis.* 74. 287–302.

Adopting parents today   123

D. Liotti (1992) Disorganised/disorientated attachment in the eitiology of dissociative disorders. *Dissociation.* 5. 196–204.

D. Liotti (1999) Understanding the dissociative process: The contribution of attachment theory. *Psychoanalytic Inquiry.* 19. 757–783.

N. Lowe, M. Murch, M. Borkowski, A. Weaver, V. Beckford with C. Thomas (1999) *Supporting Adoption: Reframing the Approach.* London: BAAF.

M. Main, N. Kaplan & J. Cassidy (1985) Security in infancy, childhood and adulthood: A move to the level of representation. In I. Bretheron & E. Waters (eds) *Growing Points in Attachment Theory and Research: Monographs of the Society for Research in Child Development.* 50. 1–2. 66–104.

E. McCullough, S, Gordon-Jones, A, Last & A. Burnell (2016) An evaluation of Neuro-Physiological Psychotherapy. An integrative therapeutic approach to working with adopted children who have experienced life trauma . *Clinical Child Psychology and Psychiatry.* 21. 4. 1–21.

E. McCullough & A. Mathura (2019) A comparison between a Neuro-Physiological Psychotherapy (NPP) treatment group and a control group for children adopted from care: Support for a neurodevelopmentally informed approach to therapeutic intervention with maltreated children. *Child Abuse & Neglect.* 97.

G. Music (2019) *Nurturing Children. From Trauma to Growth Using Attachment Theory, Psychoanalysis and Neurobiology.* London/New York: Routledge.

J. Panksepp (1998) *Affective Neuroscience.* New York: Oxford University Press.

S. Porges (1997) Emotion: An evolutionary by-product of the neural regulation of the autonomic nervous system. *Annals of New York Academy of Science.* 807. 62–77.

D. Rowe (1991) *Permanent Family Placement: A Decade of Experience.* London: BAAF.

A. Schore (2002) Advances in neuropsychoanalysis, attachment theory, and trauma research: Implications for self psychology. *Psychoanalytic Inquiry.* 22. 433–483.

J. Selwyn, W. Sturgess, D. Quinton & C. Baxter. (2006) *Costs and Outcomes of Non-Infant Adoptions.* London: BAAF.

D. Siegel (1999) *The Developing Mind: Towards a Neurobiology of Interpersonal Experience.* New York: The Guildford Press.

A. Slade. A. (2007) *Disorganized Mother, Disorganized Child. in Attachment Theory in Clinical Work with Children.* D. Oppenheim & D.G. Goldsmith (eds) New York: The Guildford Press.

M. Solms (1996) Towards an anatomy of the unconscious. *Journal of Clinical Psychology.* 5. 331–367.

M. Steele, J. Hodges, J. Kanuik, S. Hillman & K. Henderson (2003) Attachment representations and adoption: Associations between maternal states of mind and emotion narratives in previously maltreated children. *Journal of Child Psychotherapy.* 29. 187–205.

J. Thoburn (1991) Survey findings and conclusions. In J. Fratter, R. Rowe, R. Rowe, L. D. Spasford & J. Thoburn (eds) *Permanent Family Placement: A Decade of Experience.* London: BAAF.

J. Thoburn & G. Sellick (1997) *What Works in Family Placement.* Barkingside: Barnardo's.

C. Trevarthen (1993) The self born in intersubjectivity: The psychology of an infant communicating. In U. Neisser (ed.) *The Perceived Self.* New York: Cambridge University Press, pp. 121–173.

J. Triseliotis, M. Borland & M. Hill (2000) *Delivering Foster Care.* London: BAAF.

124 *Adopting parents today*

H. van der Kolk & B. van der Kolk (1987) Traumatic antecedents of borderline personality disorder. In B. van der Kolk (ed.) *Psychological Trauma*. Washington DC: American Psychiatric Press, pp. 111–126.

B. van der Kolk (2014) *The Body Keeps the Score: Mind, Brain and Body in the Transformation of Trauma*. London: Penguin Random House.

J. Vaughan, E. McCullough & A. Burnell (2016) Neuro-Physiological Psychotherapy: The development and application of an integrative, wrap-around service and treatment program for maltreated children placed in adoptive and foster care placements. *Clinical Child Psychology and Psychiatry* 21. 4. 1–14.

9 Reproductive adoption

We are at the foothills of a revolutionary change in our thinking about what constitutes a family and what a child needs for its psychic growth and well-being. In this last chapter I am going to explore briefly two issues in the complicated world of reproductive technology that touch back on the issue of adoptive and birth mothers. We have already seen the lengthy debate that took place about whether a legally adopted baby's origins should be kept secret. There has been a similar issue as to whether sperm or egg donors should be anonymous, and until quite recently the donor has remained unknown to their potential child.[1] A second problem has arisen over the use of surrogate mothers to carry the child of the infertile couple.[2] And here we see a new form of adoption. The surrogate mother is the legal mother who has to agree that her child shall be adopted by the woman whose child she is carrying. At the very least, all these new forms of fertility treatment throw into question the familiar tenet within psychoanalytic theory of the 'parental couple' in exclusive sexual intercourse. If a child can be conceived without sexual intercourse in a petri-dish and carried by a woman who is not the child's mother, where lie the baby's ontological roots? Do these different ways of being brought into the world alter the way we need to think about the psychological development of the child's internal world? Whatever the answer, reproductive technology has opened up some unfamiliar territory and as one fertility doctor said, 'Who the hell knows how it is going to turn out?'[3]

IVF (In Vitro Fertilisation) or ART (Assisted Reproductive Technology) offer at least five ways in which a baby can be created today. There is IVF treatment, where a mother's and father's egg and sperm are fertilised in petri-dish and returned to the mother's womb; secondly the mother can be impregnated with a donor sperm; if that does not work, the donor egg can be impregnated by the father's sperm and returned to the mother; fourthly, there are situations where the father's sperm and surrogate mother's egg are fertilised and returned to the surrogate mother; and finally the father's sperm and donor egg can be fertilised in a petri-dish and returned to the surrogate mother.[4] These forms of fertility treatment have become valued alternatives to adopting a baby for couples who find themselves infertile. At the same time, it has also enabled gay and lesbian couples to start their own families as questions are no longer asked about their suitability to become parents. They can also assert their reproductive rights.[5] All these cases of

126 *Reproductive adoption*

fertility treatment have not only filled a gap that has been created by the dearth of new-born babies to adopt but it has also made possible a rainbow of new family constellations and kinship structures. However, all couples, whatever their sexual orientation, still face the complex laws, roles and relationships that arise from the new ART techniques and in particular lesbian and gay couples may have an added difficulty because they are also 'simultaneously pioneering new languages, laws, roles, and relationships.'[6]

I am going to step back and touch on the history of fertility in the hope that it may help us to understand why fertility treatment has needed to keep the identity of sperm and egg donors hidden. In our Western culture there has been a far-reaching myth that a child could be produced without a man and a woman having sexual intercourse beginning with the story in Genesis where Adam gave birth to Eve from his rib. Greek civilisation has given us another influential myth that has underpinned our European culture in which Zeus gave birth to Athena, who sprang out of his head. In this case, Zeus had swallowed Athena's mother, Metis, and then carried Athena within him until she was full-term.[7] Perhaps the most influential myth in Western culture is the Christian belief that Jesus was not born from ordinary sexual intercourse but as the result of Mary being given a message from the angel Gabriel. All these differing myths conjure up the idea that babies could be born without human coupling and they have played an important part in our cultural imagination over the last two centuries.[8] Today these myths may have unconsciously given confidence to the early pioneers in human fertility treatment.

The mystery about how a child came into being started to be resolved by the eighteenth century, as scientific research began to more confidently assert that the male sperm and the female ovum had separate identities and therefore had separate functions. This knowledge, and the development of endocrinology, eventually led to opening the door on to the concept of artificial insemination and in particular the artificial insemination of animals. In Italy in 1780, Lazzaro Spallanzani (1729–1799) successfully impregnated a dog with the sperm from another dog.[9] This led a little later to an important development in Scotland by John Hunter (1728–1793) who was able to fertilise a woman with her husband's sperm.[10] More controversially in 1884 William Pancoast (1834–1897) in the US inseminated a woman with a donated sperm that both husband and wife thought was the husband's sperm.[11] The significant point here is that the far more complex problems of human insemination developed from animal insemination.

It was a revolutionary moment when it was recognised that animals could be impregnated by artificial insemination and that it could be used commercially. When I was a child growing up in rural England in the late 1940s, and long before human IVF was in the popular press, animal insemination was widely used for breeding horses and cattle. It was rare to find a bull running with cows in the fields. By the 1930s it had become possible to successfully freeze the sperm of bulls, a process known as cryopreservation that preserved the vitality of the sperm over time.[12] The frozen sperm could be used later to impregnate many hundreds of cows. In the case of dairy farming a bull that had a track

Reproductive adoption 127

record of producing heifers who had a high milk yield was the one that would be chosen. This choice of sperm was very satisfactory to the farmer who could thereby not only increase his milk yield but also increase his income.

It is clear that this method of artificial insemination of animals is a form of eugenics but it has not been trammelled by ethical considerations. It has, however, had an unexpected downside. The undoubted reward of producing cows who could increase a farmer's milk yield led in turn to the need for higher crop yields to feed these cows, and then there followed the need to fertilise the land to increase the crops. So, ineluctably, artificial insemination has been a silent part of the capitalist economics of growth and consumerism that is being openly challenged today as to whether it promotes either animal or human well-being.[13] As we shall see, this pull towards economic growth has become part of human reproduction programmes and has encouraged the commercialisation of human infertility through sperm banks, egg banks and surrogacy. In Thompson's (2006) far-ranging exploration of reproductive technology, *Making Parents,* she suggests that capitalism has moved from production to reproduction where 'now bodies reproduce things that make profit.'[14]

To return for a moment to my childhood, the artificial insemination of the cows on the dairy farm where I grew up was not without a certain amount of drama. When a cow was on heat a man would arrive, always in a white van, to inseminate the cow. His long clean black boots and white gown would give him an aura of medical authority. The sperm was chosen and put into a long tube that was then inserted into the reluctant and troubled cow, often accompanied by exasperated epithets from the man who was known in our family as 'the bull in the bowler hat.'[15] This dramatic moment that took place on the dairy farm of my childhood has its counterpart in the accounts of many couples who have undergone fertility treatment. Whether artificial insemination is used with animals or human beings, 'the subject of human reproduction raises huge emotions' as no other 'spare part' medical intervention is capable of doing, such as the donation of a heart or kidney.[16] These intense emotions are not only experienced by those who undergo IVF treatment, they are also aroused in those, like myself, who try to think about the process and imagine the physical and psychological stress that some infertile couples are prepared to endure in the hope of having a child. Miriam Zoll (2013) in her memoir, *Cracked Open,* records a particularly difficult journey that she and her husband underwent as they spent thousands of dollars on fertility treatment that failed. The failure, it has to be said, was largely due to her age. She was already forty when she started treatment and all the evidence is now indicating that at that age there is a high risk of failure.[17] Ironically, the wheel then turned back and Zoll ends her book with the thought that 'the cultural promotion of reproductive medicine as the primary solution to infertility has often overshadowed the ancient and established role that adoption has always played in helping couples build their families.'[18]

As I have already suggested, there is no doubt that IVF and ART have given a life-enhancing chance to infertile couples and gay and lesbian couples who now have the possibility of producing a genetically related baby. Its beauty, if it is

128   *Reproductive adoption*

successful, is that it not only bypasses the lengthy process of adoption but many people are now accepted for treatment who might have been turned down for adoption, such as gay or lesbian couples. In 1978 in the UK the first test-tube baby Louise Brown was born and became a household name. Thanks to the skill of Robert Edwards, Patrick Steptoe and Jean Purdy they were able to 'harvest' the eggs of Mrs Brown and then fertilise them in a petri-dish with her husband's sperm before re-inserting the embryo into Mrs Brown.[19] From that moment on an imaginative, scientific, commercial and popular revolution took place that far surpassed the success of adoption. Not only did IVF transcend the biological difficulty of infertility in either men or women but sexual intercourse was no longer the necessary condition for creating a child. The commercialisation of human infertility had begun. In 1972 Steptoe and Edwards had set up the British Fertility Clinic that was privately run. Then, following the world-wide success of Louise Brown's birth, Edwards and Steptoe in 1980 set up the privately run Bourn Clinic near Cambridge that was sold to Ares-Serono in 1987, a multi-national pharmaceutical company that supplied fertility drugs for assisted human reproduction. Overnight, as it were, human infertility became a potentially profitable commercial enterprise.[20]

Once it was possible to freeze human sperm, the first sperm bank was opened in Minnesota in the US in 1970 and there followed the Repository for Germinal Choice in California that was opened in 1980. The latter offered the sperm of exceptional men, such as 'Nobel Prize Winners and Olympic Athletes.'[21] In Denmark the Cryos International Sperm Bank was created in 1991 and the sperm that was on offer came from young men who were studying at the nearby University. Their sperm was deemed to be of high quality and because the donors were Scandinavian their progeny were expected to be 'tall, blond and blue-eyed' which was hugely popular. As a result '… ten thousand pregnancies have been achieved' in 1991 though the donors have remained anonymous.[22] One of most extreme of these surreal sperm banks was the creation of the Northeastern Cryobank in Boston. There can be found 165,000 vials of sperm donated by the ideal fit man, who is not too old, or young, or too tall or short, with no sexual deviant proclivities or carrying hereditary disease. The sperm of these perfect men is sold via a glossy photographic catalogue showing them as though they were male models.[23] Today there are many other sperm banks to found across the US with the largest sperm bank in California, the Cryobank, where millions of sperm are stored in hundreds of cylinders. At this institution there is a catalogue in which the donor history is recorded though there is no legal mandate yet in the US for a donor's history.[24] The catalogue can include childhood photos of the donor as well as his generational history going back three generations. There may even be a recording of the donor's voice as well as an account of his interests and 'poetry, songs, essays, drawings,' and so, if you choose this sperm bank, you will be able to have access to the mystery sperm that has produced you.[25]

It is hard not to feel a chilling sense of a 'brave new world' when reading about the creation of these commercially viable sperm banks, even though it has meant that there are many thousands of children that have been created in this

Reproductive adoption 129

way and they have brought lasting happiness to their newly created families. One difficult legacy that these sperm banks have created is the ethical and legal issue of fertilised embryos that are not used. Whose are they? And do they have a right to life? These issues are troubling to legislators but do not touch on my argument. There are, however, other difficulties. One way of thinking about the revolution that has followed from IVF is to say that from the moment that it succeeded, 'the facts of life' no longer held us in their firm embrace. The nineteenth century nuclear family of Freud's day may be seen as a twentieth century phenomenon that has been superseded by today's rainbow families.[26]

Following the birth of Louise Brown scientists across the world gained new insight into how sperm and ovum could be fertilised in a petri-dish, with the result that other test-tube babies soon followed. The earliest in the US was, Elizabeth Jordan Carr, born in 1981 and Amandine was born in France in 1982.[27] The doctor who succeeded in producing Amandine, as it were, was Jacques Testart. He later wrote about this momentous occasion in the following way:

> Alone with this living thing, at the end of the night, I often dreamt that there perhaps was "our" first child and that right now, it was coming into being for the first time. Never did I think it would be a boy, quite obviously, I knew it was female.[28]

The highly charged futuristic prose with which Testart described his night vigil waiting for 'our' first child to be fertilised, was hiding a more personal disquiet. After the birth of Amandine he gave up reproductive research for two reasons. 'He claimed that many of his colleagues were taking part in a sustained campaign of disinformation, not telling the public how slim the chances of a successful pregnancy and birth really were.' And he went on to say that '... it was the beginning of eugenics – of parents being able to select desirable characteristics in their offspring, with the richest being able to create an *uber*-class of strong, beautiful, intelligent, flawless children.'[29]

Winston (2006), one of the early pioneers in IVF treatment, has challenged Testart's first point about the slim chance of a successful IVF pregnancy with a counter-argument that 'humans are naturally infertile,' [30] and so if you compare IVF treatment with the ordinary method of conception, IVF treatment is more successful. In his IVF department at Hammersmith hospital Winston states that 'The average pregnancy rate ... at present is about 26%' and this is 'five times better than a single shot at sex' in normal circumstances.[31] This is an important fact to remember in the face of the physical stress and the emotional turmoil that is aroused by IVF treatment. But Testart's second point still remains; fertility treatment may have brushed too close to eugenics, and when fertility doctors recommended donors should remain anonymous, they may have an uneasy feeling that fertility treatment is perilously close to a selection process, for after all only the 'best' sperm and 'healthy' eggs are selected and banked.

It is a contentious issue as to whether there was an underlying anxiety that fertility treatment needed to keep itself out of the public eye, because it came too

130 *Reproductive adoption*

close to eugenics. As if in answer to that difficulty, in 1982 the Government did set up an inquiry into fertility treatment with a Committee of Inquiry into Human Fertilisation and Embryology chaired by Dame Mary Warnock. Their report in 1984 made several recommendations. There should be a statutory licensing authority and embryo research should be limited to an embryo under fourteen days old. They also recommended that donor anonymity should be maintained and human surrogacy should be prohibited.[32] The donor anonymity raised familiar questions that had accompanied the sealed adoption records, though now the debate was about the ontological status of the sperm and egg. This led in the UK to the Human Fertility and Embryology Act of 1990 (HFEA) and by 1991 it included that donors needed to be registered. However, it was not until 2005 that a modification of the act allowed children over the age of eighteen to find out if they were donor children and donors could no longer remain anonymous.[33]

It is this lengthy twenty-year debate about donor anonymity that has echoes of the debate about the sealed records of adopted children. In 1926 when the adoption laws were being drawn up, it was imagined that no respectable family who had adopted a child would want its 'lower class' mother breaking into their drawing room and disrupting their life with unseemly knowledge about the child's origins. Now, the problem rested upon the premise that a donor who later marries, would not want this embodied egg or sperm suddenly walking into his or her marriage unannounced and unwelcomed, nor would he or she want their natural children to be confronted by unknown siblings. There is, of course, a qualitative difference between being a potential child, such as is the case of a sperm or an egg, and a living child ready for adoption, but what is similar in both cases is the belief that secrecy and anonymity should be protected lest the truth should come out that the child is not fully the 'natural' child of his or her parents.

There have been other concerns about the need for secrecy about fertility treatment. One concern has been to protect parents from any sense of shame at their infertility, but this ignores what is in the best interests of the child. There have been many IVF children who have felt uncomfortable in their family, and as with some adopted children, they have wondered about their identity. Their discomfort has been matched by a new-found openness in society where they can give voice to their anxiety and it is quite acceptable to ask 'who do you think you are?' and expect to find answers, through DNA testing or on the internet. This has meant that the anonymity of a donor's identity has come under serious challenge from those who believe they have a right to know their genetic history, and this has close parallels to the way the sealed records of adoption were gradually opened up in most countries, though not in all states in the US.

It is worth remembering that there has been another powerful argument that has fuelled the question as to why donors need to be kept anonymous in fertility treatment, and this cannot be equated to the same anxiety that led to the sealed records of adopted children. There has been a fear that donors will not give their sperm or eggs if their possible future child could find them. The donor's intention when they donated these parts of themselves was motivated financially and they did not want to be encumbered by the thought of a future child.[34] This argument

Reproductive adoption 131

has been used to support donor anonymity and is not without good foundation because once the new act was implemented donations of sperm and egg began to dry up and some fertility clinics in the UK had to close. One unintended consequence has been that it has increased the number of people travelling to other countries for fertility treatment.[35]

Winston (2006) would take issue with my argument that IVF treatment and adoption procedures confront the child with similar existential questions about identity. He believes that '[i]t is pointless to make comparison, as many in favour of lifting anonymity have done, with the feelings of adopted children.' The reason he gives is that 'donor-conceived children' were not given away by their biological parents, which of course is true, and furthermore most 'donor-conceived children are likely to feel more loved, more wanted, more special, because the parents who have brought them up were prepared to go to such lengths to conceive them.'[36] This argument is well supported by other research that parents who go through lengthy fertility treatment are 'very committed when their longed-for child eventually arrives.'[37] Nevertheless, Winston undermines his argument when he cites the case of the portrait artist Stuart Pearson Wright whom he interviewed; and the case shows how there are similar existential and emotional questions that arise from donor anonymity as with the sealed records of adoption.

Stuart Pearson Wright had his origins concealed from him and it was only when he grew up that he learned that his father had been a sperm donor and that he had two half-siblings. As an artist he had spent a lot of time painting self-portraits and one particularly striking self-portrait had half his face missing. In conversation with Winston he comments 'I look at every single face I pass or see on the tube and I'm always looking ... to see them [his half-siblings] or my father ... that would fill in so much of the jig-saw puzzle.' Until meeting Pearson Wright, Winston had championed the need to keep donors' identities anonymous, yet, when he met Pearson Wright and after seeing how troubled Pearson Wright was, he reflected, 'I wondered how much damage I had done during the course of my career in pursuing treatment by donor insemination.'[38] Another way of putting that might be to say that Pearson Wright's pain was that he was lied to or deceived by not being told that he was the child of anonymous donor insemination. Surely what is at issue here is the contradictory emotions that are inevitably created in a family when you are not straightforwardly your mother's and father's child. This is not to say that fertility treatment should be avoided because it causes existential problems, but it is to say that if parents try to hide their child's origins this not only contravenes the child's human right to know about its genetic origins but secrets have a way of creeping out and disturbing the family system in a more destructive way, whether you are anonymously adopted or an anonymously donated IVF child.

> When I was a girl I would sneak down the hall late at night once my parents were asleep. I would lock myself into the bathroom, climb onto the Formica counter, and as close as possible to the mirror until I was nose to nose with my own reflection ... I was looking for something I couldn't have possibly articulated.[39]

132 *Reproductive adoption*

These were the opening words of Dani Shapiro's (2019) autobiography *Inheritance*. They were not, however, the words of an adopted daughter wondering about who she was, or why she felt different from her adopted family, but they were the words of an IVF child who also felt different from her mother and father but she could not understand why this was so. She had no reason to suspect that she might not be her parents' biological child except she did not look like either of them as she had blonde hair and blue eyes and both her parents were dark-haired. Her father was a Jew and her mother had converted to Judaism at their marriage. Shapiro's striking 'Aryan' features meant that throughout her early life she had to explain that she was Jewish in spite of her looks. It was only in her thirties, when her father was dead, that, through DNA testing with her supposed half-sister – her father's daughter by a previous marriage – that she discovered that she was unrelated to her half-sister and therefore could not be her father's child. The striking physical difference from either her mother or her father, that had caused her to look in the mirror 'to find a truer face just beneath my own,' was now explained.[40] She was her mother's child but her biological father was an unknown sperm donor.

The knowledge that she was not her father's daughter caused her much anguish and distress because she had adored him and had internalised a belief that she was descended from a line of distinguished Jewish Rabbis. She spoke Hebrew and had accompanied her father, throughout her childhood, to all the orthodox services throughout the year and was deeply imbued with her supposed Jewish heritage. Now she had to come to terms with the fact that her Jewish origins were a lie. With remarkable fortitude she does succeed in integrating the fact that she had a father who parented her and yet he was not her biological father. Ambiguously, she acknowledges this contradiction when she dedicates her book: 'This book is for my father.'

Her strength seems to have come from her confidence that she was adored by her father and she never doubted her love for him. She had experienced, however, an unhappy and lonely childhood with a mother who seemed to care little for her and whom she described as having a personality disorder. In some ways this helped her, not least because she wanted to find out why her mother was so angry. Once Shapiro knew she was not her father's child she could understand how heroic her father had been. He had willingly allowed his wife to be fertilised by another man's sperm, and the sperm donor was clearly not Jewish, because he wanted above all else to give his wife a child. This also helped her understand better her mother's anger with a husband who had been unable to provide her with a child. She was sad that her father had not known how to convey this fact to her and instead she had to witness an increasingly discordant marriage. The price of fertility treatment?

Fortuitously, through the internet, Shapiro did meet up with her biological father. He had been a medical student who had donated his sperm to the unregulated and dubious Farris Institute for Parenthood at Penn in the 1960s. Once she'd found him and met him she had an answer to her search for 'the truer face beneath my own' and like all the best fairy stories they have both found great

Reproductive adoption 133

delight in their contact with each other. She is also able to appreciate that 'I came from two men – my dad and Ben – who were honourable to the core.'[41] Ben is a distinguished doctor who has spent a lot of his time concerned with medical ethics, though not it seems about the ethics of donor sperm!

I have taken Shapiro's account of her discovery that she was not her father's child because it seemed to show that an IVF child can experience anxieties about her or his identity that resonates with the accounts that some adopted children have given. Both Shapiro and many of the adopted children mentioned in previous chapters, have felt that they were looking into a mirror for something they could not see or articulate. Something made them feel different. Something made them disquieted. At this point I am reminded of Kirk's (1985) argument that there is a different kinship system that is created when you adopt a child and most children intuitively pick this up and know they are not exactly their parents' child. It does not follow that adoption is detrimental, but the difference between being a naturally born child and an adopted one needs to be accepted and known if it is to be psychically integrated. The complicated kinship systems that are created in fertility treatment need to be openly acknowledged and accepted, even though the complexity of the kinship affiliations are more diffused and are still being defined.

This brings me to my final consideration about surrogate mothering that has gained increasing support as a solution to failed fertility treatment. Surrogate mothers began to appear on the fertility treatment horizon in the 1980s when it became possible to successfully freeze eggs. Young fertile women could have some of their eggs harvested and frozen and kept in an egg bank. These fertile eggs could then be used to help women who were infertile.[42] In the case of a surrogate mother, who had contracted with a couple to carry the other woman's baby, she could either have her own egg fertilised by the sperm of the man through straightforward artificial insemination, known as 'traditional' or 'partial' surrogacy, or she could agree to carry the egg of an anonymous donor, also fertilised by the man, or a sperm donor, and have that fertilised embryo inserted and this is known as 'gestational' surrogacy.[43] Some couples prefer 'gestational' surrogacy as the surrogate will have no genetic link to the child she is carrying.

There are many issues surrounded surrogacy, not least the psychological consequences for the child who has a surrogate mother. What might it mean to a child who is born from a mother who has always intended to hand him or her over to its adopted mother? Does the child, as in the case of the adopted child, experience a loss? Linked to this question about the child of a surrogate mother, there is a question about the surrogate mother's own children. Surrogate mothers are usually selected once they have had their own family, on the assumption that they will not be carrying a child that they will want to keep. However, there does not seem to be research on the effect that the birth of a 'surrogate baby,' that is then given away, might have upon the existing children of the surrogate mother. What unconscious fantasies might such children have when they realise their 'half-sibling' is given away by their mother? Once the question is posed in this way, it is easy to see that surrogate mothering is enormously complex and at the very least it has some familiar echoes to that of the birth mother and the baby she gives up for adoption.

134 *Reproductive adoption*

It has not been easy, legally, emotionally or socially, to become a surrogate mother. Before it became an acceptable method of fertility treatment there were battles in court as the legality of the procedure was clarified. The most famous case in the US, in 1985, was one that is known as Baby M.[44] Mary Beth Whitehead, who was married and had two children, was watching a popular TV programme by Phil Donahue. He was introducing the idea of surrogacy on his programme and the idea of becoming a surrogate mother filled Mary Beth's imagination. Many other surrogate mothers have responded in this way to popular TV programmes or articles that have celebrated the positive contribution that a surrogate mother makes to an infertile couple. Whitehead contacted Noel Keane's Infertility Treatment Centre in New York and a contract was drawn up that she would carry the child of Bill Stern through artificial insemination that would fertilise her own egg. Betsy Stern, Bill Stern's wife, would then adopt the child that Mary Beth had carried. The legal battle that took place when the baby girl was born was that Mary Beth had changed her mind. She was not prepared to hand over her child even though she had agreed to do so by signing a contract. Much debate centred around the legal and binding force of the contract and in the end Bill Stern won custody of the baby, though the court, in 1988, did allow Mary Beth supervised contact with her child.

It is hard not to characterise this case in patriarchal terms; Stern won because his sperm had a stronger natural right than Mary Beth's egg. In fact, the case was complicated by many other competing forces and arguments, not least the judicial and the psychoanalytic ones that the Sterns could mobilise against the lesser force of the one counsel that Mary Beth could afford. Two of the prime witnesses that the Sterns used to further their claim that they would be better parents to adopt this child than its natural mother, were the well-known adoption experts, Dr David Brodzinsky and Dr Marshall Schechter. Their later books *The Psychology of Adoption* (1990) and *Being Adopted: The Lifelong Search for Self* (1993) have been much-respected guides to the problems that adopted children face,[45] yet in the case of Mary Beth they were confident that she was not the best person to bring up her child. 'Mrs Whitehead had difficulty accurately reading her daughter's (Baby M.) behaviour as well as separating her own needs from those of her daughter,' wrote Brodinsky in his report on her. 'Mrs Whitehead has a Narcissistic Personality Disorder … [A] Narcissistic Personality Disorder [includes] a preoccupation with grooming and remaining youthful … Mrs Whitehead … dyes her hair very frequently to remain youthful.' Schechter used this observation to confirm her unsuitability for motherhood. At the very least these well-known adoption experts, who in their published work make clear the difficulties that adopted children face, reveal, in the case of Baby M, the way we can all be persuaded in the emotional heat of the moment to use evidence to further a popular argument. The popular forces were against Mary Beth, and helped by the media, the American nation was divided between the few who supported Mary Beth and the majority who were against her.[46]

One result of the case of Baby M was that paid surrogacy was outlawed in many states in the US, as it could be seen as promoting the sale of babies, though

Reproductive adoption 135

a surrogate mother's expenses could be paid; that of course does not mean that *de facto* surrogacy is not taking place. In 1994, when Ragone was researching her book on *Surrogate Motherhood* in the US, she discovered one surrogate mother programme that estimated in 1988 that 'between 5,000 and 10,000 surrogate births ... were private arrangements.'[47] At the same time as the furore around Baby M was being fought in the courts in the US, in 1985 the UK was confronted with a similar case. Kim Cotton was a sixty-year-old woman who agreed to carry anonymously an infertile couples' baby for which she was paid £6,500. Immediately the Government brought in a bill outlawing paid surrogacy, but Kim Cotton nevertheless formed an organisation called Childlessness Overcome Through Surrogacy (COTS) that she started in 1988, which helps people through the legal parameters of surrogacy.[48]

The arguments continue between those like Kim Cotton who are passionate in their belief that surrogate mothers are a creative solution to the tragedy of couples who are infertile. Cotton and her followers believe that surrogate mothers do not suffer when they hand over the baby they have carried and presumably they believe that the baby does not suffer either. Others, like Mary Beth Whitehead, are now opposed to surrogate mothering as a result of the personal suffering it caused her when she gave up her donor-inseminated baby. Whitehead found support in another surrogate mother, Elizabeth Kane, who was in fact the first recognised surrogate mother in the US.[49] She, like Whitehead, had been inspired to become a surrogate mother by reading an article in a popular magazine. She was artificially inseminated with the sperm of the putative father at a fertility clinic in Louisville that was run by the charismatic Dr Richard L. Levin, who had made such a commercial success out of his fertility treatment that he sported a car with the number plate, 'Baby 4 U.'[50]

Several points are worth exploring in Kane's case as they do highlight some of the more complicated psychological, ethical and social issues that have become apparent as surrogate mothering has developed, and in turn this brings us back to the birth mothers of adopted children. It seems to be the case that some surrogate mothers, such as Whitehead and Kane, do experience a deep emotional pain when they are separated from the baby they have carried, whether it is genetically related to them or not. If we take the case of Kane as an example, when she was a young woman she had a child out of wedlock that she had given up for adoption; she had also experienced a miscarriage before her third child was born. She was not consciously aware of the effect of these two traumas when she became convinced that she wanted to help an infertile couple by bearing a child for them. But it became apparent to her, after she gave up 'her surrogate son,' that the loss of two previous babies had fueled the grief she felt when she gave up her baby. It needs to be noted it took her seven years of mourning before she recognised this fact. To counteract this possibility surrogate mothers are given psychological assessments by psychologists in order to rule out their vulnerability before they are taken onto a surrogate programme. Kane's losses were known to Levin and the psychologists who assessed her, but this knowledge did not prevent them from recommending her.

136   *Reproductive adoption*

There is a further point that the narrative of Kane illustrates that does not seem to have been researched. This is the effect upon the existing children of surrogate mothers when their half-sibling is given away. In the case of Kane, her three young children were puzzled and then devastated that their mother could give away their 'brother.' One of her daughters felt that her brother had died without her ever seeing him, and this in turn led her to no longer trust her mother and it permanently distanced her from a relationship with Kane. With Kane's youngest son, the 'loss' of 'his brother' has been even more dramatic; the ebullient and lively three-year-old child at the time of his 'brother's' birth, by the age of eleven was in 'a self-contained special educational classroom for learning-disabled children.' Kane was helped to see that her son had experienced an inarticulate grief and loss and a fear of death that could only be expressed through becoming 'learning-disabled.' So we see that not only had the surrogate baby that Kane gave up caused her extensive grief but it damaged her relationships with her children permanently and it affected her marriage in such a way that 'We no longer relate to each other in the manner we once did.'[51]

This is of course only one case of surrogate mothering that has caused damage to a family. There are accounts of other surrogate mothers who have handed over their babies to an infertile couple with pleasure and all the participants have celebrated this new way of creating a family and the surrogate mother has never been visited by pain or regret. But there is one more question that has not received much attention, namely the baby of the surrogate mother. Have the baby's best interests been forgotten in the rush to satisfy the needs of the infertile couple? In the absence of research on this question, I want to suggest that certain issues have gone underground in the need to simplify and normalise surrogate mothering, and I am reminded of Verrier's (2009) argument, that a baby taken away from its birth mother suffers a 'primal wound.' Following on from the case of Baby M the intention of all those participating in the surrogate procedure has been defined by sorting out who has the legal right to the child. The surrogate mother intends to hand over the child, the father intends to father the child and the infertile mother intends to adopt the child. What gets forgotten are the psychological consequences on a child who is born from a mother who intends to give him or her up at birth. Surely that is similar to the problem the adopted child faces? Why was I given up? Why was I never wanted?

A final point that I want to make about surrogate mothering is that there has been an unexpected effect. A surrogate mother, during her pregnancy, finds herself cherished and the centre of attention by both the fertility experts and the couple whose child she is bearing. When the pregnancy ends she can find herself in deep depression because she is no longer receiving this rewarding love and attention. She can feel she has lost a meaning in her life and this has led to a new phenomenon; surrogate mothers can become addicted to this way of being. One extreme example has been Carole Horlock who has had nine surrogate babies.[52] I wonder whether the addiction to surrogate mothering may be a form of mourning for the loss of the surrogate baby that the surrogate mother deals with by having another one as soon as possible. This was a point that Lettice Fisher made in

Reproductive adoption 137

1920 when considering young birth mothers who went out and immediately had another child after they had given their first child up for adoption.

Where has this exploration of the link between the sealed records of adoption and the secrecy in donor insemination and then the further exploration of surrogate mothers and their babies led me? There are clearly differences between being an adopted child and an adopted sperm or egg. To be given up for adoption involves a loss that is registered in the physical body, however successful the subsequent adoption turns out to be, and this cannot be the same for a donated sperm or egg. But what does remain the same for both an adopted child and an IVF child is a question about where they come from. Questions of identity seem to ineluctably appear in both situations, and therefore it surely must be in the best interests of the child of IVF treatment that they should know, as far as possible, who their biological father and mother were, as has been the case in adoption. When it comes to the child of a surrogate mother there can be no doubt that he or she will experience a primal loss or wound at separation from their mother, as has been argued in the case of adopted children. A difficult question is whether children who were born from a surrogate mother might face a profound psychological difficulty in internalising and integrating the fact that their mother always intended to give them away. There is also the possibility that some surrogate mothers will experience the same agonising pain of relinquishing their surrogate child, whatever their previous intentions or whatever the contract may have been, and here are familiar echoes of the birth mother who never forgot her illegitimate child that she was expected to relinquish.

Have I been mistaken to pursue the argument that adopted children and IVF babies have to come to terms with similar existential questions about their origins? I do not want for a moment to knock the extraordinary success that fertility treatment has achieved and the hope and help it has given to infertile and gay and lesbian couples. My argument, throughout this chapter, has been that fertility treatment, surrogacy and adoption need to be recognised as other ways of achieving a family, neither better nor worse, but different from families who are created through heterosexual intercourse and without difficulty. It has been a mistake for IVF donors to remain anonymous for the same reasons that it was a mistake in the case of adopted children for their birth parents to remain a mystery; secrets are damaging and destructive and as one researcher said, there is 'a potentially negative impact of keeping circumstances of conception secret from the child.' Yet in spite of this knowledge the debate about anonymous donors continues and 'constitutes one of the most contentious aspects of the practice of assisted reproduction today.'[53]

The new kinship structures created by fertility treatment need to be celebrated in new ways and not hidden in shame. Without openness we will not be able to discover whether these rainbow families create good enough internalised structures for the well-being of their children. All we can say at present is that 'There is no research on children born through surrogacy … children born through surrogacy differ in ways that may be detrimental to their emotional well-being as they grow up'[54] but we do not yet know. Perhaps the last words on the subject of surrogacy should come

138 *Reproductive adoption*

from one of our best known and respected pioneers in the field of fertility treatment, Robert Winston: 'Parenthood, whether natural or assisted, is a life-changing event accompanied by strong and conflicting feelings, and it would be irresponsible to ignore them,' and then he adds, '… surrogacy can offer hope to parents and fulfillment to those who help them.'[55]

Notes

1 Since 2005 'the donors of sperm, eggs and embryos would lose the right to anonymity.' Winston (2006) p. 278.
2 It has been argued that 'surrogate motherhood is not an infertility treatment but a means by which a man can have a biological child.' Marsh & Ronner (1996) p. 312, n. 2.
3 Robert Nachtigall, quoted in Mundy (2007) p. 20.
4 I am grateful to Faye Carey for suggesting I show these multiple ways of assisted pregnancy.
5 From 2005 in the UK, and in Sweden, Austria, Switzerland, the Netherlands and parts of Australia, there has been a mandated registry of all donors. This has been partly influenced by the United Nations declaration in 1989 that every child has 'as far as possible the right to know … his or her parents' as well as the right not to be 'deprived of some or all of the elements of his or her identity.' Quoted in Mundy (2007) p. 182.
6 Goldberg & Brushwood Rose (2009) p. 8. I wish to thank Faye Carey for suggesting I read their book.
7 Jacobs (2017): 'Zeus' giving birth to Athena forms the belief or fantasy that is elevated to the status of law and in fact the patriarchal order … depends upon it.' p. 31.
8 See Carey (2019) in her essay on Freud's omnipotent fantasy of 'parthogenesis on the Parthenon' suggesting that there is a universal unconscious fantasy that we have created ourselves.
9 Winston (2006) p. 80.
10 ibid. p. 238
11 ibid. p. 240.
12 ibid. p.190.
13 The last hundred years of classical economic theory has increasingly been challenged by economists such as Raworth (2017) in *Doughnut Economics*. Raworth argues that there is cuckoo in the nest of the economic theory that extols the virtue that prosperity should be measured by GDP (Gross Domestic Product). See also Coyle (2019) *G.D.P: A Brief but Affectionate History*, Jackson, (2019) *Prosperity Without Growth* and Partington (2019) (see *Guardian* article 17.5.2019) who are challenging the belief that the natural world can sustain infinite growth.
14 Thompson (2006) p. 11.
15 An epithet coined by my uncle Rupert Gleadow.
16 Winston (2006) p. 253.
17 ibid. 'The age of the women is critical. Women much over forty seldom have more than a 5 per cent chance of success, and are more likely to fail at any stage.' p. 134.
18 Zoll (2013) p. 188.
19 Winston (2006) pps. 96–97.
20 Marsh & Ronner (1996), Pfeffer (1993), Winston (2006). It is tempting to remind the reader that Jean Purdy's name was left out on a plaque honouring Edwards and Steptoe, even though she was one of the scientists whose work contributed to the birth of Louise Brown (*The Guardian*, 10.06.2019).
21 Winston (2006) pps. 191–192. See also Mundy (2007). It was estimated, in 2005, that the pharmaceutical industry had a $3 billion business world-wide selling products that are essential to reproductive technology, p. 4.

Reproductive adoption   139

22 Winston (2006) pps. 243–244.
23 Daniels (2006) pps. 73–74.
24 Shapiro (2019) pps. 230–231.
25 ibid. pps. 230–231.
26 Bowlby (2013) p. 4. Today we can no longer with confidence say in the words of William Wordsworth, 'the child is father of the man.' p. 106.
27 Marsh & Ronner (1996) p. 241
28 Bowlby (2013) p. 38, n. 2.
29 Winston (2006) pps.103–104. As I was putting the finishing touches to this chapter, an article appeared in *The Guardian* (14.08.2019): 'A new sperm separation technique may one day allow prospective parents undergoing IVF to choose whether they have a boy or a girl before fertilisation takes place ... Sperm can be selected based on whether they will result in female (XX) or male (XY) offspring when used to fertilise an egg.' The article went on to say, this '... work could also prove useful in agriculture. "In a dairy farm, the value of a female dairy cow is much higher than a male".'
30 Winston (2006) p. 508, n. 5.
31 ibid. pps. 273–278.
32 ibid. pps. 278–287.
33 ibid. p. 107.
34 Leve (2016) In the US egg donors could earn between $5–$10,000. Sperm donors considerably less.
35 Winston (2006) p. 280.
36 ibid. p.282.
37 Golombok (2000) p. 36. Ragone (1994).
38 Winston (2006) pps. 285–286.
39 Shapiro (2019) p. 3.
40 ibid. p.3.
41 ibid. p. 288.
42 Winston (2006).
43 Ragone (1994), Winston (2006).
44 Chesler (1988). Brodzinsky & Schechter state the aim of their book *The Psychology of Adoption* (1990) is 'to provide us with some workable models ... that should help us to conceptualise ... the daily experiences ... of the adopted child to being "different", to being unsure of his identity ... and to having his sense of being constantly undermined by the endless uncertainties of belonging.' p. vii.
45 Ragone (1994) p. 88
46 ivfbabble.com.
47 Kane (1988).
48 Winston (2006) p.310.
49 Kane (1988) p. 280.
50 Winston (2006) p. 32.
51 Kane (1988) p. 280.
52 Golombok (2001) p. 21.
53 Golombok (2000) p. 39.
54 Winston (2006) p. 320.
55 ibid. p. 320.

References

R. Bowlby (2013) *A Child of One's Own: Parental Stories*. Oxford: Oxford University Press.

D. Brodzinsky & M. Schechter (eds) (1990) *The Psychology of Adoption*. New York/ Oxford: Oxford University Press.

140 *Reproductive adoption*

D. Brodzinsky, M. Schechter & R. Henig. (1993) *Being Adopted. The Lifelong Search for the Self.* New York: Random Books.

F. Carey (2019) Derealisation. In J. Burke (ed.) *Psychoanalytic Perspectives on the Shadow of the Parent: Mythology, History, Politics and Art.* London/New York: Routledge.

P. Chesler (1988) *Sacred Bonds: Motherhood Under Siege.* London: Virago Press.

P. Coles (2018) *Psychoanalytic and Psychotherapeutic Perspectives on Stepfamilies and Stepparenting.* London/New York: Routledge.

D. Coyle (2019) *GDP: A Brief but Affectionate History.* Princeton/Oxford: Princeton University Press.

C. Daniels (2006) *The Science and Politics of Male Reproduction.* Oxford/New York: Oxford University Press.

S. Goldberg & C. Brushwood Rose. *And Baby Makes More.* London/Ontario: Insomniac Press.

S. Golombok (2000) *Parenting. What Really Counts?* London/Philadelphia: Routledge.

S. Golombok (2001) Follow up studies of children born after assisted reproduction. *Human Reproduction Update.* 7. 1. 21–22.

T. Jackson (2019) *Prosperity Without Growth. Foundations for the Economy of Tomorrow.* London/New York: Routledge.

A. Jacobs (2017) Rethinking Matricide. In R. Mayo & C. Moutsou (eds) *The Mother in Psychoanalysis and Beyond.* London/New York: Routledge.

E. Kane (1988) *Birth Mother.* San Diego: New York, London: Harcourt Brace Jovanovich, Publishers.

H.D. Kirk (1985) *Adoptive Kinship. A Modern Institution in Need of Reform.* USA/Canada: Butterworth & Co.

M. Leve (2016) The bodies and bits of (re)production: Dilemmas of egg 'donation' under neoliberalism. In K. Gentile (ed.) *The Business of Being Made: The Temporalities of Reproductive Technologies, in Psychoanalysis and Culture.* London/New York: Routledge.

M. Marsh & W. Ronner (1996) *The Empty Cradle.* Baltimore/London: The John Hopkins University Press.

L. Mundy (2007) *Everything Conceivable: How Assisted Reproduction Is Changing Men, Women, and the World.* New York: Alfred. A. Knopf.

R. Partington (2019) Is it time to end our fixation with GDP and growth. *The Guardian.* 17. 05. 2019.

N. Pfeffer (1993) *The Stork and the Syringe. A Political History of Reproductive Medicine.* Cambridge: Polity Press.

H. Ragone (1994) *Surrogate Motherhood. Conception in the Heart.* Boulder, San Francisco/Oxford: Westview Press.

K. Raworth (2017) *Doughnut Economics. Seven Ways to Think Like a 21st-Century Economist.* London: Random House Business Books.

D. Shapiro (2019) *Inheritance. A Memoir of Genealogy, Paternity and Love.* London: Daunt Books.

C. Thompson (2006) *Making Parents. The Ontological Choreography of Reproductive Technologies.* Cambridge, Massachusetts/London: The MIT Press.

R. Winston (2006) *A Child Against All Odds.* London: Bantam Books, Transworld Publishers.

M. Zoll (2013) *Cracked Open. Liberty, Fertility, and the Pursuit of High-Tech Babies: A Memoir.* Massachusetts: Interlink Books.

Index

Adie, K. 100n20

adopted children: access to background information about 53, 65, 88, 90, 112; adoption experience of 7, 90, 96–8, 100, 100n20; attachment to birth mother 113–14; behaviour of 112, 117; cultural perception of 18n20, 92, 95–6; danger of incest 16; debates about late placement of 115; *vs.* donor-conceived children 137; emotional problems of 87, 92–3, 112, 117; feelings about adoption 6–7; genetic disorders of 114; identity confusion 11, 13, 69, 96–7, 100n19, 137; legal rights of 88; mental state of 16; myths about 4, 17; non-searching 95–6, 100n19; primal wound idea and 93–4, 101n27; psychological problems of 1–2, 89, 90, 98; public perception of 98; relation with adopting parents 87, 94, 95, 111–13; relation with birth parents 59–60, 68, 69–70, 107; search for biological parents 89, 90, 91–2; sexuality of 115; statistics of 73n53; *vs.* stepchildren 1; studies of 134

Adoptees' Liberty Movement Association (ALMA) 91

adopting parents: adopting experience of 7; attachment behaviour of 105; feeling of guilt of 44n24; relations with adopted children 105, 108, 109–10, 111–13, 115; therapeutic help for 116–17, 118; violence towards 121n72

adoption: anxieties of 17; attachment theory and 92–3, 94, 97, 100n5; birth fathers and 66, 67–8; birth mothers and 55; of children of drugs or alcohol addicts 104–5; criticism of 69; damaging effect of 70; economic aspect of 80; efficacy of 43; emotional trauma of 46, 51, 52, 93; evolution of ideas about 5, 38, 42–3, 52, 53, 86, 115–16; *vs.* fertility treatment 125–6, 127–8; forced 5, 50–1, 52; as form of abandonment 93; *vs.* foster care 77–8, 80; as hope to achieve family 137; interest of children and 78; inter-racial and inter-country 96; kinship structures of 88; legal practices of 38, 79, 92, 100n24; of new-born babies 104; present-day approaches to 106–7, 108; problem of openness of 69; problems of late 104, 108–10, 121n43; as reasonable course of action 71; regulation of 43; same sex couples and 125, 127–8; studies of 86–7, 88–9; success rate of 87; termination of at-risk 115

Adoption Act of 1926 5, 38, 46, 47

adoption agencies 14, 16, 51, 115, 121n43

adoption circle 75

Adoption Contact Register 65

adoption records: changing attitude towards 91; restricted access to 53, 87–8, 89, 90, 92, 113, 130

adoption societies 37–8

adoption triangle 6, 75

Adoption UK 116

adoptive kinship 88

Aeschylus: 14

Agnew, T. 29, 30

Ainsworth, M. 66,

Ainsworth, M. & Eichenberg, C. 105n6, 120n12

Ainsworth, M., Behar, M., Waters, E. & Wall, S. 105

Alice, Princess, Countess of Athlone 37

ALMA, 91

Amandine (test-tube child) 129

American War of Independence 60

142 *Index*

Andrew, C.: establishment of adoption
society 36, 37, 42; legislative initiative
of 5, 38; support of illegitimate children
36, 37; views of adoption 38, 40,
44n21, 46
Andrew, T. 36
Andrews, J. 82n40
Archbishop's Advisory Board for
Preventive and Rescue Work 37
Archer, C. & Burnell, A. 46n6, 56n6,
92n27 104, 107n23, 109, 116, 120n15
Arms, S. 18n19
ART (Assisted Reproductive Technology)
125, 127
artificial insemination 126–7
Athena, Greek goddess 126, 138n7
attachment behaviour: types of 105
attachment disorders 42, 106, 109–10
attachment theory 2–3, 5, 7, 42, 105,
106, 108
avoidant attachment 105

BAAF 81n36, 84n37
'baby farming' 29
Baby M case 134–5, 136
Bernardo Homes 36–7
Barnardo, T. J. 28, 31n43, 36–7
bastards: adoption of 21–2; association
with fornication 21; debates about the
care of 26; etymology of the word 21;
inheritance rights 22; practice of
murdering 23; social problem of 22–3;
stigma of 21
Bastardy Act 39
Bazalgette, Joseph 75
Beckford, V. 121n72
Bean, P. & Melville, J. 28n40, 28n43,
28n45
Beebe, B., & Lachmann, L. 42n42 105
Bertocci, D. 89
biological parent: concept of 108
Bion, W. 5, 41–2
birth mothers of illegitimate children:
attachment to abandoned children 55–6;
'Badge of Shame' of 72n13; categories
of 54, 55, 56; emotional trauma of
13–14, 46, 51, 53; fertility problems of
51; perception of adoption by 55,
73n49; reunion with abandoned children
55; societal attitudes towards 5, 46–7,
52, 53, 54, 56; survey of 53–4, 55;
synchronized interactions with babies
120n14; testimonies of 52, 53, 54, 65
birth records: access to 65, 88, 100n11

Blackstone, W. 24n17
Blackwood, Justice, 76
Blincoe, R. 5, 27–8, 30
Boer War, 35
borderline personality disorder 106, 109
Borkowski, M. 121n72
Boswell, J. 16n18
Boswell, S. & Cudmore, L. 83
Bouchet, M. E. du 61
Bowen, C. Sir, 77
Bowlby, J.: attachment theory of 2–3, 5, 7,
42, 86, 105, 106, 108–109; 129 109
Bowlby, R. 13, 14n13 17n2, 18n13
Brack, A 30n48 30n49
Bretherton, I. & Waters, E. 123
Brief Encounter (film) 50
Briggs, A. 104
British Psychoanalytic Society 41
Brodzinsky, D. M. Schechter, M. D. &
Heinz, R. M. 18n20
Brodzinsky, D. M & Schechter, M. D.
134n44
Bower, M. & Solomon, R. 82n37 82n38
Brown, A.: childbirth experience 50;
confinement in Magdalene Laundry 50;
emotional trauma of 52; forced
separation from a child 50–1;
marriage of 51
Brown, J. 27
Brown, L. 128, 129, 138n20
Burdett-Coutts, A. 35
Burdett, F. 27, 31n37
Burke, J. 126
Burnell, A. 5 6n6, 107, 119, 120n15;
115, 116
Butler, J. 34–5, 43n9

Canham, H. 18n16
Carey, R. 76, 77, 138n8
Carey, F. 125, 126n6, 126n8
Carr, E. J. 129
Category D (disorganised/disorientated)
attachment 105, 106, 109
Cecil, D. 28n8
Chamberlain, N. 40
Charles II, King of England 22, 61
Charles I, King of England 61
Chessler, F. 134n44
Chesterfield, P. D. S., Earl of 6, 61, 62, 64
Child Guidance Clinics 92
child labour: regulations of 27, 30; in
Workhouses 26, 27–8
Childlessness Overcome Through
Surrogacy (COTS) 135

Index 143

child migration policy 28–9
children: brain development of 3, 41, 118;
impact of upbringing on behaviour of
3–4; physical and mental well-being of
33–4, 36, 41; poverty of 31n11; removal
from families 56n6; slavery of 26–7,
28–9; wartime mortality of 34; *see also*
adopted children; donor-conceived
children; foster children; troubled
children; unwanted children
Children Adoption Association 36
Children's Acts 77, 106–7, 108
child to parent violence (CPV) 121n72
Clapton, Gary 6, 65–67, 69–70, 71
Clarke, W., Sir 38
Clement of Alexandria 16
Cline, Foster 105, 108; 109
Coogan, D. 119n72
Coleridge, S. T. 41
Coles, Gary 6, 65–69, 73n53
Coles, Allegra 10
Coles, P.: 13, 23 101n30
Colpus, E. 39
Committee of Inquiry into Human
Fertilisation and Embryology 130
Connolly, T. 64n19
Contagious Diseases Act
(1886) 43n9
Cookson, C. 52
Coram, T 13
Cosmopolitan (magazine) 57n19
Cotton, K, COTS, 135
Coyle, D. 127n13
Crichton-Miller, H. 41
Crusade of Rescue (adoption agency) 51
Cries International Sperm Bank 128

Daniels, C. R. 128
Davies, H. 94–5
de Zulueta, F. 118n68
Delaware Forest School 36
Denny, A. 48
Deutsch, H. 90, 108
Dickens, C. 5, founder of rescue home 35,
27–8
Dickinson, E. 3
disruptive attachment disorder 42
D O H 66, 119n68, 121n72
D O E 107n20
Donahue, P. 134
donor-conceived children: *vs.* adopted
children 137; experience of anxiety of
133; identity confusion of 130, 131–2,
137; kinship systems and 133; personal

accounts of 132–3; search for biological
father 132–3
Dozier, M. 100n5
Dyer, Mrs. 76
Dwork, D. 33

economic theory of growth 127, 138n13
Education Act (1870) 33
Edwards, J. 23n11
Edwards, R. 128, 138n20
Emmanuel, R. 79
endocrinology 126
eugenics 37, 127, 129, 130
Euripides: plays of 6, 11, 13–14
Exodus 11n1 11n3

Factory Acts 31n37
Fairbairn, R. 42
family crisis 49–50
'Family Futures' organisation 7, 115–16,
117, 118–19
Farris Institute for Parenthood, 132,
fatherhood: society's concept of 66, 67
fathers of illegitimate children:
autobiographies of 65; emotional
suffering of 66, 68, 70, 71; literary
works about 66–9; moral condemnation
of 63, 70; personal accounts of 66;
relations with abandoned children 5–6,
25, 31n20, 59–63, 65, 68–71, 73n49;
societal attitudes towards 59–60, 64;
stereotypes about 65; study of 68,
69–71, 72n45
Fawcett, M. 34
Feder, L. 18n13
'The Female Mission to the Fallen' 35
feminism 50
fertility: development of scientific
understanding of 126
fertility treatment: anxiety about 8, 129–30;
benefits of 127–8; commercialization of
128–9, 138n21; concerns over secrecy
of 130; cross-country 131; donor
anonymity in 130–1, 137; ethical issues
of 129, 131; first successful experiment
with 128; forms of 125; gender selection
and 139n29; history of 126; as hope to
achieve family 137; kinship structures
created by 137–8; legal issues of 129; in
private clinics 128; regulations of 130,
138n5
Fessler, A. 50, 53
Flint, J. 21
Field, J. 2

144 *Index*

Filius nullius 5, 24, 31n18, 65, 76
Finnegan, F. 49n11
Fisher, F. 7, 90 91, 92
Fisher, H.A.L. 39
Fisher, L. 7; background of 38–9; influence of 42; marriage of 39; position at N.C.A.A. 39–40; social activism of 5; support of women's welfare 39; views of adoption 41, 46; views of mother-child relations 40–1; views of young birth mothers 43, 136–7
Fisk, N. 120n17
Flint, C. 21
foetus: cortisol level in 120n17
foster care: *vs.* adoption 77–8, 80; children's account about 79–80; definition of 75; economic component of 80, 81; history of 76; legal foundation of 79; long-term quasi-adoptive 80–1; psychological problems created by 78; public debate about 80; re-evaluation of 82–3; regulations of 80, 82; stigmatisation of 78
foster carers: in adoption circle, role of 75; assumptions about 83; attachment to foster children 77–8, 81, 83; custodial responsibility of 76–7; in Euripides' play, depiction of 6; financial need of 81, 82, 84; legal rights of 76, 77, 79, 81; need of psychological support for 83–4; as parents, self-perception of 83; shortage of 82, 84n35
foster children: behaviour of 81, 82, 121n68; career prospects of 81; grief and disturbance of 82; legal protection of 77; multiple care givers of 78, 79; relations with foster parents 81, 83; statistics of 84n35
Fostering and Adoption Team 101n27
Franklin, B. 6, 60, 61, 64, 72n4
Franklin (née Read), D. 60
Franklin, W. 60–1, 64
Freud, A. 108
Freud, S. 5, 14n15, 18n16, 41, 91, 129, 138n8
Froebel, F. 41

gay and lesbian couples: reproductive rights of 125–6
General Magdalene Asylum, Donneybrook, 48
Gentile, K. 130
George I 61
George II 61

Gerhardt, S. 46n1, 56n1
Gibbs, I. 82, 83
Giggs, M. 21, 22
Giggs, O. 21
Giggs, T. 21
Gleadow, R. 127n15.
Goldberg, R. 18n16
Goldberg, S. & Brushwood Rose, C. 126
Goldstein, J., Freud, A. & Solnit, J. 88n11, 108
Golombok, S, 131 136n58
Gordon-Jones, S. 118n66
Goody, Jack 42
Graham-Dixon, S. 34, 35, 36, 38, 39
Greenmail, L. 110
Gregory, Pope 48
Guite, M. 41
Guntrip, H. 42

Haley, A. 100n24
Halifax, E. W., Earl 61
Hall, E. 18n13
Hall, W. 38
Hamblin, A. 72n13
Hamilton, V. 18n16
Hanway, J. 25
Harley, J. 22
Harton Workhouse 25
Hawthorne, N. 63–4, 72n19
Health and Morals of Apprentices Act (Peel's Act) 33
Henry VIII, King of England 22
Herbert, E. W. 60
Hibbs, E. D. 58
Hindle, D. & Schulman, G. 93
Hill, O. 38
Home for Rest in Liverpool 34
Hopkirk, J. 22, 24, 25, 26, 26, 35
Horlock, Carole 136
Houghton Report 88
Howe, D. 65, 73n53, 107, 110
Howe, D. & Feast, J. 65, 71, 88–89
Howe, D., Sawbridge, P. & Hinings, D. 71, 80
Hug-Helmuth, Hermine 59, 92
Hughes, D. 102
Human Fertility and Embryology Act of 1990 (HFEA) 130
Humphreys, M. 28
Hunter, J. 126

Ilbert, C. 38
illegitimate children: adoption of 21–2, 38; belief in hereditary defect of 37; cultural

stigma around 87; deprivation of rights of 24; in feudal society 22; fictional characters of 63–4; in Greek mythology 4; inhumane treatment of 26; legal status of 5, 24–5, 31n18, 59; mortality rate of 25, 34, 35, 44n29; parliamentary debates about 37; prejudice against the adoption of 6, 21, 36, 37; relations with birth fathers 5–6, 25, 59, 61–4, 68–71; religious beliefs about 60; search for fathers 65; societal attitudes towards 4–5, 10, 22, 23, 34–6, 46, 60, 64–5, 70; statistics of 26, 34, 43n6; *see also* bastards
incest 15–16, 18n19
Independent Inquiry into Child Sexual Abuse 29
Infant Life Protection Bill (1871) 76
infants *see* new-born babies
infertility 13–14, 18n12
Ion (Euripides): depiction of mother-son relations 4, 12–13, 18n6, 18n13; emotional trauma of birth mother 13–14; foster-parenting theme 6, 12, 14, 75; plot 11–13; problem of paternity in 13
Ireland: asylums for disruptive women in 48–9; Church and State relations in 48; Magdalene Laundries in 5, 49
IVF (In Vitro Fertilisation) 125, 127, 128, 129, 130, 138n17
IVF babies *see* donor-conceived children

Jacobs, A. 126n7
Jackson, T. 127n13
James I, King of England 23
Jenkins, A. 79, 80
Jenkins, C. 79, 80
Jewish refugee children: prejudice against 35–6
Jones, K. 25, 52
Jordan, J. 34
Judd, Dorothy 44n24

Kay, J. 18n17
Kane, E. 8, 135–6
Keane, N. 134
Keating, J. 18n17, 25n18, 25n23, 33, 36, 37, 38, 39, 40, 41, 42
Kendrick, J., Lindsey, C. & Tollemache, L. 2, 79, 92
Kimble Loux, A. 7; on adopting families 119; adoption story of 111–15; 109, 111; relations with adopted children 114–15, 116

Kirk, D. 7, 87–8, 92, 133
Klein, M. 5, 41, 92
Krystal, H. 120n11
Kyle, F. 46, 53, 70–1, 72n45

Langdon, M. 36
Laub, D. & Auerhahn, A. 105n11
Leichnam, H. M. 109
Leve, M. 130
Levin, R. L. 135
Lifton, B. 7, 90–92, 108
Lifton, R. 91
Liotti, D. 106, 120n13
Liverpool Society for the Prevention of Cruelty to Children 30
Loewald, H. 72n22
London Female Penitentiary 35
Lopez, C-A & Herbert, E. W. 60
Loreto Convent Mother and Baby Home 50, 51
Loux, Mark 111
Lowe, N., Murch, M., Borkowski, M., Weaver, A., Beckford, V., with Thomas, C. 121n72
Lyster, Dr. 34, 35

MacLean, G. & Rappen, U. 59
Macleod, J. 84
Magagna, Jeanne 2n3
Magdalene Asylums 47–8, 49
Magdalene Laundries 49, 50–51
Main, M., Kaplan, K. & Cassidy, J. 105
Main, M. & Goldwyn, R. 9, 105
marital faithfulness: propaganda of 50
Marris, P, 122
Marsh, M, & Rommer, W, 125, 128–129
Mary Magdalene, Saint 47, 48
Mason, John 86
Maxton-Graham, K. 18n17
McCarthy, R. L. 48
McCullogh, E. & Madura, A. 121n66
McCullough, E., Gordon-Jones, S., Last, A., & Burnell, A. 121n66
McWhinnie, M. 6, 25n23, 35, 47, 86, 87, 88
Me-K Ando: adoption story of 96–7
Megee, M. & Alexander, L. 25
Melbourne, W. L., Viscount 22
Melosh, B. 18n17
Mental Deficiency Act of (1913) 35
Milburn, A. 42
monasteries: dissolution of 22
Montessori, M. 41
More, J, 21

146 *Index*

More, T., Sir 22
Moses, prophet: exodus from Egypt 11; story of adoption of 10–11
Mother and Baby Home 47
mother-child relationships 39–40, 42
Mundy, L. 125, 128n21
Murch, M. 121n72
Murray, G. 12, 13, 14, 17, 18n6
Museum of the Coram Foundling Hospital 13
Music, G. 7, 92n27 101n27, 105, 106, 121n62

Nafisi, A. 8n5
Natchigall, R. 125n3
'National Baby Week' 33–4
National Children Adoption Association (N.C.A.A.) 37–8, 46
National Council for the Unmarried Mother and her Child (N.C.U.M.C.) 5, 39–40, 41, 43, 46
National Society for the Prevention of Cruelty to Children 30
NeuroPhysiological Psychotherapy (NPP) 118
neuroscience of the brain 3, 38, 105, 106, 118
new-born babies: of addict parents 104–5; adoption of 104; attachment with mothers 42, 105–6, 120n14; brain development of 105–6
Newill, H. 37
New Zealand: debates on adoption in 69
Newman C. 58
Nobody's Child (BBC Radio broadcast) 21
Northeastern Cryobank 128
Novy, M. 18n13
NPN (Natural Parents Network) 116
nuclear family: *vs.* adopting family 88

Oedipus myth: moral of 4, 17; mother-son relations in 14–15; problem of incest in 15–16; studies of 18n16; theme of self-deception 16–17
Oppenheim, D. & Goldsmith, D. F. 100n5 111n40
Orphan Voyage 91
O' Riordan, S. & Leonard, S. 57n18
Overseas Adoption Line 104

PAC 116
Pancoast, W. 126
Pankhurst, E. 26
Panksepp, J. 120n13

Parker, Val 57n32
Paton, J. 7, 91, 90
Patchick, D. J. 43n14
Patrick, A. & Barrett-Lee, L. 48–51
Peel, R., Sir, 35
Peters, E. 61,
Pfeffer, N. 138n20
Phillips, J. 21
Pinchbeck, I. & Hewitt, M. 22, 23, 24, 25, 26 29, 30, 33, 41, 75, 92
Plath, S. 50
Porges, S. 120n13, 120n19
Poor Law Acts 23, 24, 25, 26, 33, 39, 41
poor people: societal attitudes towards 23
Post-Adoption Centre (PAC) 101n27, 116
post-adoption societies 104, 115, 116
Prevention of Cruelty to Children Act 29
primal wound: concept of 93–4, 108
Prynn, B. 59
prostitution: popular beliefs about 35
Protestant Mother and Baby Homes 5
psychoanalytic theories: popularity of 41–2
psychological parent: concept of 108
Purdy, J. 128, 138n20
Puritan belief system: repression of sexuality by 64

Ragone, H. 134–135, 139n37
Raworth, K. 138n13
reactive attachment disorder 109
Repository for Germinal Choice 128
reproductive technology 8, 125–6, 127, 130
rescue homes 35, 49
resilience: concept of 3–4
resistant (ambivalent) attachment 105
Robinson, J. 46
Romantic Movement 41
Roots (film) 100n24
Roper, M. 22
Rose, J. 28
Rowe, J. 58
Rowe, J. & Lambert, L, 79–82
Rustin, M. 101n27, 101n33
Rustin, M. & Rustin, M. 18n13, 93, 101n27
Rutter, M. 3
R. v. Nash 76–7
Ryan Report 49

Salem Witch Hunts 64
Sawbridge, P. 71
Schechter, M. & Bertocci, D. 89
Schellabarger, S. 61
Schore, A. 46n1, 93, 105n7, 106n14, 120n14

Index 147

Schofield, G., Beek, M., Sargent, K., W. with Thoburn, J. 77–78, 81
Schulenburg, Melusine von der 61
Schulman, G. 93
Scotten, R. 107
Sean Ross Abbey 49
secure attachment 42, 105, 106
Selwyn, J., Sturgess, W., Quinton, D. & Baxter, C. 107, 109–110
Siegal, D. 120n13
separation: trauma of 2, 3, 7
Sexton, A. 2, 25
sexual morality 23–4, 34, 64
Shapiro, Dani 131–3
Shorter Oxford Dictionary 21
Silverstone, Jennifer 43n14.
Sinclair, I., Gibbs, I. & Wilson, K. 76–77, 80
Sinclair, I., Baker, C., Wilson, K. & Gibbs, I. 78, 79, 81, 82, 83
Sixsmith, M. 49
Slade, A. 111
slave trade 27
Smith, B., Surrey, L. & Watkins, M. 94
Smith, J. M. 48–49
Smith, S. 30
Society for the Prevention of Cruelty to Children (US) 29–30
Solms, M. 120n13
Solomon, R. 82
Sophocles 4, 14
Spallanzani, L. 126
sperm banks 128–9
sperm donors 128, 130, 138n1, 138n5
Springford, Kate 119n1
Stanhope (née Peters), E. 62
Stanhope, P. 61–2
Steele, M. 83
Steele, M., Kabuki, J., Hodges, J., Hillman, S. & Henderson, K. 100n5, 120n39, 111
Steiner, J. 16
Steptoe, P. 128, 138n20
Stern, B. 134
Stobbs, Tanya 1, 8
Suchet, M. 101n30
surrogate motherhood: concept of 125, 138n2; cost of 135; criticism of 135; emotional trauma of 134, 135–6, 137; impact on family 136, 137, 138; legal issues of 134–5; promotion of 134, 135; psychological consequences of 8, 133, 135–7; selection of mothers for 133; as solution to failed fertility treatment 133, 134; statistics of 135

Tavistock Clinic 2, 5, 41, 79
Teichman, J. 21, 24, 26, 76
Testart, J. 129
test-tube babies 128, 129
Thane, P. & Evans, T. 23, 35, 46
Thoburn, J. & Sellick, G. 121n43
Thomas, C. 121n72
Thompson, C. 127
Tizard, B. 21, 79
trauma: childhood histories of 121n68; clinical approaches to 121n62; theories of 41–2, 115, 117, 118
Treacher, A. & Katz, I 54, 102
Trevarthen, C. 120n13
Triselotis, J. 93
Triselotis & Russell, 89
Triseliotis, J., Feast, J. & Kyle, F. 46, 52–55, 65–71, 72n45, 88, 89n12, 95, 97
troubled children: attachment disorder of 105, 109–10, 120n15; behaviour of 110, 113–14, 118; borderline personality disorder of 113; cortisol level in 106, 120n15; legacy of past abuse and neglect in 106, 109–10; multi-disciplined approach to study of 119; psychological problems of 104–5; rehabilitation into original family 107; relations with adopting parents 110; therapeutic help for 109, 118–19; unconditional love to 109
Tyne & Wear Workhouse 52

UN Convention on the Rights of the Child 88
Universal Credit 23, 31n11
unmarried mothers: custodial responsibility for illegitimate children 24–5, 31n18; economic support for 23, 39; House of Correction for 23; rescue homes for 5, 34–5, 47–8; societal attitudes towards 4–5, 23–4, 35, 39–40, 48, 50, 52, 63, 104; vulnerability of 50
unwanted children: disposal of 75, 76; legislative protection of 76; prevention of cruelty towards 29–30; promotion of adoption of 36; systems of caring for 28, 29; transportation to overseas colonies 28–9, 31n43

van der Kolk, H. & van der Kolk, B. 105n11
van der Kolk, B, 42, 110, 119n68
Vaughan, J., McCullough, E. & Burnell, A. 118, 119

148   *Index*

Vernant, Jean-Pierre & Vidal-Naquet, P. 18n16

Verrier, Nancy 14n12; adopting experience of 94; idea of primal wound 93, 94, 98, 108, 136; on reconnection with biological mother 89, 93

Wadia-Ells, S. 69n49
Waller, J. 25, 26, 27, 30n1
Warnock, M. 130
Waters, Mrs. 29, 75
Wayne-Carp, E. 94, 100n24
Wegar, K. 102
Weider, H. 18n16
Whitehead, M. B. 134, 135
Who Do You Think You Are? (TV programme) 95
Wieder, H. 18n16
Wilde, O, 10
Williams Syndrome 114

Wilson, K. 82, 83
Winnicott, D. 42
Winston, R. 125–131, 133, 133n43, 135–136
Winterson, J. adoption experience of 7, 93, 98–9, 100 100n20; meeting with birth mother 99; suicidal breakdown of 99
women: deprivation of rights of married 24; societal expectations from 34, 49–50, 57n19
Wordsworth, W. 41 129n26
Workhouses: administration of 26; child labour in 25, 26, 27; conditions in 25–6, 27; establishment of the first 25; illegitimate children in 4; infant mortality in 25; in literary works 27–8; standard of nutrition in 25
Wright, S. P. 131

Zeus 126, 138n7
Zoll, M. 127